Biological Sciences (continued)

Excretory System

Kidneys

<u>Structure and functions</u>
The kidneys are composed of several layers, and are each covered by a fibrous capsule, called the renal capsule. The outer layer of the kidneys is the cortex, which contains the major (upper) portion of the nephrons. The middle layer of the kidneys is the medulla, which is composed of the triangular-shaped pyramids, and the renal columns. The pyramids contain the collecting tubules and the loops of Henle, the lower portion of the nephrons. These tubules run nearly parallel to one another, and give the pyramids a grain that leads to their points, or papillae. The renal columns are regions between the pyramids through which blood vessels run to and from the cortex. The papilla of each pyramid projects into a funnel-shaped area, known as the calyx. The calyces (plural of calyx) collect the urine that is released from the papillae, and allow it to drain into a large area, known as the renal pelvis, and then into the ureters. The nephrons are the functional units of the kidneys: they individually and collectively perform the functions of the kidneys.

<u>Blood supply</u>
The blood supply to the kidneys is paramount to their function. The two kidneys receive between 15-20% of the body's systemic blood flow at rest. The renal arteries branch into lobar, and then interlobar arteries, which pass through the renal columns in the direction of the renal cortex. Arcuate arteries branch into the cortex, and lead to the interlobular arteries, which evenly distribute the blood supply throughout the cortex to the afferent arterioles that serve the nephrons. Blood flow that leaves the nephrons returns through veins of the corresponding names.

Glomerulus

The processes in the glomerulus are as follows:
- The filtration coefficient is high because of a high permeability and a large surface area.
- The reflection coefficient is high (about 1.0), and the filtrate is a true ultrafiltrate, as the glomerular capillaries are essentially impermeable to protein (oncotic pressure in the filtrate is zero).
- The hydrostatic pressure in the capillaries is high, and does not decrease much along the length of the capillary.
- Because of the large loss of fluid, and the impermeability to protein, the oncotic pressure in the capillary increases along its length. This increased oncotic pressure is important in the reabsorption from the proximal tubule into the peritubular capillaries.
- There is a net outward filtration pressure, often along the whole length of the capillary.

<u>Renal tubule</u>

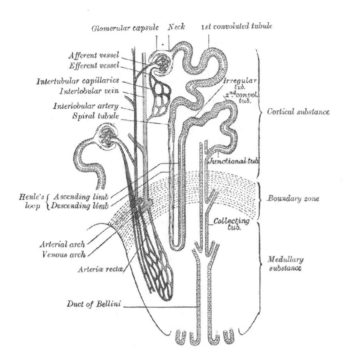

Glomerulus

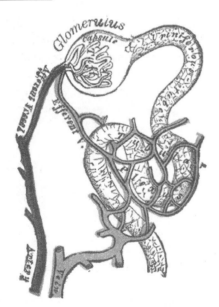

Proximal convoluted tubule

A large amount of nutrients and water are filtered from the blood in the glomerulus. It is necessary to reabsorb most of the nutrients and water, but leave wastes in the tubule, or death would result from dehydration and starvation. Selective reabsorption occurs in the proximal convoluted tubule. Glucose, vitamins, important ions, and most amino acids are reabsorbed from the tubule back into the capillaries near the proximal convoluted tubule. These molecules are moved into the peritubular capillaries by active transport, a process that requires energy. Cells of the proximal convoluted tubule have numerous microvilli and mitochondria, which provide surface area and energy. When the concentration of some substances in the blood reaches a certain level, the substance is not reabsorbed; it remains in the urine. This process prevents the composition of the blood from fluctuating by regulating the levels of glucose and inorganic ions, such as sodium, potassium, bicarbonate phosphate, and chloride. Urea remains in the tubules.

Descending and ascending aspects of the loop of Henle
The descending loop of Henle is highly permeable to water. Water moves out of the tubule by osmosis, and into the medullary interstitial fluid for reabsorption. The descending limb epithelial cells do not have the appropriate protein channels on them for active water transport. In the ascending loop of Henle, the sodium-potassium pumps work non-stop to pump sodium out into the medullary interstitial fluid. This is a major contributing factor to the reason why the medullary interstitial fluid has a solute concentration gradient. As the positive ions leave the ascending limb cells, the negative ions, such as chloride, tend to follow.

Note: The ascending limb is NOT permeable to water. This is unusual, as most cells will allow some water to slip through at any time. However, these cells are specialized to prevent it. Even their tight junctions between cells are excessively tight so that water will not slip between the cells.

Early distal convoluted tubule and collecting tubules

Early distal convoluted tubule (DCT)
- Reabsorption of sodium ions.
- Reabsorption of calcium ions.
- Reabsorption of chloride ions.
- Reabsorption of H_2O (regulated by vasopressin).

Collecting tubules (CT)
- Reabsorption of sodium ions.
- Secretion of hydrogen ions (for blood pH homeostasis).
- Secretion of potassium ions.
- Reabsorption of H_2O (regulated by vasopressin).

Both the DCT and the CT are involved in the reabsorption of water.

Renal plasma flow

$$RPF = \frac{(U_x \times V)}{(P_a - P_v)}$$

Where:
U_x = The urine concentration of solute X.
V = The urine flow rate.
P_a = The arterial plasma concentration of the substance X.
P_v = The venous plasma concentration of the substance X.

However, in practice, it is very difficult to measure the P_v of a substance since catheterization of the renal vein is required, which is an uncommon procedure. Therefore, *para*-aminohippurate (PAH) is used because nearly 100% is secreted in the urine. Using PAH, P_v can be eliminated, and the effective RPF (eRPF) can be calculated as follows:

$$eRPF = \frac{(U_{PAH} \times V)}{P_{PAH}}$$

Where:
U_{PAH} = The urine concentration of PAH.
P_{PAH} = The arterial plasma concentration of PAH.

Note: Renal blood flow (RBF) = $\dfrac{RPF}{(1 - [Hematocrit])}$

Renal clearance

As substances in the blood pass through the glomeruli, they are filtered to different degrees. The extent to which they are removed from the blood is called "clearance". The clearance is the number of liters of plasma that are completely cleared of a substance by the kidneys per unit time (mL/min). The idea of complete clearance is hypothetical since almost no substance would be completely cleared. However, clearance measurements are extremely important clinically.

The clearance (C_x) of a substance (X) is given by the following equation:

$$C_x = \frac{U_x \times V}{P_x}$$

Where:
U_x = The concentration of X in the urine in mg per mL (or mmol/L).
P_x = The concentration of X in the plasma in mg per mL (or mmol/L).
V = The urine flow rate in mL per minute.

If a substance is completely cleared (hypothetical), then clearance equals the glomerular filtration rate (GFR). This means that the substance had neither been secreted nor reabsorbed during its passage down the renal tubule. If the clearance is < GFR, then net reabsorption has occurred. Any solute that is fully reabsorbed has a clearance of zero. Solutes that have a clearance > GFR have undergone net secretion, as well as filtration.

Net filtration pressure

NFP = $\Delta P - \Delta \pi$
Where:
ΔP = Hydrostatic pressure gradient.
$\Delta \pi$ = Oncotic pressure gradient.

The NFP can be calculated by subtracting the factors that promote filtration from the factors that oppose filtration. Specifically, the NFP can be calculated as follows:

NFP = GBHP – CHP –BCOP
Where:

GBHP = Glomerular blood hydrostatic pressure.
CHP = Capsular hydrostatic pressure.
BCOP = Blood colloid osmotic pressure.

Under typical conditions, the NFP is positive on the order of 10 mmHg, favoring filtration.

Free water clearance

$$C_{H_2O} = V - C_{osm}$$

Where:
V = The urine flow rate.

C_{osm} = The osmolar clearance = $U_{osm} \times \dfrac{V}{P_{osm}}$

Dilute urine, excreted in the absence of antidiuretic hormone (ADH), can be thought of as being made up of two fluid volumes:
- A volume that contains the urine solutes at the same concentration as in plasma, and called the osmolar clearance (C_{osm}).
- Pure water excreted with no solutes, called positive free water clearance (V).

Concentrated urine, produced in the presence of ADH, can be thought of as the difference between two volumes:
- The volume of plasma from which the urinary solutes derive (C_{osm}).
- The (smaller) volume of urine actually excreted (V).

The difference, C_{osm} – V, represents water free of solutes, retained in the body due to the action of ADH. This is called the negative free water clearance, or tubular free water reabsorption.

Total body weight, extracellular fluid, and intracellular fluid

Total Body Weight (TBW)
TBW = ECF + ICF
Where:
ECF = Extracellular fluid volume.
ICF = Intracellular fluid volume.

Extracellular Fluid
ECF = IV + PV
Where:
IV = Interstitial volume.
PV = Plasma volume.

Muscle and Skeletal Systems

Classification of muscles

A muscle cell not only has the ability to propagate an action potential along its cell membrane, as does a nerve cell, but also has the internal machinery to give it the unique ability to contract. Most muscles in the body can be classified as striated muscles in reference to the fact that when observed under a light microscope the muscular tissue has light and dark bands or striations running across it. Although both skeletal and cardiac muscles are striated and therefore have similar structural organizations, they do possess some characteristic functional differences. In contrast to skeletal muscle, cardiac muscle is a functional syncytium. This means that although anatomically it consists of individual cells the entire mass normally responds as a unit and all of the cells contract together. In addition, cardiac muscle has the property of automaticity, which means that the heart initiates its own contraction without the need for motor nerves. Nonstriated muscle consists of multi-unit and unitary (visceral) smooth muscle. Visceral smooth muscle has many of the properties of cardiac muscle. To some extent it acts as a functional syncytium (e.g., areas of intestinal smooth muscle will contract as a unit. Smooth muscle is part of the urinary bladder, uterus, spleen, gallbladder, and numerous other internal organs. It is also the muscle of blood vessels, respiratory tracts, and the iris of the eye.

Skeletal muscles

In order for the human being to carry out the many intricate movements that must be performed, approximately 650 skeletal muscles of various lengths, shapes, and strength play a part. Each muscle consists of many muscle cells or fibers held together and surrounded by connective tissue that gives functional integrity to the system. Three definite units are commonly referred to:
- Endomysium – Connective tissue layer enveloping a single fiber.
- Perimysium – Connective tissue layer enveloping a bundle of fibers.
- Epimysium – Connective tissue layer enveloping the entire muscle.

Differences between skeletal and cardiac muscles

Skeletal muscle is found attached to the bones for movement. Its cells are long, multi-nucleated cylinders. They acquired this characteristic because they develop from the fusion of small, single cells into long units. The cells may be many inches long, but they vary in diameter, averaging between 100 and 150 microns. Skeletal muscle cells are independent cells that are separated from one another by connective tissue, and must each be stimulated by the axons of nerves. Cardiac muscle is the muscle found in the heart. It is composed of much shorter cells than skeletal muscle, and these cells branch to connect to one another. These connections are by means of gap junctions, called intercalated disks, which allow for electrochemical impulses to simultaneously pass to all of the connected cells. This causes the cells to form a functional network, called a syncytium, in which the cells function as a single unit.

Smooth muscle

Visceral muscle is located within the walls of internal organs and blood vessels. Visceral muscle is called smooth muscle because it has no striations, and is thus smooth in appearance. It is organized as layers within the mucous membranes of the respiratory and digestive systems, as distinct bands within the walls of blood vessels, or as sphincter muscles. Single unit smooth muscle is also connected into syncytia, similar to cardiac muscle, and is partly myogenic. Within the walls of the stomach, intestines, and blood vessels, smooth muscle cells form multi-unit muscle tissue that is regulated by the autonomic nervous system, and thus involuntary. Such multi-unit smooth muscle tissue is responsible for the continual rhythmic contractions of the stomach and the intestines.

Muscle attachment and function

For coordinated movement to take place, the muscle must attach to either bone or cartilage or, as in the case of the muscles of facial expression, to skin. The portion of a muscle attaching to bone is the tendon. A muscle has two extremities, its origin and its insertion.

Muscle movement

The following are terms to describe movement:
- Flexion – Bending, most often ventrally to decrease the angle between two parts of the body; it is usually an action at an articulation or joint.
- Extension – Straightening, or increasing the angle between two parts of the body; a stretching out or making the flexed part straight.
- Abduction – Movement away from the midsagittal plane (midline); to adduct is to move medially and bring a part back to the mid-axis.
- Circumduction – Circular movement at a ball and socket (shoulder or hip) joint, utilizing the movements of flexion, extension, abduction, and adduction.
- Rotation – Movement of a part of the body around its long axis.
- Supination - Refers only to the movement of the radius around the ulna. In supination the palm of the hand is oriented anteriorly; turning the palm dorsally puts it into pronation. The body on its back is in the supine position.
- Pronation – Refers to the palm of the hand being oriented posteriorly. The body on its belly is the prone position.
- Inversion – Refers only to the lower extremity, specifically the ankle joint. When the foot (plantar surface) is turned inward, so that the sole is pointing and directed toward the midline of the body and is parallel with the median plane, we speak of inversion. Its opposite is eversion.
- Eversion – Refers to the foot (plantar surface) being turned outward so that the sole is pointing laterally.
- Opposition – One of the most critical movements in humans; it allows us to have pulp-to-pulp opposition, which gives us the great dexterity of our hands. In this movement the thumb pad is brought to a finger pad. A median nerve injury negates this action.

Muscle names

Position and location:
- Pectoralis major and minor – Pectoral region of thorax; major is larger.
- Temporalis – Temporal region of head.
- Infra- and supraspinatus – Below and above spine of scapula.
- External and internal intercostals – Intercostal spaces.

Principal action:
- Pronators (e.g., pronator quadratus) – Refers to palm down and supinator to palm up; quadratus refers to the shape.
- Flexors and extensors – Flexors and extensors of digits.
- Levator scapulae – Elevator of the scapula (shoulder).

Shape:
- Trapezius – Trapezoidal in shape.
- Rhomboid major and minor – Rhomboidal in shape.

Number of divisions (heads) and position:
- Biceps brachii – Two-headed muscle in anterior brachium.
- Triceps brachii – Three-headed muscle in posterior brachium.

Size, length, and shape:
- Flexor pollicis longus and brevis – Long and short flexors of the thumb.
- Rhomboid major and minor – Major is larger in size; rhomboidal in shape.

Attachment sites:
- Sternocleidomastoid – Extends from sternum and clavicle to the mastoid process.
- Sternohyoid – Extends from sternum to hyoid bone.

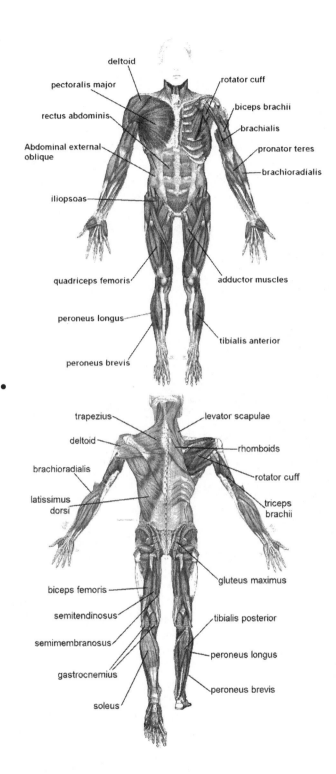

Muscles of mastication

The muscles of mastication (chewing) are inserted into the mandible, and are innervated by the motor root of V3:

- Temporalis – Closes jaw.
- Masseter – Closes jaw.

- Medial (internal) pterygoid – Closes jaw and moves jaw from side to side (opposite).
- Lateral (external) pterygoid – Opens, protrudes, and moves jaw from side to side (opposite).

The pterygoid muscles are so named because they arise from the medial and lateral sides of the lateral pterygoid plate of the sphenoid bone. The lateral pterygoid muscle can open the jaw because it inserts into the neck of the mandible, and into the articular disc. Upon contraction, it pulls the head of the mandible anteriorly, causing it to hinge on the articular disc in such a way that the jaw opens. Alternating action of the pterygoids on both sides can move the jaw from side to side. Thus, with proper synchronization, these muscles produce the grinding movements of chewing. The buccinator, although a muscle of facial expression (innervated by VII), aids in maintaining the position of food within the oral cavity during chewing. The temporo-mandibular joint is a double synovial joint with an intervening disc. It has two functions: the upper part functions as a gliding joint, and the lower part functions as a hinge joint. This joint is frequently damaged when the teeth are misaligned.

Borders of the abdomen

The borders of the abdomen are as follows:
- Superior – The diaphram.
- Inferior – Continuous with the pelvis.
- Anterior – The lower part of the thoracic cage superiorly, as well as the musculature of anterior abdominal wall.
- Posterior – The lumbar vertebrae and intervertebral discs, the 12th rib, the quadratus lumborum muscles, the psoas, and the iliac crest.

Hesselbach's triangle

The following are the boundaries of Hesselbach's triangle:
- Lateral edge of the rectus abdominus.
- Inferior epigastric vessels.
- Inguinal ligament.

Hernias that occur within the triangle are said to be direct, while hernias that occur lateral to the triangle borders are said to be indirect.

Umbilical, diaphragmatic hiatal, and femoral hernias

Umbilical hernia
During development, there is a natural herniation of the bowel into the umbilical cord. The bowel returns to the abdominal cavity before birth. However, on occasion, the linea alba fails to fuse properly, resulting in a weak area that is subject to herniation (congenital umbilical hernia). An umbilical hernia in adults occurs when the umbilicus becomes greatly stretched, allowing omentum or intestines to pass through it. This condition is referred to as an acquired umbilical hernia.

Diaphragmatic hiatal hernia
An abnormal opening in the diaphragm that permits herniation of abdominal viscera into the thoracic cavity. Congenital diaphragmatic hernias are present at birth (hernias of

Bochdalek), and are due to a failure of the diaphragm to develop properly. Acquired diaphragmatic hernias are located at the esophageal hiatus, and usually result in a portion of the stomach protruding into the thoracic cavity.

Femoral hernia
A protrusion of abdominal viscera or omenta into the femoral canal lateral to the lacunar ligament. Because of the sharp concave edge of this ligament, these hernias are subject to strangulation (compression that results in a loss of blood supply, which could lead to gangrene).

Groin hernias

The Nyhus classification of groin hernias is as follows:
- Type I – Indirect inguinal hernia. The internal inguinal ring is normal (i.e., pediatric hernia).
- Type II – Indirect inguinal hernia. The internal inguinal ring is dilated with the posterior inguinal wall intact.
- Type III:
  - Direct inguinal hernia. Posterior wall defects.
  - Indirect inguinal hernia. The internal ring is dilated with a large medial encroachment on the transversalis fascia of the Hesselbach's triangle (i.e., massive scrotal sliding hernia).
  - Femoral hernia.
- Type IV – Recurrent hernia.
  - Direct.
  - Indirect.
  - Femoral.
  - Other.

Skeletal system

The skeletal system of vertebrates is an *endoskeleton*—that is, it is within the body—as compared to an *exoskeleton*, which is characteristic of arthropods. The human skeletal system provides the following:
- Support.
- Protection of vital organs.
- Sites for muscle attachment.
- Storage site of body calcium and phosphates.
- Sites for blood cell formation.

The *human skeleton* consists of bone and cartilage. The bones form the main rigid structure of the skeleton. The human skeleton consists of about 206 bones, some of which are fused while others are joined together at sites that permit various degrees of movement. The sites of junction, or articulation, whether movable or immovable, are known as *joints*. The human skeleton is divided into an *axial skeleton* and an *appendicular skeleton*.

Adult human skeleton

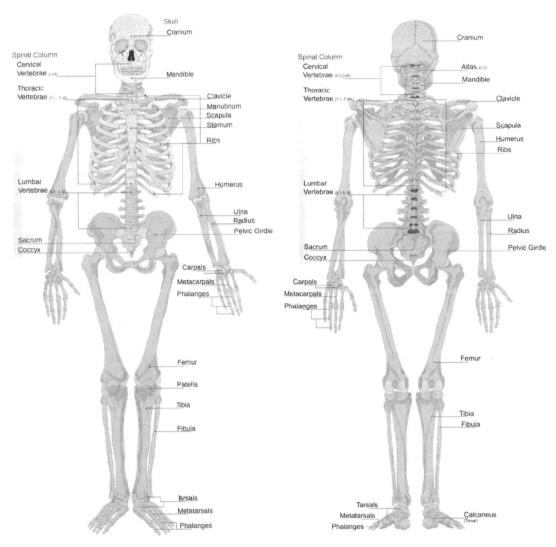

Axial skeleton

The axial skeleton consists of 80 bones forming the trunk (spine and thorax) and skull.

Vertebral column

The main trunk of the body is supported by the spine, or vertebral column, which is composed of 26 bones, some of which are formed by the fusion of a few bones. The vertebral column from superior to inferior consists of 7 cervical (neck), 12 thoracic and 5 lumbar vertebrae, as well as a sacrum, formed by fusion of 5 sacral vertebrae, and a coccyx, formed by fusion of 4 coccygeal vertebrae.

Ribs and sternum

The axial skeleton also contains 12 pairs of *ribs* attached posterior to the thoracic vertebrae and anterior either directly or via cartilage to the *sternum* (breastbone). The ribs and sternum form the *thoracic cage*, which protects the heart and lungs. Seven pairs of ribs articulate with the sternum (*fixed ribs*) directly, and three do so via cartilage; the two most inferior pairs do not attach anteriorly and are referred to as *floating ribs*.

Skull

The skull consists of 22 bones fused together to form a rigid structure which houses and protects organs such as the brain, auditory apparatus and eyes. The bones of the skull form the *face* and *cranium* (brain case), and consist of 6 single bones (*occipital, frontal, ethmoid, sphenoid, vomer* and *mandible*) and 8 paired bones (*parietal, temporal, maxillary, palatine, zygomatic, lacrimal, inferior concha* and *nasal*). The *lower jaw* or *mandible* is the only movable bone of the skull (head); it articulates with the temporal bones.

Other parts

Other bones considered part of the axial skeleton are the *middle ear bones* (*ossicles*) and the small U-shaped *hyoid bone* that is suspended in a portion of the neck by muscles and ligaments.

Appendicular skeleton

The *appendicular skeleton* forms the major internal support of the appendages—the *upper* and *lower extremities* (limbs).

Pectoral girdle and upper extremities

The arms are attached to and suspended from the axial skeleton via the *shoulder* (*pectoral*) *girdle*. The latter is composed of two *clavicles* (*collarbones)* and two *scapulae* (*shoulder blades*). The clavicles articulate with the sternum; the two *sternoclavicular joints* are the only sites of articulation between the trunk and upper extremity. Each upper limb from distal to proximal (closest to the body) consists of hand, wrist, forearm and arm (upper arm). The *hand* consists of 5 *digits* (fingers) and 5 *metacarpal* bones. Each digit is composed of three bones called *phalanges*, except for the thumb, which has only two bones.

Pelvic girdle and lower extremities

The lower *extremities*, or legs, are attached to the axial skeleton via the *pelvic* or *hip girdle*. Each of the two coxal, or *hip bones* comprising the pelvic girdle is formed by the fusion of three bones—*illium, pubis,* and *ischium*. The coxal bones attach the lower limbs to the trunk by articulating with the sacrum.

The Human Skeletal System	
Part of the Skeleton	Number of Bones
Axial Skeleton	80
Skull	22
Ossicles (malleus, incus and stapes)	6
Vertebral column	26
Ribs	24
Sternum	1
Hyoid	1
Appendicular Skeleton	126
Upper extremities	64
Lower extremities	62

Bone

Characteristics

Bone is a specialized type of connective tissue consisting of cells (*osteocytes*) embedded in a calcified matrix, which gives bone its characteristic hard and rigid nature. Bones are encased by a *periosteum*, which is a connective tissue sheath. All bone has a central marrow cavity. *Bone marrow* fills the marrow cavity or smaller marrow spaces, depending on the type of bone.

Types

There are two types of bone in the skeleton: *compact bone* and *spongy* (cancellous) bone. Compact bone lies within the periosteum, forms the outer region of bones, and appears dense due to its compact organization. The living osteocytes and calcified matrix are arranged in layers, or *lamellae*. Lamellae may be circularly arranged surrounding a central canal, the *Haversian canal*, which contains small blood vessels. Spongy bone consists of *bars, spicules* or *trabeculae*, which forms a lattice meshwork. Spongy bone is found at the ends of long bones and the inner layer of flat, irregular and short bones. The trabeculae consist of osteocytes embedded in calcified matrix, which in definitive bone has a lamellar nature. The spaces between the trabeculae contain bone marrow.

Major types of human bones:

Type of Bone	Characteristics	Examples
Long bones	Width less than length.	Humerus, radius, ulna, femur, and tibia.
Short bones	Length and width close to equal in size.	Carpal and tarsal bones.
Flat bones	Thin, flat shape.	Scapulae, ribs, sternum, and bones of cranium (occipital, frontal, parietal).
Irregular bones	Multifaceted shape.	Vertebrae, sphenoid, and ethmoid.
Sesamoid	Small bones located in tendons of muscles.	

Bone cells

The cells of bone are osteocytes, osteoblasts, and osteoclasts. Osteocytes are found singly in *lacunae* (spaces) within the calcified matrix and communicate with each other via small canals in the bone known as *canaliculi*. The latter contain osteocyte cell processes. The osteocytes in compact and spongy bone are similar in structure and function. Osteoblasts are cells that form bone matrix, surround themselves with it, and thus are transformed into osteocytes. They arise from undifferentiated cells, such as mesenchymal cells. They are cuboidal cells that line the trabeculae of immature or developing spongy bone. Osteoclasts are cells found during bone development and remodeling. They are multinucleated cells lying in cavities, *Howship's lacunae*, on the surface of the bone tissue being resorbed. Osteoclasts remove the existing calcified matrix releasing the inorganic or organic components.

Bone matrix

Matrix of compact and spongy bone consists of collagenous fibers and ground substance, which constitute the organic component of bone. Matrix also consists of inorganic material, which is about 65% of the dry weight of bone. Approximately 85% of the inorganic component consists of calcium phosphate in a crystalline form (hydroxyapatite crystals). Glycoproteins are the main components of the ground substance.

Joints

The bones of the skeleton articulate with each other at *joints*, which are variable in structure and function. Some joints are immovable, such as the *sutures* between the bones of the cranium. Others are *slightly movable joints*; examples are the *intervertebral joints* and the *pubic symphysis* (joint between the two pubic bones of the coxal bones).

Types

Joint Type	Characteristic	Example
Ball and socket	Permits all types of movement (abduction, adduction, flexion, extension, and circumduction); it is considered a universal joint.	Hips and shoulder joints.
Hinge (ginglymus)	Permits motion in one plane only.	Elbow and knee, inter-phalangeal joints.
Rotating or pivot	Rotation is only motion permitted.	Radius and ulna, atlas and axis (first and second cervical vertebrae).
Plane or gliding	Permits sliding motion.	Between tarsal bones and carpal bones.
Condylar (condyloid)	Permits motion in two planes that are at right angles to each other (rotation is not possible).	Metacarpophalangeal joints, temporomandibular.

Adjacent bones at a joint are connected by fibrous connective tissue bands known as *ligaments*. They are strong bands that support the joint and may also act to limit the degree of motion occurring at a joint.

Respiratory System

Respiratory system

The respiratory system is composed of a conduit for air and an air-blood interface for gaseous exchange in the alveoli of the lungs. Respiration refers to the gaseous exchanges that occur between the body and the environment.

Lungs

The two lungs, which contain all the components of the bronchial tree beyond the primary bronchi, occupy most of the space in the thoracic cavity. The lungs are soft and spongy because they are mostly air spaces surrounded by the alveolar cells and elastic connective tissue. The only point of attachment for each lung is at the hilum, or root, on the medial side. This is where the bronchi, blood vessels, lymphatics, and nerves enter the lungs. The right lung is shorter, broader, and has a greater volume than the left lung. It is divided into three lobes, and each lobe is supplied by one of the secondary bronchi. The left lung is longer and narrower than the right lung. It has an indentation, called the cardiac notch, on its medial surface for the apex of the heart. The left lung has two lobes. Each lung is enclosed by a double-layered serous membrane, called the pleura. The visceral pleura is firmly attached to the surface of the lung. At the hilum, the visceral pleura is continuous with the parietal pleura that lines the wall of the thorax. The small space between the visceral and parietal pleurae is the pleural cavity.

Respiratory bronchioles

Respiratory bronchioles are similar in construction to terminal bronchioles, except that the walls are periodically interrupted by alveoli, which are capable of gas exchange. When the proportion of interspersed alveoli increases to the degree where they occupy the majority of the surface of the airway, the passages are called alveolar ducts. Alveolar ducts end in clusters of alveoli, called alveolar sacs. The alveolus can be considered as the unit of gas exchange. Its walls are composed of two epithelial cell types: type-I and type-II pneumonocytes.

Type-I and Type-II pneumonocytes

Type-I Pneumonocytes are squamous pulmonary epithelial cells that form about 95% of the alveolar surface. They are extremely thin, and form part of the blood-air interface, where the gasses diffuse through the cell. Type-II Pneumocytes are cuboidal, and are generally located at the junctions between alveoli. They secrete phospholipid-rich pulmonary surfactant. Small numbers of sensory brush cells, fibroblasts, and macrophages are also present in the interstitial spaces. Alveoli are in intimate contact with capillaries of the pulmonary vasculature.

Gas exchange in the alveoli

Gas exchange takes place only in the alveoli and not in the tracheobronchial tree. The diffusion pathway for alveolar gas may be listed as follows:
1. Surfactant (lowers surface tension)
2. Alveolar epithelium
3. Interstitium (fused basement membranes)
4. Capillary endothelium (epithelium)
5. Plasma
6. Red blood cells

Oxygen transport

Oxygen is transported mainly in the form of oxyhemoglobin. The O_2 Content of Blood (OCB) can be calculated using the following equation:

$$OCB = (15 \text{ g Hb}/ 100 \text{ ml Blood}) \times (1.36 \text{ ml } O_2/\text{g Hb}) \times (O_2 \text{ Saturation Factor } (\%)) \times (0.0032 \text{ p}O_2 \text{ (torr)})$$

Four factors affect the affinity of hemoglobin for oxygen:
- pH
- Temperature
- Concentration of 2,3-diphosphoglycerate (DPG)
- Carbon dioxide

Carbon dioxide transport

While some carbon dioxide remains in plasma, most diffuses into red blood cells. Bicarbonate ions that are produced in the red blood cells diffuse into the plasma because of the concentration gradient.

Chemical regulation of respiration

The chemical stimulants of physiological importance that affect respiration are as follows:
- Increased arterial pCO_2 (hypercapnia).
- Decreased arterial pO_2 (hypoxia).
- An increased arterial hydrogen ion concentration (acidosis).

V/Q ratio

The V/Q ratio expresses the balance between alveolar ventilation and capillary blood flow. When ventilation matches blood flow, carbon dioxide is eliminated, and the blood becomes fully saturated with oxygen. In the normal lungs, gravitational forces affect the V/Q ratio; when a person stands, the V/Q ratio is 3 in the apex of the lung, and 0.6 in the base. In the overall lung, the V/Q ratio is assumed to be ideal, and equals 1. When capillary blood flow is in excess of ventilation, the V/Q ratio is less than 1, and arterial hypoxemia results. When V/Q mismatch worsens, the minute ventilation increases, which produces either low or normal arterial pCO_2. The hypoxemia that is caused by low V/Q areas is responsive to supplemental oxygen administration. The more severe the V/Q imbalance, the higher the

- 19 -

concentration of inspired oxygen that is needed to raise the arterial pO_2. In the extreme case, when V/Q equals 0, pulmonary blood flow does not participate in gas exchange because the perfused lung unit receives no ventilation. This is referred to as intrapulmonary shunting, and is calculated by comparing the oxygen content in arterial blood, mixed venous blood, and pulmonary capillary blood.

Mnemonic: "FEV ONE"
F – Fibrosing mediastinitis, E – Effusion, V – Vasculitis, O – One pulmonary artery (or hypoplasia),
N – Neoplasm, E – Embolism.

Contribution of respiration to pH regulation

The respiratory system functions as a physiological buffer, which acts rapidly and keeps pH levels from changing too much, until the slowly responding kidneys can eliminate the imbalance. The respiratory system can do this because it can excrete the volatile acid CO_2. Increased CO_2 production by metabolizing tissues is detected by chemoreceptors, which drive the respiratory system to match CO_2 exhalation to the rate of production. The pH change brought about by the change in pCO_2 also affects rate of alveolar ventilation. If pH falls below 7.4, ventilation increases. Alternatively, if pH rises above 7.4, ventilation decreases. Increased $[H^+]$ stimulates the respiratory center to increase ventilation. This results in a decrease in $[CO_2]$, and therefore decreases $[H^+]$. Alveolar ventilation rates then decrease again. The opposite occurs with decreased $[H^+]$, which will stimulate the respiratory center to decrease ventilation. In this way the respiratory system returns pH in the right direction towards normal. Respiratory pH regulation is 50-75% effective. It cannot return pH all the way back to normal when a disturbance outside of the respiratory system alters the pH.

Anatomic dead space and physiologic dead space

Anatomic dead space is the total volume of the conducting airways, from the nose or mouth down to the level of the terminal bronchioles, and averages about 150 mL in humans. The anatomic dead space fills with inspired air at the end of each inspiration, but this air is exhaled unchanged. Thus, assuming a normal tidal volume of 500 mL, about 30% of this air is "wasted" in the sense that it does not participate in gas exchange. Physiologic dead space includes all of the non-respiratory parts of the bronchial tree that are included in anatomic dead space, but also factors in alveoli, which are well ventilated, but poorly perfused, and are therefore less efficient at exchanging gas with the blood. Because atmospheric pCO_2 is practically zero, all of the CO_2 that is expired in a breath can be assumed to come from the communicating alveoli, and none from the dead space. By measuring the pCO_2 in the communicating alveoli (which is the same as that in the arterial blood), and the pCO_2 in the expired air, one can use the Bohr equation to compute the "diluting", non-CO_2-containing volume, which is, in other words, the physiologic dead space.

Bohr equation for physiologic dead space

$$\frac{V_D}{V_T} = \frac{(P_{ACO_2} - P_{ECO_2})}{P_{ACO_2}}$$

Where:

V_D = Dead space.

V_T = Tidal volume.

P_{ACO_2} = Arterial partial pressure of CO_2.

P_{ECO_2} = Expiratory partial pressure of CO_2.

Removal of inhaled products

Large particles are filtered by hairs and mucous material in the nose and respiratory tract. Air is also warmed and humidified.

Diaphragm

The diaphragm is a dome-shaped, musculofibrous septum that separates the thorax from the abdomen. Its peripheral part consists of muscular fibers that originate from the circumference of the inferior aperture of the thorax, and converge to be inserted into a central tendon. The muscle fibers may be grouped into three parts, according to their origins: the sternal, the costal, and the lumbar. The sternal part arises by two muscular slips from the dorsum of the xiphoid process. The costal part arises from the inner surfaces of the last 6 ribs. And, the lumbar part arises from the medial and lateral arcuate ligaments (lumbo-costal arches), and from crura. The medial and lateral arcuate ligaments are thickenings of transversalis fascia on the psoas and quadratus lumborum muscles. The lateral arcuate ligament forms the lateral lumbocostal arch. The crura are tendinous at their origins, and blend in with the anterior longitudinal ligament of the vertebral column.
The central tendon of the diaphragm is a strong aponeurosis situated near the center of the muscle, partially blended with the fibrous pericardium. The diaphragm receives both sensory and motor innervation from the C3, C4, and C5 through the phrenic nerve (the C3, C4, and C5 keep the diaphragm alive).

Action of muscles in respiration

- Diaphragm – Contraction causes descent of the central tendon. This decreases intrathoracic pressure and increases the volume of the thoracic cavity, resulting in air being drawn into the lungs.
- Accessory muscles used in forced respiration:
  - Scalenus Muscles
  - Sternocleidomastoid
  - Levator Costarum
  - Serratus Inferior, Posterior and Superior
  - Quadratus Lumborum
  - Intercostals: External, Internal, and Innermost

Inspiration and expiration

During inspiration the thoracic cavity expands, its volume increases, and air rushes into the respiratory tract due to the creation of negative pressure; the musculature involved is the diaphragm. Normal expiration is passive and involves no great muscular contraction.

Positive- and negative-pressure breathing

Gases flow from regions of higher pressure to those of lower pressure. For inspiration to occur, the alveolar gas pressure must be less than the atmospheric pressure. Normal breathing is a form of negative-pressure breathing.

Neuronal control and integration of breathing

Normal spontaneous breathing is under control of motor neurons (primarily the phrenic nerves), which innervate the respiratory muscles. Brain impulses regulate and modulate the process. Voluntary activity originates in the cerebral cortex, while automatic (autonomic) control originates in the pons and medulla of the brain.

Skin System

Skin

The skin and the specialized organs that are derived from the skin (i.e., hair, nails and glands) form the integumentary system.

<u>Functions</u>
The skin functions by surfacing the body and thus protecting it from dehydration, as well as from damage by the elements in the external environment. The skin also helps to maintain normal bodily activities.

<u>Structure</u>
Skin consists of the *epidermis* and the *dermis* (*corium*). Deep to the dermis, and therefore the skin, is the *hypodermis*, which is also known as the *subcutaneous* or superficial connective tissue of the body. The epidermis is derived from the ectoderm and is composed of a keratinized stratified squamous epithelium. *Thick skin* denotes skin with a thicker epidermis, which contains more cell layers when compared to *thin skin*. The epidermis ranges in thickness from 0.07 millimeter to 1.4 millimeters. In addition, the epidermis consists of specific cell layers, as follows:
- Stratum basale or germinativum.
- Stratum spinosum.
- Stratum granulosum.
- Stratum lucidum.
- Stratum corneum.

Hair

Hairs are long, filamentous keratinized structures that are derived from the epidermis of the skin. The structure of hair consists of a *shaft* and a *root*. The hair follicle consists of two sheaths: the *epithelial root sheath* and the *connective tissue root sheath*. Growth of a hair depends on the viability of the epidermal cells of the hair matrix, which lie adjacent to the dermal papilla in the hair bulb. The matrix cells abutting the dermal papilla proliferate and give rise to cells that move upward to become part of the specific layers of the hair root and the inner epithelial root sheath. Hairs are oriented at a slight angle to the skin surface, and are associated with *arrector pili muscles*. These smooth muscle bundles extend from the dermal root sheath to a dermal papilla. Contraction results in the hairs standing up and the skin surrounding the hair rising up.

Nails

Nails are translucent plates of keratinized epithelial cells on the dorsal surface of distal phalanges of fingers and toes.

Glands

Glands are specialized organs that are derived from the skin. There are two basic types of glands:
- Sebaceous glands – Sebaceous glands are *simple, branched alveolar (acinar) glands* with a *holocrine* mode of secretion.
- Sweat glands – Sweat is a watery fluid containing ammonia, urea, uric acid and sodium chloride. There are two types of sweat glands:
  - Eccrine Sweat Glands – The eccrine sweat glands are *simple, coiled tubular glands* with a *merocrine* mode of secretion.
  - Apocrine Sweat Glands – The apocrine sweat glands are *very large glands* that are thought to have a *merocrine* mode of secretion.

Reproductive System and Development

Reproductive organs

Male:
- Seminiferous tubules of the testes
- Epididymis
- Vas deferens
- Seminal vesicles
- Prostate
- Prostatic urethra
- Membranous urethra
- Penile urethra
- Glans penis

Female:
- Ovaries

- Oviduct
- Uterus
- Vagina
- The breasts (accessory organs)

Epididymis, vas deferens, and urethra

<u>Epididymis</u>
The epididymis lies in the scrotum, and is about 3.8-cm long, while the duct is actually about 6-meters long. The epididymis is subdivided into a head, a body, and a tail, which become surrounded by an increasingly thick layer of smooth muscle. The tail of the epididymis is continuous with the vas deferens. The duct is lined by a pseudostratified epithelium, in which the cells have non-motile stereocilia. The epididymis stores spermatozoa, which finish their maturation by acquiring motility here.

<u>Vas deferens and ejaculatory duct</u>
The vas deferens is a highly muscular tube that begins at the epididymis and runs into the pelvic cavity, through the inguinal canal. A total of 45-cm long, it is easily palpable in the spermatic cord, increasing the ease of vasectomy, an operation in which the vas deferens is cut, rendering the patient infertile. At its termination at the prostate, it widens a bit, forming a portion called the ampulla. At this point, it merges with the duct of the seminal vesicle to form the ejaculatory duct, which traverses the prostate to end in the urethra.

<u>Urethra</u>
The urethra is subdivided into prostatic, membranous, and penile urethral portions. The prostatic portion is the first part that traverses the prostate, and receives the ejaculatory ducts. As the urethra passes through the pelvic diaphragm, it is called the membranous part, which then enters the penis, forming the penile portion.

Leydig and sertoli cells

Leydig cells are the target cells for luteinizing hormone (LH), and increase their secretion of testosterone in response. Some of this testosterone remains locally to affect Sertoli cells, while most of it is released into the blood stream, where it circulates to affect other organs of the male reproductive system, as well as other tissues and organs. Sertoli cells are the target cells for follicles-stimulating hormone (FSH), and increase their functions in support of spermatogenesis in response. The combination of testosterone from Leydig cells and FSH results in a number of changes, such as an increase in the amount of androgen binding protein (ABP) and an increase in metabolic support for spermatocytes. ABP chaperones testosterone to developing spermatocytes and throughout the male reproductive tract.

Production and maturation of sperm

The stages in sperm production from germ cells are as follows:
- Meiosis to produce haploid cells.
- Loss of most of the cytoplasm.
- Development of the flagellum.
- Formation of the acrosomal tip, which aids in penetration of the egg.

These events require about 60 days, and occur in the seminiferous tubules, the epididymis, and the vas deferens. Sperm are stored in the vas deferens. Sperm maturation requires a temperature below core body temperature. This is possible because the testes are suspended in a scrotum that hangs outside of the main body cavity, keeping their temperature about 3 degrees Celsius cooler than the core body temperature. In addition, the scrotum has a muscular wall that contracts in cold weather to keep temperature from getting too low. Since a lower temperature is required for sperm development, raising the temperature will reduce sperm production.

Erection

Normally the penis is flaccid because the venous spaces in erectile tissues are empty as a result of constriction of the arteries supplying these spaces. As a result, blood is shunted via arteriovenous channels, thereby bypassing these regions. Upon sexual excitement, mediated by the parasympathetic nervous system, these arteries dilate, allowing the venous spaces to fill with blood, giving rise to an increase in pressure, and an enlargement of the penis, called an erection. This vasodilation is mediated by the release of nitric oxide (NO), a potent vasodilator. The parasympathetic nerves also stimulate the secretions of the bulbourethral glands, which produce mucus that not only neutralizes any acidic urine that may be present, but also results in the release of this mucus from the penis, aiding in lubrication. A variety of inputs, including both sensory and mental, can lead to the stimulation of vasodilatory parasympathetic nerves, leading to erection. Failure to achieve an erection is called impotence, which can result from a variety of factors, ranging from vascular to nerve, psychological, or even temporary factors, such as alcohol or certain drugs.

Uterus

The layers of the uterus are as follows:
- Endometrium – The lining of the mucosa.
- Myometrium – Consists of several thick smooth muscle layers that are capable of great enlargement during pregnancy.
- Epimetrium – The outer peritoneal covering (visceral peritoneum).

The parts of the uterus are as follows:
- Fundus – The part of the uterus superior to the entrance of the uterine tubes.
- Body – The bulk of the uterus between the fundus and the cervix. It contains most of the uterine cavity.
- Isthmus – A slight constriction between the body and the cervix.
- Cervix – The inferior neck of the uterus that protrudes into the vagina. It contains the cervical canal that connects the uterine cavity with the vaginal canal. The lower opening of the cervical canal is the cervical os. The cervix may be divided into supravaginal and vaginal portions.

Uterine tube

Infundibulum – The lateral, expanded portion of the uterine tube that has many small finger-like projections, called fimbriae, which are closely apposed to the ovary. It also contains an ostium that opens into the peritoneal cavity. Through the ostium, the ovum enters the uterine tube. This opening is also clinically important since it provides a possible route of infection from the vagina into the peritoneal cavity, and it affords the potential for abnormal fertilization of an ovum and a subsequent ectopic (outside of the uterus) pregnancy in the abdominal cavity.

Ampulla – The intermediate portion of the tube.

Isthmus – The medial, constricted portion of the tube.

Intramural (intrauterine) – The portion located in the wall of the uterus. It is continuous with the uterine cavity.

Blood supply of the ovaries

The ovarian artery originates from the abdominal aorta near the L2 vertebral level, and anastomoses with the uterine artery in the broad ligament. The ovarian veins drain from the pampiniform plexus of the ovary. The right ovarian vein drains directly into the inferior vena cava, while the left drains into the left renal vein. The ovaries produce eggs and secrete sex hormones (estrogen and progesterone). They are attached to the posterior aspect of the broad ligament of the uterus. In nulliparous females (females who have never borne children), they are usually located in the ovarian fossae, which are shallow depressions that are bounded by the external iliac vessels, the obliterated umbilical arteries, and the ureters. Alternatively, in parous females (females who have borne children), their position varies.

Placental barrier and relaxin

The placental barrier between maternal and fetal blood is similar in structure to the respiratory membrane in the lungs, and does not exclude alcohol, nicotine, or toxins from crossing into the fetal blood circulation. With the exception of a rare rupturing of the capillary walls, which may occur at delivery, fetal and maternal blood do not mix. The placenta also functions as an endocrine organ, producing steroid and peptide hormones, as well as prostaglandins, which play an important role in the onset of labor. By the end of the eighth week, the placenta takes over the production of progesterone and estrogen from the corpus luteum. Other hormones that are produced by the placenta include human chorionic gonadotropin, insulin-like growth factors I and II, placental lactogen, prolactin, oxytocin, and relaxin. The hormone relaxin prepares the cervix and pelvic ligaments for birth by inducing them to "relax" and become more pliable for delivery, dilating the cervix to about 10 cm. Oftentimes, labor can also be induced by physically stretching the cervix.

Breast

The anatomy of the breast is as follows:
- Cooper's ligaments – Suspensory ligaments, or connective tissue, that connects the skin to the underlying fat.
- Lactiferous sinuses – Place where the milk is stored; deep to the areola; the dilated portion of the lactiferous ducts.
- Lactiferous ducts – The ducts into which milk is secreted; directly deep to the nipple.
- Areola – Darkened region around the nipple; appears lighter in women who have not borne a child; contains sebaceous glands that secrete protective substances (not milk) during pregnancy.

- Mammary glands – Lobules of glandular tissue that arise from the lactiferous ducts; any deep tissue that is not fatty is glandular tissue.

Menstrual cycle

The following are the phases of the menstrual cycle:
- Day 1 – The menstrual cycle begins (bleeding starts).
- Day 5 – Sperm can live for 7 days in the female.
- Day 12-16 – A mature egg is released from an ovary into the fallopian tubes.
- Day 16-21 – The egg moves towards the uterus. The egg must be fertilized during this time period or menstruation will result.
- Day 24 – The endometrial lining deteriorates.
- Day 28 – The cycle ends, and bleeding begins again with Day 1.

Embryogenesis

Week 2 - week 40 of fetal development are as follows:
- Week 2 – Conception is the moment when the sperm penetrates the ovum. Once fertilized, the ovum is called a zygote, until it reaches the uterus 3 to 4 days later. A bilaminar disk forms during week 2.
- Week 4 – The embryo may float freely in the uterus for about 48 hours before implantation. Upon implantation, complex connections between the mother and the embryo develop in order to form the placenta. The neural plate and the primitive streak form from 3 to 8 weeks. In addition, the heart starts to beat during week 4.
- Week 6 – The embryo is about 1/5 of an inch in length. The tiny heart is beating. The head, mouth, liver, and intestines begin to take shape. And, brain waves are produced by week 6.
- Week 10 – The embryo is now about one inch in length. The limbs, hands, feet, fingers, toes, and facial features become apparent. The nervous system is responsive, and many of the internal organs begin to function. In addition, male or female characteristics begin to appear.
- Week 14 – The fetus is now three-inches long, and weighs almost an ounce. The muscles begin to develop, and eyelids, fingernails, toenails, and sex organs form. Spontaneous movements can be observed.
- Week 18 – The fetus is now about five-inches long. The fetus blinks, grasps, and moves its mouth. Hair grows on the head and body.
- Week 22 – The fetus now weighs approximately half a pound, and spans about 10-inches from head-to-toe. Sweat glands develop, and the external skin has turned from transparent to opaque.
- Week 26 – The fetus can now inhale, exhale, and even cry. Eyes have completely formed, and the tongue has developed taste buds. Under intensive medical care, the fetus has over a 50% chance of survival outside of the womb.
- Week 30 – The fetus is usually capable of living outside of the womb, and would be considered premature at birth.
- Week 40 – This marks the end of the normal gestational period. The child is now ready to live outside of its mother's womb.

Gastrulation

Gastrulation is a dramatic restructuring of the animal embryo during the gastrula phase. Gastrulation varies in different phyla. The following description concerns the gastrulation of triploblasts, or animals with three embryonic germ layers. At the beginning of gastrulation, the embryo is hollow, with an animal pole and a vegetal pole. The cells of the vegetal pole begin to divide and bud inwards, forming a hollow called the archenteron (literally, primitive gut) on the outside surface of the gastrula. Some of the cells of the vegetal pole detach and become mesenchymal cells. The mesenchymal cells divide rapidly, migrate to different parts of the blastocoel, and form filopodia (extensions of the cellular membrane) that help to pull the tip of the archenteron towards the animal pole. Once the archenteron reaches the animal pole, a perforation forms, and the archenteron becomes a digestive tract, passing all the way through the embryo. The three embryonic germ layers have now formed. The endoderm, consisting of the archenteron, will develop into the digestive tract. The ectoderm, consisting of the cells on the outside of the gastrula that played little part in gastrulation, will develop into the skin and the central nervous system.

Pectinate line

The pectinate line is the division of the hindgut anal canal (endoderm) and the ectoderm by an invagination of the skin. The upper anal canal, superior to the pectinate line, is endodermal hindgut. The lower anal canal, inferior to the pectinate line, is ectoderm. They are both supplied by different vessels, nerves, etc. The pectinate line can be identified by looking for the anal columns, longitudinal folds of mucosa that demarcate the upper anal canal.

Derivatives of the ectoderm, mesoderm, endoderm, and notochord

The ectoderm will ultimately form:
- Surface ectoderm – The adenohypophysis, and epithelial components of the skin.
- Neuroectoderm – The brain and spinal cord, CNS neurons, and the pineal gland.
- Neural crest – The autonomic nervous system, Schwann cells, and the pia mater.
- The sensory organs in the body and special sensory organs in the head.

The mesoderm will form:
- Most of the skeleton.
- The heart and blood vessels.
- The kidneys.
- The linings of internal body cavities.
- The spleen and adrenal cortices.

The endoderm will form the gut tube epithelium and its derivatives. The notochord will form the vertebral column.

Key fetal structures that turn into adult structures

Fetal Structure	Adult Structure
Umbilical Arteries	Median Umbilical Ligament
Notochord	Nucleus Pulposes
Ductus Arteriosus	Ligamentum Arteriosum
Foramen Ovale	Fossa Ovalis
Allantois, Urachus	Median Umbilical Ligament
Ductus Venosus	Ligamentum Venosum
Umbilical Vein	Ligamentum Teres Hepatis

Umbilical cord

The umbilical cord is the flexible, cord-like structure that connects a fetus, at the abdomen, to the placenta. It contains two umbilical arteries and one vein that transport nourishment to the fetus, and remove its wastes. The length of the umbilical cord varies from no cord (achordia) to 300 cm, with diameters of up to 3 cm. Umbilical cords are helical in nature, with as many as 380 helices. An average umbilical cord is 55-centimeters long, with a diameter of 1-2 cm and 11 helices to the fetal left. 6% of cords are shorter than 35 cm, and 94% of cords are shorter than 80 cm. Causes of differences in cord length are unknown. Cords with a single umbilical artery occur in fewer than 1% of singletons, and 5% of cases with at least one twin. The incidence of single umbilical artery can be underestimated with gross examination of the cord, especially if the portion close to the placenta is examined, because the arteries often fuse close to the placenta. Single umbilical arteries are found twice as often in Caucasian women than in African and Japanese women. Diabetes increases the risk significantly. Two-vessel cords are also found more frequently in fetuses aborted spontaneously. And, the male-to-female ratio is 0.85:1. Single umbilical artery is believed to be caused by atrophy of a previously normal artery, presence of the original artery of the body stalk, or agenesis of one of the umbilical arteries.

Blood flow through the fetal heart

Blood from the mother enters the fetus through the vein in the umbilical cord. It goes first to the liver, and splits into three branches. The blood then reaches the inferior vena cava, a major vein that is connected to the heart. Blood enters the heart through the right atrium, the chamber on the upper right side of the heart. Most of the blood flows to the left side through a special fetal opening between the left and right atria, which is called the foramen ovale. Blood then passes into the left ventricle (lower chamber of the heart), and then to the aorta (the large artery that exits from the heart). After exiting the heart through the aorta, the blood is circulated to the head and upper extremities. The blood then returns to the right atrium of the heart via the superior vena cava. About one-third of the blood that enters the right atrium does not flow through the foramen ovale, but instead stays in the right side of the heart, and eventually flows into the pulmonary artery. Since the placenta does the work of exchanging oxygen (O_2) and carbon dioxide (CO_2) through the mother's circulation, the fetal lungs are not used for breathing. Thus, instead of circulating the blood to the lungs, the fetal circulation shunts (bypasses) most of the blood away from the lungs.

Heart development

The heart begins development by the fusion of two separate heart tubes into a single heart tube. As this tube elongates, it develops dilations and constrictions, which will become parts of the atria and ventricles of the adult heart. The primitive heart initially has only a single atrium and ventricle. The atria become distinct from the ventricles by development of endocardial cushions and atrioventricular valves. Endocardial cushions are swellings that grow out from the dorsal and ventral walls of the single heart tube in the area that marks the separation of the tube into atrium and ventricle. The valves develop by a very complicated process in the region of these endocardial cushions. Separation of the single atrium into right and left atria involves the development of partitions called septa. The 1st septum, called the septum primum, grows down from the wall of the common atrium, and ultimately fuses with the endocardial cushion, separating the primitive atrium into a right and left side. For a very brief time before it fuses, there is a small opening between the two chambers, called the foramen (ostium) primum. Before this foramen closes, perforations occur higher up on septum primum that join to form another opening, called the foramen (ostium) secundum. A 2nd septum, called the septum secundum, grows down on the right side of the 1st septum, and covers the foramen secundum.

Blood pressure before and after birth

Before birth, blood pressure is greater in the right atrium than in the left, and the blood passes freely from the right atrium to the left atrium through the foramen ovale. However, after birth, because of an increase in pressure in the left atrium, the septum primum is forced against the foramen ovale, fuses to the septum secundum, and effectively prevents blood from passing between the two chambers. Division of the single ventricle, into right and left ventricles, occurs when the muscular interventricular septum grows up from the floor of the ventricle, and fuses with the endocardial cushions that mark the boundary between atria and ventricles. The membranous part of the interventricular septum marks the site of this fusion, and is the last region of the ventricular wall to close.

Neural tube

The neural tube is the embryonal structure that gives rise to the brain and spinal cord. During gestation, the human neural tube gives rise to three vesicles: the rhomboencephalon, the mesencephalon, and the prosencephalon. Formation of the neural tube is the result of an invagination of the ectoderm following gastrulation. This process is induced by signaling molecules that are produced in the notochord and the basal plate. Normally, the closure of the neural tube occurs around the 30th day after fertilization. However, if something interferes, and the tube fails to close properly, a neural tube defect will occur. Among the most common tube defects are anencephaly, encephalocele, and spina bifida. The incidence of a neural tube defect is 2.6 in 1,000 individuals worldwide.

Meckel's diverticulum

A Meckel's diverticulum is a common congenital (present before birth) formation that consists of a small pouch, called a diverticulum, which is located off of the wall of the small intestine. The diverticulum may contain stomach or pancreatic tissue. A Meckel's diverticulum is a remnant of structures within the fetal digestive tract that were not fully reabsorbed before birth. Approximately 2% of the population has a Meckel's diverticulum, but only a few develop symptoms. Symptoms include diverticulitis, or bleeding in the intestine. Symptoms often occur during the first few years of life, but can occur in adults as well. The tests for Meckel's diverticulum include a stool smear for occult blood (stool guaiac), hematocrit, or hemoglobin, and a technetium scan. Surgery to remove the diverticulum is recommended if bleeding develops. In rare cases, the segment of small intestine that contains the diverticulum is surgically removed, and the ends of intestine are sewn back together. Iron replacement may be needed to correct anemia. And, if bleeding is significant, a blood transfusion may be necessary.

Genetics

Mendelian concepts

Gregor Mendel discovered the concept of genetics and the inheritance of traits by carefully analyzing the numerical proportions of hybrid plant species in his garden. He found it essential to work with as great a number of plants as possible in order to overcome chance. His research enabled him to detect three principles of heredity:
- Mendel's first law: Mendel's first law is the principle of uniformity. It states that if two plants that differ in just one trait are crossed, the resulting hybrids will be uniform in the chosen trait. This depends upon whether the traits are the uniform feature of either one of the parents' traits (a dominant-recessive pair of characteristics) or whether it is intermediate.
- Mendel's second law: Mendel's second law is the principle of segregation. It states that the individuals of the second filial (F2) generation will not be uniform, but that the traits will segregate. Depending upon whether it is a dominant-recessive crossing or an intermediate crossing, the resulting ratios will be 3:1 or 1:2:1. According to this principle, hereditary traits are determined by discrete factors (now called genes) that occur in pairs, one of each pair is inherited from each parent. The concept of independent traits explains how a trait can persist from generation to generation without blending with other traits. It also explains how the trait can seemingly disappear and then reappear in later generations. The principle of segregation was consequently of the utmost importance for understanding both genetics and evolution. Mendel's law of segregation essentially has three parts:
  - Alternative versions of genes account for variations in inherited characteristics. This is the concept of alleles.
  - Alleles are different versions of genes that impart the same characteristic. For example, each human has a gene that controls height, but there are variations among these genes in accordance with the specific height the gene "codes" for.
  - For each characteristic, an organism inherits two genes, with one derived from each parent. This means that, when somatic cells are produced from two gametes, one allele comes from the mother, and one from the father.

  If the two alleles differ, then the dominant allele is fully expressed in the organism's appearance. The other, although inactive, still segregates during gamete production.
- Mendel's third law: Mendel's third law is also called the principle of independent assortment. It states that every trait is inherited independently of the others: the

two alleles of an organism separate during gamete formation, and randomly reunite during fertilization. This allows for new combinations of genes to arise that did not previously exist, thus ensuring variation. We know today that this principle is only valid in the case of genes that are not coupled; i.e., genes that are not located on the same chromosome.

Ploidy and euploidy

Ploidy indicates the number of copies of the basic number of chromosomes. The basic number of chromosomes in an organism is called the monoploid number (1x). The ploidy of cells can vary within an organism. In humans, most cells are diploid (2x, containing one set of chromosomes from each parent), though sex cells (sperm and oocytes) are haploid (0.5x). In contrast, tetraploidy (4x, four sets of chromosomes), a type of polyploidy, is not uncommon in healthy plant species. Euploidy is a species' normal number of chromosomes per cell. For example, the euploid number of chromosomes in a human cell is 46.

Allele, penetrance, and expressivity

Allele
An allele is a particular version of a given DNA sequence, implying more than one possible version or copy. All existing alleles result from a process of evolution, with either gradual or drastic change. There can be more than two possible alleles for a given gene locus, but only two at a time, in a given diploid individual. Multiple alleles can mean many different possible combinations and phenotypes for individuals.

Penetrance
Penetrance is the percentage of individuals with a genotype who actually show the trait. If only 80% of people with the genotype actually develop the trait, then you could pass on a trait without showing it, even if the trait is dominant.

Expressivity
Expressivity is the degree to which the trait is expressed. For example, a genetic defect causing mental retardation, such as Fragile X, can result in individuals with a very wide range of intellect, and you cannot predict the degree of expression.

Polygenic traits

The distribution of individuals within a population with different trait values for polygenic (quantitative) traits typically forms a bell-shaped curve. There are three main ways that selection can act on a population, given a distribution of traits such as this:
- Directional selection – The situation in which one extreme form of the trait has highest fitness.
- Stabilizing selection – The situation in which the average form of the trait has higher fitness than does either extreme.
- Disruptive selection – The situation in which both extreme forms of the trait have higher fitness than does the average.

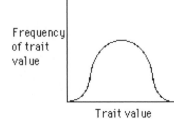

- 32 -

The results of selection on quantitative traits generally make sense: the forms that have highest fitness become most common. As shown, directional selection results in a change in the mean value of the trait toward the form that has the highest fitness. Stabilizing selection results in the loss of the extreme forms of the trait, which means that there is a decrease in genetic variation. Eventually, genetic variation may be lost, as all individuals will have the alleles for the average trait value of the highest fitness. At that point, any phenotypic variation would depend on direct environmental effects rather than on genetic differences among individuals, and the heritability of the trait would be zero, or at least very low. Disruptive selection results in an increase in both extremes, and a loss of intermediate forms. Over a long period of time, directional selection will result in a shift in the frequency of individuals with different traits until the average form has highest fitness. At this point, the situation becomes one of stabilizing selection, and the extreme forms of the trait will be lost. So, directional selection will eventually lead to a situation where genetic variation will be lost (heritability will become zero) and all individuals will have the alleles for the highest fitness form of the trait.

Autosomal dominant diseases

Autosomal dominant (AD) diseases are those in which both heterozygous and homozygous dominant individuals express the abnormal phenotype. One copy of the mutant gene is sufficient for expression of the abnormal phenotype. In fact, in many AD diseases, the homozygous genotype is incompatible with life. Some examples of AD diseases include familial hypercholesterolemia, Huntington's disease, achondroplasia, and Marfan syndrome. Several distinct characteristics of AD inheritance include the following:

- Every individual has an affected parent (except in cases of new mutations or incomplete penetrance).
- Males and females are equally likely to inherit the allele and be affected. This is because these alleles are on autosomes, for which each male and female has two copies (in contrast to X-linked diseases).
- The recurrence risk (the probability that a genetic disorder that is present in one patient will recur in another family member) for each child of an affected parent is 50%. For a dominant disorder, only one copy is necessary for development of the disease. Therefore, if one parent is heterozygous for a particular gene, their offspring will either inherit the gene, or they will not, with each outcome equally likely.
- Normal siblings of affected individuals do not pass the trait on to their offspring. If an affected individual's siblings are not affected, they do not carry the mutation and cannot pass it on to their own offspring.

Autosomal recessive diseases

Autosomal recessive (AR) diseases are those in which only individuals whom are homozygous for the mutant allele develop the disease. Those who are heterozygous are phenotypically normal. Some examples of AR diseases include cystic fibrosis, sickle cell anemia, Tay-Sachs, and albinism. Several characteristics of AR diseases include the following:

- Males and females are equally likely to be affected. This is because these are genes on autosomes, of which each male and female has two copies. Sex-linked disorders show different patterns in this respect, since males are XY and females are XX.
- The trait is often found in clusters of siblings, but not in their parents or offspring.
- The more rare a trait is in the general population, the greater the chance that it was from a co-sanguineous mating (inbreeding). If the trait is rare, the probability of two unrelated individuals both carrying the gene, mating, and then having an affected child is very low. If two individuals have a common ancestor, the likelihood that they both carry the same mutated allele is higher than the probability in the general population (assuming that their common ancestor carried the mutation).
- All offspring of an affected person are obligate carriers. Since the affected person is homozygous for the mutated allele, all of their children will inherit one copy of it, and will be carriers of the mutation.

Phenylketonuria

Phenylketonuria (PKU) is an inherited error of metabolism that is caused by a deficiency in the enzyme phenylalanine hydroxylase. Loss of this enzyme results in mental retardation, organ damage, unusual posture, and can severely compromise pregnancy (in cases of maternal PKU). Classical PKU is an autosomal recessive disorder that is caused by mutations in both alleles of the gene for phenylalanine hydroxylase (PAH), which are found on chromosome 12. In the body, PAH converts the amino acid phenylalanine into tyrosine. Mutations in both copies of the gene for PAH mean that the enzyme is inactive, or is less efficient, and the concentration of phenylalanine in the body can build up to toxic levels. In some cases, mutations in PAH will result in a phenotypically mild form of PKU, called hyper-phenylalanemia. Both diseases are the result of a variety of mutations in the PAH locus. In the cases where a patient is heterozygous for two mutations of PAH (i.e., each copy of the gene has a different mutation), the milder mutation will predominate.

X-linked recessive diseases

X-linked recessive diseases are diseases in which a female must have two copies of the mutant allele in order for the mutant phenotype to develop. Many X-linked recessive disorders are well known, including color blindness, hemophilia, and Duchenne muscular dystrophy. Typical features of X-linked recessive inheritance are as follows:
- They are never passed from father to son.
- Males are much more likely to be affected because they only need one copy of the mutant allele to express the phenotype.
- Affected males get the disease from their mothers, and all of their daughters are obligate carriers because they must inherit the father's X-chromosome, which contains the mutant allele.
- Sons of heterozygous females have a 50% chance of receiving the mutant allele.
- These disorders are typically passed from an affected grandfather to 50% of his grandsons.

Mitochondrial inheritance

Mitochondria are cellular organelles that are involved in energy production and conversion. They have a small amount of their own mitochondrial DNA (mtDNA). Although it is a relatively small proportion of our total DNA, it is still subject to mutation, and several diseases that are associated with mutations in mtDNA have been found, such as exercise intolerance, Leber's optic atrophy, and Kearns-Sayre syndrome. The inheritance patterns of mtDNA are unique because mtDNA is inherited almost entirely maternally. This is because the relatively large ovum has many copies of mitochondrial DNA, but the sperm has very few copies, and most of these are lost during fertilization. Due to this unique feature of mtDNA inheritance, there are a couple constraints on the inheritance patterns of mtDNA disorders:

- All children of affected males will not inherit the disease.
- All children of affected females will inherit it.

DNA mutations

The following are types of DNA mutations:
- Point mutation – A simple change in one base of a genetic sequence.
- Frame-shift mutation – A mutation where one or more bases are inserted or deleted, shifting the reading frame of the genetic sequence, and potentially altering or inactivating one or more genes.
- Deletion – A mutation that results in a missing segment of DNA. These may affect only a single gene, or may affect numerous genes.
- Insertion – A mutation that results in the addition of an extra segment of DNA. These can also cause frameshift mutations, and generally result in the production of nonfunctional proteins.
- Inversion – A mutation where an entire section of DNA is reversed. A small inversion may involve only a few bases within a gene, while longer inversions involve large regions of a chromosome containing several genes.
- DNA expression mutation – There are many types of mutations that do not change a protein itself, rather they change where and how much of a protein is made. These types of DNA mutations can result in proteins being made at the wrong time, or in the wrong cell type.
- Silent mutation – The mutation does not alter the peptide sequence.
- Neutral mutation – The mutation codes for a functionally similar amino acid.
- Missense mutation – The mutation codes for a functionally different amino acid.

Analytic methods

Hardy-Weinberg equilibrium
The Hardy-Weinberg equilibrium is the principle that genotype frequencies in a population remain constant unless outside disturbing influences are introduced. In general, if two individuals mate who are heterozygous (i.e., Aa) for a trait, we find the following:
- 25% of their offspring are homozygous for the dominant allele (AA).
- 50% are heterozygous like their parents (Aa).
- 25% are homozygous for the recessive allele (aa), and thus express the recessive phenotype.

Using these principles, the Hardy-Weinberg equilibrium provides us with the following equations to determine the frequencies of particular genotypes:

$A^2 + 2Aa + a^2 = 1$

- 35 -

A + a = 1
Where:
A^2 = The fraction of the population that is homozygous for p.
a^2 = The fraction of the population that is homozygous for q.
2Aa = The fraction of the population that is heterozygotes.

Probability
Probability events are possible outcomes of some random processes.

Examples of events:
- You pass 320.
- The genotype of a random individual is Bb.
- The weight of a random individual is less than 150 pounds.

We can define the probability of a particular event, say A, as the fraction of the outcomes in which event A will occur. In written form, we can denote the probability of A by Pr(A) or Prob(A).

For example, when flipping a coin once, the only possible outcomes are heads or tails. If Pr(Heads) is 0.75, then that means that there is a 75% chance that the coin will land on heads. Therefore, Pr(Tails) has to be 0.25, since Pr(Tails) = 1 - Pr(Heads) = 0.25.

Useful rules of probability are as follows:
- Probabilities are between zero (never occur) and one (always occur) – Pr(A) lies between zero and one for all A.
- Probabilities sum to one – The sum of probabilities of all mutually exclusive events is one. For example, if there are *n* possible outcomes, then Pr(1) + Pr(2) + ... + Pr(*n*) = 1. Therefore, Pr(1) = 1 - (Pr(2) + ... + Pr(*n*)).

The AND and OR rules are as follows:
- AND rule – If A and B are independent events (knowledge of one event tells us nothing about the other event), then the probability that BOTH A and B occur is Pr(A and B) = Pr(A) Pr(B). Therefore, probabilities are multiplied with the AND rule.
- OR rule – If A and B are exclusive events (non overlapping), then the probability that EITHER A or B occurs is Pr(A or B) = Pr(A) + Pr(B). Therefore, probabilities are added with the OR rule.

For example, suppose that we are rolling a set of fair dice, and flipping a fair coin. What is the probability of rolling an even number on the dice?

A single roll of a set of fair dice has the possible outcomes of 1, 2, 3, 4, 5, or 6 for each of the die, each with the same probability: 1/6. Rolling an even number means that a 2 OR 4 OR 6 is rolled. These three events (2, 4, 6) are non overlapping, and hence exclusive, so we can use the OR rule, giving Pr(Roll Even) = Pr(2) + Pr(4) + Pr(6) = 3/6 = 1/2.

What is the probability of rolling a 5, and then getting a heads in the coin flip?

The dice roll and coin flip are independent events, as the outcome of one does not influence the outcome of the other. Hence, Pr(Heads AND Roll 5) = Pr(Heads) x Pr(5) = 1/2 x 1/6 = 1/12.

Conditional Probability: Conditional probability can be used to compute joint probabilities when A and B are NOT independent (i.e., knowing that A has occurred provides information on whether or not B has occurred). The joint probability of A and B, Pr(A,B), is the product of the probability of B, Pr(B), and the probability of A given B, Pr(A|B). Therefore:

Pr(A,B) = Pr(A|B) Pr(B)
Where:
Pr (A|B) = The conditional probability of A given B = Pr(A,B)/Pr(B).

A and B are said to be independent of one another if Pr(A|B) = Pr(A), so that knowing event B occurred provides us with no information about event A.

An important use for conditional probabilities is to compute the probability of some complex event by conditioning on other events. For example, suppose that event A occurs under one of three other mutually exclusive events, say B, C, and D. Then, Pr(A) = Pr(A|B) x Pr(B) + Pr(A|C) x Pr(C) + Pr(A|D) x Pr(D). For another example, suppose that there are three genotypes with different disease risks, where event A is having the disease, and B, C, and D are three different genotypes. Then, Pr(A|D) is the risk of the disease for genotype D, and so forth. The overall risk of the disease is just the weighted risk over all genotypes.

Disease relative risks: What is the risk that you will have a disease given that your sibling (brother/sister) has the same disease?

This is quantified by the disease relative risk, RR, where:
1. RR = Prob(Sib 1 Affected |Sib 2 is Affected)/Prob(Random Individual Affected).
2. RR = The increase in your risk over that for a random individual.

Note: RR = 1 if Prob(Sib 1 Affected|Sib 2 is Affected) = Prob(Random Individual Affected); i.e., you have no increased risk given a relative has the disease.

Therefore, the disease relative risk is the increase in the conditional probability for a sibling (or other relative) vs. a random individual.

For example, consider diabetes: The probability that a random individual (from the US population) has type-1 diabetes is 0.4 percent. This is also referred to as the population prevalence, K. However, the frequency of diabetes in families with an affected sibling is 6 percent. The resulting relative risk that an individual has diabetes, given that its sibling does, is 6/0.4 = 15.

What is the probability that a pair of sibs both have diabetes?

Pr(Both Siblings Affected) = Pr(2nd Affected|1st is Affected) Pr(1st Affected)
Where:
(2nd Affected|1st is Affected) = RR x K, as RR = Pr(2nd Affected|1st is Affected)/K

Pr(Both Siblings Affected) = (RR x K) x K = (K^2) x RR = 0.06 x 0.004 = 0.00024. Hence, the population frequency of families with both siblings affected is 15 times more common than would be expected by chance (i.e., if the disease is independent of family membership, which is K^2).

Example: Rheumatoid Arthritis

Consider the following data for individuals with rheumatoid arthritis (from del Junco et al, 1984):

	Disease	**No Disease**	**Total**
Siblings of Affected Individuals	21	475	496
Spouses of Affected Individuals	12	661	673

1. Prob(2nd Sibling Affected|1st is Affected) = 21/496 = 0.042
2. Prob(Random Affected) = 12/673 = 0.018
3. Relative Risk, RR = 0.042/0018 = 2.374

Evolution

Evolution

Evolution is the change in gene (allele) frequencies over time. Evolution takes place at the population level, not at the individual level. In other words, populations evolve over time, but individuals do not. In terms of evolution, a population is a group of interbreeding individuals of the same species that share a common geographical area. A species is a group of populations that have the potential to interbreed in nature and produce viable offspring. And, a gene pool is the sum total of all of the alleles within a population. The four processes of evolution are as follows:

- Mutation – Changes in the nucleotide sequences of genomic DNA. Mutations provide new alleles, and are therefore the ultimate source of variation.
- Recombination – The reshuffling of the genetic material during meiosis (i.e., prophase I & metaphase I).
- Natural selection – Differential reproduction, with the fittest species surviving for future reproduction.
- Reproductive isolation – Geographical isolation of a population, allowing for interbreeding only within that population, and the eventual adaptation of that population to their particular environmental surroundings.

Note: Mutation and recombination provide natural variation, which is the raw material for evolution.

Hardy-Weinberg law

Prior to the beginning of the 20th century, biologists believed that natural selection would eventually result in the dominant alleles eliminating the recessive alleles. Therefore, over a period of time, genetic variation would eventually be eliminated in a population. As a challenge to this belief, a geneticist, Punnett, was asked to explain the prevalence of blue eyes in humans despite the fact that it is recessive to brown. However, he was unable to do so, and therefore recruited a mathematician colleague, named Hardy, to explain it. Coincidentally, a physician, named Weinberg, also came up with an explanation similar to Hardy's, thus forming the Hardy-Weinberg law. The Hardy-Weinberg law states that the frequencies of alleles within a population will remain constant unless acted upon by outside agents or forces. In the absence of outside forces, populations are non-evolving and are said to be in Hardy-Weinberg equilibrium. The following forces will disrupt Hardy-Weinberg equilibrium causing evolution to occur:

- Mutation – By definition, mutations change allele frequencies, causing evolution.
- Migration – If new alleles are brought in by immigration, or old alleles are taken out by emigration, then the frequencies of alleles will change, causing evolution.
- Genetic drift – Random events that occur due to a small population size. Random events have little effect on larger populations.
- Nonrandom mating – For each allele in the population to have an equal chance of uniting with any other allele, and thus for the proportions in the population to remain the same, each individual in the population must have an equal chance of mating with any other individual in the population at random. However, most mating in nature is not random because most individuals choose their partner. Sexual selection is an example of nonrandom mating in which mates are selected on the basis of physical or behavioral characteristics.
- Natural selection – For a population to be in Hardy-Weinberg equilibrium there can be no natural selection, which means that all genotypes must be equal in reproductive success. However, according to Darwin's reasoning:
  - All species reproduce in excess of the numbers that can survive; however, adult populations remain relatively constant. Therefore, there must be a severe struggle for survival.

All species vary in many characteristics; and, some of the variants confer an advantage or disadvantage in the struggle for life. Therefore, natural selection favors the survival and reproduction of the more advantageous variants, and the elimination of the less advantageous variants. Since one or more of these events are always acting upon natural populations, the Hardy-Weinberg equilibrium sets up conditions that are very unlikely to occur in nature. Therefore, evolution is occurring in most natural populations.

Genetic drift

Intense natural selection or a disaster can cause a *population bottleneck*, which is a severe reduction in population size that reduces the diversity of a population. The survivors have very little genetic variability and little chance to adapt if the environment changes. Consider a population of 1 million almond trees with a frequency of r at 10%. If a severe ice storm wiped out half of the population, leaving 500,000, then it is very likely that the r allele would still be present in the population. However, suppose that the initial population size of almond trees were 10 (with the same frequency of r at 10%). In this case, it is likely that the same ice storm could wipe the r allele entirely out of the small population. For another example, by the 1890's, the population of northern elephant seals was reduced to only 20 individuals by hunters. Even though the population has increased to over 30,000 since then, there is no genetic variation in the 24 alleles sampled. A single allele has been fixed by genetic drift and the bottleneck effect. In contrast, southern elephant seals have wide genetic variation because their numbers have never reduced by such hunting.

The bottleneck effect, combined with inbreeding, is an especially serious problem for many endangered species because great reductions in their numbers have reduced their genetic variability. This makes them especially vulnerable to changes in their environments and/or diseases. Sometimes a population bottleneck or migration event can cause a *founder effect*. A founder effect occurs when a few individuals that are unrepresentative of the gene pool start a new population. For example, a recessive allele causes the homozygous recessive condition, dwarfism. In Switzerland, the condition occurs in 1 out of 1,000 individuals, while amongst the 12,000 Amish now living in Pennsylvania the condition occurs in 1 out of 14 individuals. This higher frequency is because all of the Amish are descendants of 30 people whom migrated from Switzerland in 1720, and those 30 individuals carried a higher than normal percentage of genes for dwarfism.

Natural selection

Natural selection is differential reproduction where the fittest species survive environmental challenges. Organisms with more advantageous gene combinations secure more resources, which allow them to leave more progeny. It is a negative force: nature selects against, not for. There are three types of selection:

- Stabilizing selection – Selection maintains an already well adapted condition by eliminating any marked deviations from it. As long as the environment remains unchanged, the fittest organisms will also remain unchanged. For example, fur color in mammals varies considerably but certain camouflage colors predominate in specific environments. Stabilizing selection accounts for "living fossils", which are organisms that have remained seemingly unchanged for millions of years.
- Directional selection – Favors one extreme form over others, which eventually produces a change in the population. Directional selection occurs when an organism must adapt to changing conditions. Industrial melanism in the peppered moth (Biston betularia) during the industrial revolution in England is one of the best document examples of directional selection: when increased soot from the industrial revolution darkened the lichens on tree trunks that the light-colored moths used as a camouflage, the population of the lighter-colored moths decreased rapidly, and the frequency of the dark allele increased from less than 1% to over 98% in just 50 generations. Since the 1950's, attempts to reduce industrial pollution in Britain have resulted in an increase in numbers of light moths.
- Disruptive selection – Occurs when two or more character states are favored. For example, African butterflies (Pseudacraea eurytus) range in color from orange to blue. Both the orange and blue forms mimic other foul tasting species (models), so they are rarely eaten. Natural selection eliminates the intermediate forms because they do not look like the models.

Ultimately, natural selection leads to *adaptation*, which is the accumulation of structural, physiological, or behavioral traits that increase an organism's fitness.

Fitness

Darwin marveled at the "perfection of structure" that made it possible for organisms to do whatever they needed to do to stay alive and produce offspring. He called this perfection of structure *fitness*, by which he meant the combination of all traits that help organisms survive and reproduce in their environment. Fitness is now measured as reproductive success, or the number of progeny left behind who carry on the parental genes. Those who fail to contribute to the next or succeeding generations are unfit.

Diploidy and heterozygosity

Diploidy and heterozygosity help to maintain genetic variation. Even though only exposed alleles (those that cause a phenotypic difference) are subject to natural selection in sexually reproducing organisms, heterozygous diploid organisms may be a repository of rare recessive alleles. Recessive alleles provide "genetic insurance" should the environment change.

Sickle cell anemia

Sickle cell anemia is a potentially fatal disease that results from homozygous recessive alleles that code for one of the four polypeptide chains of hemoglobin, the oxygen-transporting molecule in human blood. The mutant form of hemoglobin causes the red blood cells to collapse, forming a variety of odd shapes, including some that are sickle shaped. As a result, their oxygen carrying capacity is much reduced, and they tend to clog up tiny capillaries. Affected individuals exhibit a variety of symptoms, and they usually have considerably shortened lives. Despite the lethality of the allele, it occurs at frequencies as high as 40% in some parts of tropical Africa. By contrast, it occurs at less than 5% in African Americans, and at 0.1% in Caucasian Americans. The high frequency in tropical Africa is maintained because the heterozygous condition confers resistance to malaria, and natural selection has acted to preserve it in areas traditionally high in malaria.

Note: The same trait may be an advantage in one environment, yet a disadvantage in another.

Adaptive radiation

Adaptive radiation is the evolution of a single evolutionary stock into a number of different species. Starting with a single common ancestor, adaptive radiation allows for the evolution of a variety of species that are adapted to particular elements of their environments. An example of this is the differences in beak sizes and shapes of the 14 different finch species that Darwin discovered in the Galapagos Islands: each species were adapted to different food sources.

Convergent and divergent evolution

Convergent evolution is the independent acquisition over time of similar characteristics in unrelated species that are subject to similar selection pressures (convergence of analogous traits). Divergent evolution is the evolution of differences among closely related species because of differing selection pressures in their particular environments (divergence of homologous traits).

Example of convergent evolution
Spiny anteaters, pangolins and giant anteaters all eat a diet of mainly ants and termites. Each of these animals lives on a different continent and is basically unrelated to each other. Each of them has a long, sticky, wormlike tongue and big claws to dig with. So, despite the

fact that each of them has come from a different ancestor, they resemble each other and make a living in a similar way (i.e., they eat ants). Therefore, while the ancestors of these animals were different, these animals have evolved similar ways to exploit a resource that is hard to eat.

<u>Example of divergent evolution</u>
Male wolf spiders can use vibrations or visual signals to attract and mate with females. In two species that came from a common ancestor that used visual and vibratory signals, one uses a visual signal while the other uses vibrations (beating its legs on the ground). One lives in a flat habitat, in which vision is not obscured at all, and uses visual signals; the other lives in a complex forest habitat, in which you cannot see very far, and it uses vibrations to signal. These two species have diverged in their signaling behavior because of different selective pressures acting upon them.

Comparative anatomy

Comparative anatomy is the study of similarities and differences in the anatomy of different organisms, and is very similar to evolutionary biology. Comparative anatomy classifies organisms based upon their anatomical structures, and indicates whether various organisms share a common ancestor. An example of comparative anatomy is the presence of similar bone structures in the forearms of humans, cats, whales, and bats. While it is likely that they all once shared a common function, they all serve different functions today, even with common structural parts: humans–hands, cats–paws, whales–fins, and bats–wings. This occurs due to descent from a common ancestor, with modifications due to random mutations and natural selection, allowing each organism to better adapt to their particular environment.

Homology and analogy

Two major concepts in comparative anatomy are homology and analogy. Homology (homologous traits) refers to similar characteristics in two animals that are a result of common ancestry (descent). Analogy (analogous traits) refers to similarity (or equivalence) in function, morphology, etc. that has arisen independently (i.e., similar selective pressures have resulted in similar traits in unrelated taxa). Animal species that come from the same ancestor are usually similar (i.e., they share characteristics). This is homology, or similarity, as a result of descent. On the other hand, if different species evolve similar traits to adapt to similar environments, then this is analogy as the result of convergent evolution (i.e., they are similar because it is a good trait, not because of descent).

Anatomical terminology

Anatomical Plane	Orientation
Sagittal	Plane parallel to the sagittal suture; divides the body into left and right portions.
Coronal	Plane that divides the body into dorsal (front) and ventral (back) portions.
Transverse	Axial plane that divides the body into cranial (head) and caudal (tail) portions.

Anatomical Term	Direction
Ipsilateral	On the same side.
Contralateral	On the opposite side.
Superficial	On the outside surface.
Deep	Away from the surface.
Intermediate	Between two structures.
Visceral	Associated with organs within body cavities.
Parietal	Associated with the wall of the body cavity.
Axial	Toward the central axis.
Abaxial	Away from the central axis.
Rostral	Toward the nose/mouth.
Caudal	Toward the tail/posterior (or feet in humans).

Directional Term	Defined Axis	Synonym	Direction
Anterior	Anteroposterior	Rostrocaudal Craniocaudal Cephalocaudal	From head to tail (opposite end).
Posterior			
Dorsal	Dorsoventral		From the spinal column (back) to the belly (front).
Ventral			
Left (lateral)	Left-Right	Dextrosinistral Sinistrodextral	From left to right.
Right (lateral)			
Medial	Mediolateral		From the center of the body to one side or the other.
Lateral			
Proximal	Proximodistal		From the tip of an appendage to where it joins the body.
Distal			

Lines of orientation in the thorax

1. Midsternal line – The midline of the body.
2. Lateral sternal line – A vertical line along the lateral sternal margin.
3. Midclavicular line – A vertical line, parallel to the midsternal line, which runs through a point midway between the center of the jugular notch and the tip of the acromion.
4. Midaxillary line – A line that passes vertically from the apex of the axilla down the lateral wall of the thorax.
5. Midscapular line – Runs vertically through the apex of the inferior angle of the scapula.

Vertebral levels

1. Jugular (suprasternal) notch – At the same horizontal level as the lower border of the body of the 2nd thoracic vertebra.
2. Sternal angle – At the level of the disc between the 4th and 5th thoracic vertebrae.
3. Xiphisternal junction – At the level of the intervertebral disc between the 9th and 10th thoracic vertebrae.

Organic Chemistry

Periodic Table of the Elements

	IA	IIA	IIIB	IVB	VB	VIB	VIIB	VIII	VIII	VIII	IB	IIB	IIIA	IVA	VA	VIA	VIIA	0
1	1 H																	2 He
2	3 Li	4 Be											5 B	6 C	7 N	8 O	9 F	10 Ne
3	11 Na	12 Mg											13 Al	14 Si	15 P	16 S	17 Cl	18 Ar
4	19 K	20 Ca	21 Sc	22 Ti	23 V	24 Cr	25 Mn	26 Fe	27 Co	28 Ni	29 Cu	30 Zn	31 Ga	32 Ge	33 As	34 Se	35 Br	36 Kr
5	37 Rb	38 Sr	39 Y	40 Zr	41 Nb	42 Mo	43 Tc	44 Ru	45 Rh	46 Pd	47 Ag	48 Cd	49 In	50 Sn	51 Sb	52 Te	53 I	54 Xe
6	55 Cs	56 Ba	57 • La	72 Hf	73 Ta	74 W	75 Re	76 Os	77 Ir	78 Pt	79 Au	80 Hg	81 Tl	82 Pb	83 Bi	84 Po	85 At	86 Rn
7	87 Fr	88 Ra	89 + Ac	104 Rf	105 Ha	106 106	107 107	108 108	109 109	110 110								

• Lanthanide Series	58 Ce	59 Pr	60 Nd	61 Pm	62 Sm	63 Eu	64 Gd	65 Tb	66 Dy	67 Ho	68 Er	69 Tm	70 Yb	71 Lu
+ Actinide Series	90 Th	91 Pa	92 U	93 Np	94 Pu	95 Am	96 Cm	97 Bk	98 Cf	99 Es	100 Fm	101 Md	102 No	103 Lr

Organic chemistry

Organic chemistry is a subdiscipline of chemistry that involves the study of the structures, properties, and reactions of carbon-based compounds, hydrocarbons, and their derivatives. In addition to carbon, these compounds may be composed of hydrogen, nitrogen, oxygen, phosphorus, silicon, sulfur, and the halogens. Organic compounds are numerous and diverse, have an enormous range of applications, and form the basis for almost all life processes.

Organic versus inorganic compounds

Organic	Inorganic
Volatile	Non-Volatile
Low Melting Point	High Melting Point
Low Boiling Point	High Boiling Point
Covalent or Van der Waals Bonding	Ionic Bonding
Insoluble in Water	Soluble in Water
Slow Reactions	Fast Reactions

Carbon

The special role of carbon in chemistry is the result of a combination of factors, including the number of valence electrons on a neutral carbon atom, the electronegativity of carbon, and the atomic radius of carbon atoms. The following are the physical properties of carbon:
- Electronic Configuration – $1s^2\ 2s^2\ 2p^2$
- Electronegativity – 2.55
- Covalent Radius – 0.077 nm

Carbon has four valence electrons, $2s^2\ 2p^2$, and it must either gain four electrons or lose four electrons in order to reach the noble-gas configuration. The electronegativity of carbon is too small for carbon to gain electrons from most elements in order to form C^{4-} ions, and too large for carbon to lose electrons in order to form C^{4+} ions. Therefore, carbon forms covalent bonds with a large number of other elements, including the hydrogen, nitrogen, oxygen, phosphorus, and sulfur atoms that are found in living systems. Because they are relatively small, carbon atoms can come close enough together to form strong double bonds (C=C), or even triple bonds (C ≡ C). Carbon also forms strong double and triple bonds to nitrogen and oxygen. It can even form double bonds to elements, such as phosphorus or sulfur, which do not form double bonds to themselves.

Catenation

Carbon atoms are unique amongst all of the elements that are found in nature. In particular, they can form long-chain molecules. The ability of carbon to form long chains is called catenation. Carbon chains are formed because carbon atoms form tetravalent bonds with other carbon atoms. This structure can be repeated endlessly without disturbing the stability of the bonds or the compounds formed. The chains can also form branches, sub-branches, and rings. In addition, the rings can have more rings attached to them. The list is endless. Most amino acids are long-chain carbon molecules.

Carbon compounds are classified into two groups:
- Open-chain compounds, or aliphatic compounds.
- Closed-chain compounds, or cyclic compounds.

Organic compounds that form carbon-carbon chains are called aliphatic compounds, such as alkanes, alkenes, and alkynes. They are found in animal and vegetable fats, and do not have a strong aroma. Organic compounds that form closed rings are called cyclic compounds, such as benzene, vanillin, and phenol. Aromatic compounds are cyclic compounds that contain a 6-carbon ring with alternating double and single bonds. As their name suggests, they give off a very strong aroma.

> ➤ **Review Video: <u>Catenation</u>**
> Visit ***mometrix.com/academy*** and enter ***Code: 295775***

Covalent bonds

When a carbon atom forms a compound, it always forms covalent bonds. There are two types of covalent bonds: sigma bonds and pi bonds. When the covalent bond is linear, or aligned along the plane containing the atoms, the bond is known as sigma (s) bond. Sigma bonds are strong and the electron sharing is at its maximum. Methane, CH_4, is a good example of sigma bonding, and it has four of them. When the covalent bond is parallel, formed by the overlap of two p-orbital lobes, the bond is known as a pi bond. Relative to sigma bonds, pi bonds are usually weaker because they have less orbital overlap due to their parallel orientation. Single bonds are composed solely of sigma bonds, while double and triple bonds are composed of one sigma bond and either one or two pi bonds, respectively.

Hydrocarbons

Hydrocarbons are made up of carbon and hydrogen atoms only. Carbon forms sigma and pi bonds. Chains with all sp^3 hybridization have all single bonds (saturated, 1 sigma), and saturated hydro-carbons are called alkanes. Chains with sp^2 hybridization have double bonds (unsaturated, 1 sigma and 1 pi), and unsaturated hydrocarbons with even 1 double bond, but without triple bonds, are called alkenes. Chains with sp hybridization have triple bonds (unsaturated, 1 sigma and 2 pi), and unsaturated hydrocarbons with even 1 triple bond are called alkynes. Thus, there are three types of hydrocarbons:
- Alkanes – Saturated, connected with 1 sigma bond.
- Alkenes – Unsaturated, connected with 1 sigma and 1 pi bond.
- Alkynes – Unsaturated, connected with 1 sigma and 2 pi bonds.

The golden rule for remembering whether a given hydrocarbon is an alkane, an alkene, or an alkyne is to first count the number of carbon and hydrogen atoms that are present in the molecular formula, and then calculate the result as follows:
- If the number of hydrogen atoms is 2 more than 2x the number of carbon atoms, then the compound is an alkane.
- If the number of hydrogen atoms is same as 2x the number of carbon atoms, then the compound is an alkene.
- If the number of hydrogen atoms is 2 less than 2x the number of carbon atoms, then the compound is an alkyne.

The prefixes and suffixes of hydrocarbons are standardized by IUPAC.

<u>Hydrocarbon prefixes and their carbon-atom relationship</u>

Number of Carbon Atoms	Prefix Used
1	Meth-
2	Eth-
3	Prop-
4	But-
5	Pent-
6	Hex-
7	Hept-
8	Oct-
9	Non-
10	Dec-

Straight-chain hydrocarbons are named by combining the prefix for the number of carbon atoms in the chain together with the suffix "-ane" for alkanes, "-ene" for alkenes, or "-yne" for alkynes.

Naming of hydrocarbons with three or more carbon atoms

For hydrocarbons with three or more carbon atoms, branching of the chain is a clear possibility. The IUPAC rules for naming these hydrocarbons are as follows:
- Find the largest chain of carbon atoms.
- Name it similar to straight-chain hydrocarbons. This is called the parent hydrocarbon.
- Find the alkyl group of the branches, or the side chains.
- Number the carbon atoms in the straight chain so that the alkyl groups of the side chain come attached to the smallest-numbered carbon atom of the main chain.
- The position of the alkyl group gets the number of the carbon atom it is attached to.
- The IUPCA name is written first with the number of the side chain, then its alkyl group, and then the parent hydrocarbon.

> ➤ **Review Video: The Basics of Hydrocarbons**
> *Visit mometrix.com/academy and enter Code: 824749*

Alkyl groups

In inorganic chemistry, radicals are atoms or groups of atoms that always stay together in a reaction (e.g., –OH, –SO$_4$, etc.). In organic chemistry, radicals exist but in the form of groups of carbon and hydrogen atoms. A group that is formed by the removal of one hydrogen atom from an alkane molecule is called an alkyl group (e.g., the methyl group is represented as CH$_3$–, while the ethyl group is represented as C$_2$H$_5$–). The structures of the methyl and ethyl groups are shown below.

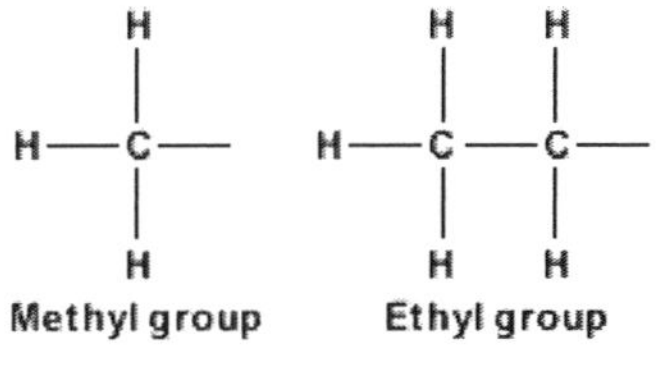

Methyl group   Ethyl group

Aliphatic compounds

Aliphatic compounds are derived from parent hydrocarbons. A hydrocarbon is a compound that is composed of hydrogen and carbon only. By replacing one or more of the hydrogen atoms from a hydrocarbon with a reactive atom from a group of atoms, X, a new compound can be formed. For example, a hydrocarbon R–H can be made to become R–X, where R is the carbon-hydrogen grouping, and X is a functional group. A functional group is an atom, or a group of atoms, which defines the function or the mode of activity of a given carbon compound, R–X. The functional group also determines the properties of the compound. However, aliphatic functional groups cannot be aromatic.

Standard organic functional groups

Functional Group	Name	Example
——OH	Hydroxyl	CH_3CH_2OH (ethanol)
–F, –Cl, –Br, and –I	Alkyl Halide	CH_3Br (methyl bromide)
——NH_2	Amine	CH_3NH_2 (methyl amine)
$\begin{array}{c} \vert \\ -\!\!-C-\!\!- \\ \vert \end{array}$	Alkyl	$CH_3CH_2CH_3$ (propane)
C=C	Alkenyl	$CH_3CH = CH_2$ (propene)
——O——	Ether	CH_3OCH_3 (dimethyl ether)
$\begin{array}{c} O \\ \parallel \\ -\!\!-C-\!\!H \end{array}$	Aldehyde	CH_3CHO (acetaldehyde)
$\begin{array}{c} O \\ \parallel \\ -\!\!-C-\!\!- \end{array}$	Ketone	CH_3COCH_3 (acetone)
$\begin{array}{c} O \\ \parallel \\ -\!\!-C-\!\!OH \end{array}$	Carboxylic Acid	CH_3CO_2H (acetic acid)
$\begin{array}{c} O \\ \parallel \\ -\!\!-C-\!\!O-\!\!- \end{array}$	Ester	$CH_3CO_2CH_3$ (methyl acetate)
$\begin{array}{c} O \\ \parallel \\ -\!\!-C-\!\!Cl \end{array}$	Acyl Chloride	CH_3COCl (acetyl chloride)
$\begin{array}{c} O \\ \parallel \\ -\!\!-C-\!\!NH_2 \end{array}$	Amide	CH_3NH_2 (acetamide)

Isomers

Organic compounds that have similar chemical formulas, but different structures, are called isomers. For example, a molecule of butane (C_4H_{10}) can have two structures or configurations: *n*-butane, which is a straight-chain structure, and isobutane, which is a branched-chain structure. Thus, *n*-butane and iso-butane are isomers of each other. A molecule of pentane (C_5H_{12}) can have three different structures: *n*-pentane, iso-pentane, and neo-pentane, all of which are isomers of each other. Because of differences in their structures, and therefore their electronic configurations and bondings, isomers exhibit different physical and chemical properties.

Characteristics of isomers are as follows:
- Isomers occur in organic compounds that have more than 3 carbon atoms.
- Organic compounds with 4 carbon atoms have 2 isomers, those with 5 carbon atoms have 3 isomers, those with 6 carbon atoms have 4 isomers, etc.
- As the number of carbon atoms increase, the ways in which the atoms can be arranged can become very complex: straight chains with branches, and branches with sub-branches, can increase the complexity. For example, an organic compound that has 10 carbon atoms will have 75 isomers.

> ➤ **Review Video: Basics of Isomers**
> *Visit **mometrix.com/academy** and enter **Code: 809623***

Organic compounds

Groups
In order to simplify the complexity of organic compounds, they are classified into groups. Just as elements within a group in the periodic table exhibit similar properties, organic compounds that show similar structures, and thus physical and chemical properties, are put together within a group, called a homologous series. They are arranged in increasing order by their molecular weights. In general, a homologous series is a group of organic compounds that have similar structures and chemical properties. The members of the homologous series differ from each other by their number of methylene ($-CH_2-$) groups only. The homologous series for alkanes is methane, ethane, propane, *n*-butane, etc. The series for alkenes is ethene, propene, butene, etc. And, the series for alkynes is ethyne, propyne, butyne, etc.

Key points
The following are key points for organic compounds:
- Atoms prefer filled valence shells. This rule explains why atoms make bonds, and the type of bonds that are created.
- If a molecule must have an unpaired electron (a.k.a. radical), then it is better to have the unpaired electron distributed over as many atoms as possible through resonance, inductive effects, and hyperconjugation.
- If a molecule must have a charge, then it is better to have the charge distributed over as many atoms as possible through resonance, inductive effects, and hyperconjugation.

- Most reactions involve nucleophiles (molecules with a location of particularly high electron density) attacking electrophiles (molecules with a location of particularly low electron density).
- Steric interactions (atoms bumping into one another) can prevent reactions by keeping the reactive atoms away from one another.
- There must be a reason for a reaction to take place.
- Delocalization ("dispersion of electron density") is always stabilizing, which is why it happens.
- The more reasonable the resonance structures that you can draw, the more stable the species, since this implies that more resonance can take place.
- In valid substitution reactions, you must have a good leaving group. Good leaving groups are the conjugate bases of strong acids (both organic and inorganic).
- You cannot have a positively charged (+) cation in a basic (pH > 10) solution. Only neutral atoms and C^-, N^-, or O^- are allowed.
- You cannot have a negatively charged (-) anion in an acidic (pH < 3) solution. Only neutral atoms and C^+, N^+ or O^+ are allowed.
- If conjugate bases are negatively charged (i.e., with an O^-, C^-, or N^-), then they will be stabilized by electron-withdrawing effects.
- Hydrolysis is the splitting of a bond in a molecule (usually a C–O or C–N bond) by the addition of molecules of water "across" the broken bond.
- Hydration is the addition of molecules of water "across" a double bond (i.e., C=C, C=O, C=N, etc.).

> ➤ **Review Video: Basics of Organic Compound Groups**
> *Visit **mometrix.com/academy** and enter **Code: 889859***

Analyzing organic compounds

Common techniques for analyzing organic compounds

Technique	Nature	Effect
Ultraviolet (UV) Spectrometry	Absorption of radiation in the UV region of the electromagnetic spectrum.	Affects the molecular energy levels of the electrons in atomic and molecular orbitals.
Visible Spectrometry	Absorption of radiation in the visible region of the electromagnetic spectrum.	Affects the energy levels of the electrons in atomic and molecular orbitals.
Infrared (IR) Spectrometry	Absorption of radiation in the IR region of the electromagnetic spectrum.	Changes the vibrational states of the bonds in the molecules.
Mass Spectrometry	This is the exception: it does not involve either absorption or emission of radiation.	The molecule is ionized and broken apart, and then the masses of the fragments (also ions) are measured.
Nuclear Magnetic Resonance (NMR) Spectrometry	Absorption of radiation.	Changes the spin state energy of the nuclei of the hydrogen atoms.

Ultraviolet and visible spectroscopy

Organic molecules absorb light in the ultraviolet region of the electromagnetic spectrum. However, organic molecules with conjugated double bonds tend to absorb light at relatively long wave-lengths. In some cases, the wavelengths fall in the visible region, resulting in highly colored species. Alkenes, for example, are found entirely in the visible region. Commonly, basic biochemical assays, such as Bradford and Lowry assays, utilize the conjugation of organic molecules with transition metals to alter the color of ionic solutions, which in turn affects the absorption of light in the visible region. The differences in absorption, when compared to the absorption of standards of known concentration, can be used to measure the quantities of such organic molecules.

IR Spectroscopy

Infrared (IR) radiation of a molecule causes the excitation of the vibrations of covalent bonds within that molecule. These vibrations include the stretching and bending modes. An IR spectrum shows the energy absorptions as one 'scans' the IR region of the electromagnetic spectrum. Most of the information that is used to interpret an IR spectrum is obtained from the functional group region. In practice, it is the polar covalent bonds than are IR "active", and whose excitation can be observed in an IR spectrum. In organic molecules, these polar covalent bonds represent the functional groups. Hence, the most useful information that can be obtained from an IR spectrum regards what functional groups are present within the molecule (NMR spectroscopy typically gives the hydrocarbon fragments). Remember that some functional groups can be "viewed" as combinations of different bond types. For example, an ester, CO_2R, contains both $C = O$ and $C - O$ bonds, and both are typically seen in an IR spectrum of an ester.

Mass spectrometry

Mass spectrometry involves the measurement of masses of organic compounds and their constituents. In the case of proteins, the peptides are initially digested with specific proteases, and the masses of the individual fragments are then measured and combined into a spectrograph to create a specific fingerprint for that protein. Since no two proteins are identical, the specific mass spectrograph for each protein is unique. This technique can therefore be utilized to determine the identity of unknown proteins within a sample.

NMR spectroscopy

Nuclear magnetic resonance (NMR) spectroscopy is used to determine the numbers and types of atoms that molecules are composed of by exploiting the magnetic properties of atoms and measuring their atomic spins. When interpreting NMR spectroscopy data, the number of signals indicates the number of different types of protons, but be careful about overlapping signals. Downfield shifts mean that the protons are deshielded. Integration only indicates the ratios of the numbers of protons. The signal shape indicates the dynamics of the proton environments. Splitting of a signal into a doublet, triplet, quartet, etc. is due to spin-spin coupling between the nuclei with non-zero nuclear spins. Remember that the multiplicity (doublet, triplet, quartet) <u>does not</u> indicate the number of protons on that carbon: the number of protons is given by the integration. Signal splitting arises <u>only for coupling</u> between nonequivalent nuclei. Hence, ethane is a singlet, and the methyl group of ethanol is only split by the adjacent methylene group.

Liquid-liquid extraction

Liquid-liquid extraction, also known as solvent extraction or partitioning, is a technique for separating compounds based upon their relative solubilities in two different immiscible solvents, typically water and an organic solvent. Generally, when an organic compound is to be isolated from an aqueous solution, the solution is thoroughly mixed with an organic solvent and then centrifuged to separate the two solvents. By then isolating the organic solvent layer, the organic compound can be isolated from the remaining non-organic compounds in the aqueous solution. One example of this technique that is commonly used in life-science and biochemistry laboratories to separate nucleic acid and protein mixtures is called a phenol-chloroform extraction. In phenol-chloroform extractions, a chaotropic agent, such as guanidinium thiocyanate or Trizol, is used to lyse cells while maintaining the integrity of the RNA and DNA in the extracts by denaturing any RNases or DNases. Subsequently, the cell lysates are thoroughly mixed with a phenol:chloroform mixture and then centrifuged to separate the aqueous and organic phases. Following separation, the polar nucleic acids will be found in the aqueous phase (chloroform), while proteins will be found in the organic phase (phenol). To further extract DNA or RNA from the chloroform mixture, nucleic acids can be precipitated using isopropanol and/or ethanol followed by centrifugation. The proteins can be extracted from the phenol mixture by precipitating them using ice-cold acetone and centrifugation.

Distillation

Distillation is a technique for separating liquid mixtures based upon their different volatilities in a boiling solution. Using distillation, a mixture of liquids in a still flask is boiled at a temperature just above the boiling point of the chemical of interest, and the vapor is then allowed to pass through a series of condensation tubes and finally condensed in a collection flask. When the boiling points of the different liquids are relatively close to one another, a fractionating column can be utilized, filled with trays, dishes, wire mesh, or even steel wool, in order to increase the surface area of the column so that the vapor has a greater chance of condensation. Since the higher boiling point liquids will condense more easily at the lower temperatures, the fractionating column allows any impure vapors to condense in the column and return to the flask, while the chemical of interest is allowed to pass through the fractionating column and into the condensation tubes. Distillation is used in a large number of commercial applications. For example, crude oil is distilled to separate it into fractions for specific uses, such as gasoline, kerosene, heating oil, motor oil, and even asphalt. Water is distilled to separate the liquid from impurities, such as salt and other chemicals. And, fermented solutions are also distilled in order to concentrate the alcohol from the initial fermented mash.

Chromatography

Chromatography is a name for a collection of techniques to separate solutions based upon their different rates of travel through a stationary phase. Because different molecules have different sizes and charges, different stationary phases can be utilized to retard the flow of different solutions through the stationary phase based upon these characteristics. In chromatography, the substance of interest is called an analyte, and the graphical output is called a chromatogram, which contains peaks of variable intensities at different time points representative of the different components of the mixture and their rates of travel through the stationary phase.

Common chromatographic techniques include the following:
- Paper chromatography – Separates mixtures of solutes based upon size. In this technique, a strip of chromatography paper is placed into a solvent, the solvent is allowed to flow through the paper, and the solutes in the solvent travel through the paper at different rates dependent upon their size, with smaller molecules traveling faster than larger molecules.
- Thin-layer chromatography – Functions similar to paper chromatography, except that a stationary thin layer of absorbent material, such as silica gel, alumina, or cellulose, is used rather than paper.
- Ion-exchange chromatography – Separates mixtures passed through an ionic-resin-filled column based upon charges. The ionic resin may be cationic or anionic.
- Size-exclusion chromatography – Separates mixtures based upon size, with larger molecules moving more quickly than smaller molecules. Using resins filled with small pores, the smaller molecules are retained longer in the resin, while the larger molecules are not retained and pass more quickly through the resin.
- Gas-liquid chromatography – Utilizes gas, such as argon, as the mobile phase. In gas-liquid chromatography, a liquid mixture containing the analyte is injected into a very long, coiled capillary column, and is forced through the column under very high temperature and pressure. As the substance is eluted through the column, smaller molecules travel more quickly than larger molecules.

Alkanes

Alkanes have the general formula C_nH_{2n+2}. In alkanes, the carbon atoms form 4 single bonds (or s (sigma) bonds) to 4 different atoms, and are referred to as saturated hydrocarbons, or paraffins, because they contain no multiple bonds. The simplest hydrocarbon, methane, contains a single carbon atom bonded to 4 hydrogen atoms (CH_4). The alkanes are named by adding the ending "ane" to their root names, such as methane, ethane, propane, etc. The following table gives the names and compositions of the first ten alkanes.

Names and formulas for the alkanes

Formula	Name	Functional Group
CH_4	Methane	CH_3-
C_2H_6	Ethane	C_2H_5-
C_3H_8	Propane	C_3H_7-
C_4H_{10}	Butane	C_4H_9-
C_5H_{12}	Pentane	$C_5H_{11}-$
C_6H_{14}	Hexane	$C_6H_{13}-$
C_7H_{16}	Heptane	$C_7H_{15}-$
C_8H_{18}	Octane	$C_8H_{17}-$
C_9H_{20}	Nonane	$C_9H_{19}-$
$C_{10}H_{22}$	Decane	$C_{10}H_{21}-$

Structural formulas for the alkanes

Methane, ethane, and propane: The structural formulas, which are the actual arrangements of different atoms in space of these substances, are shown below.

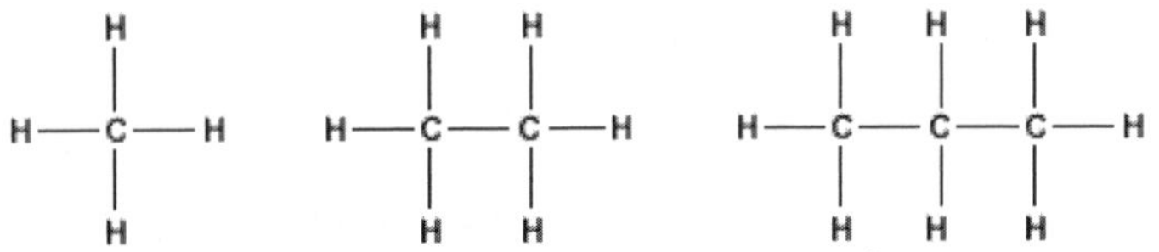

Structural formulae of some saturated hydrocarbons (or alkanes).
They all contain single bonds.

C_2H_6: Since C_2H_6 contains 2 carbon atoms, its prefix is "eth". With 6 hydrogen atoms, the compound conforms to the formula, C_nH_{2n+2}, and is thus an alkane with the suffix "ane". Therefore, C_2H_6 is the molecular formula for ethane. The structural formula for ethane is as follows:

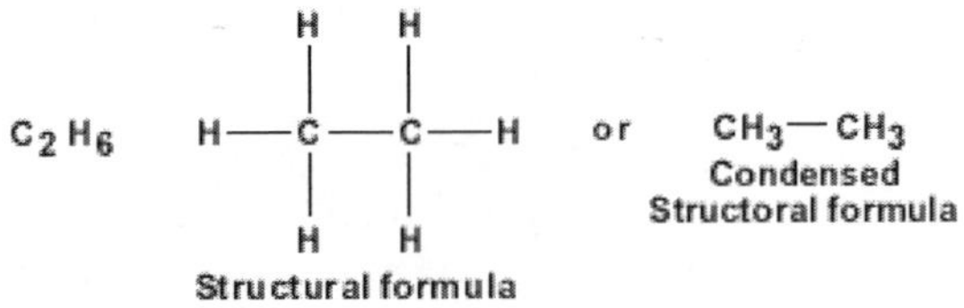

The carbon atoms are saturated, with each having four bonds attached to different atoms.

Butane:

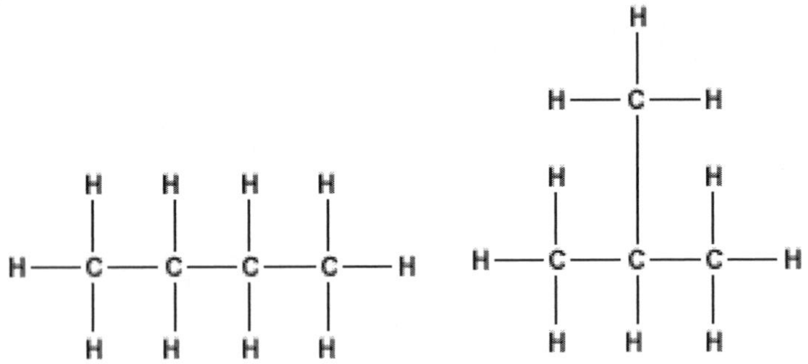

The straight-chain butane is called normal butane, or n-butane.

Pentane: Pentane (C_5H_{12}) can be represented by three different structural formulas:
- The simple straight-chain pentane is called n-pentane.
- Pentane with one branched chain is called isopentane, or 2-methylbutane.
- Pentane with two branched chains is called neopentane, or 2,2-dimethylpropane.

Properties of the alkanes
- Physical state – Lower molecular weight alkanes are gases at room temperature (i.e., methane, ethane, propane, and butane). Higher alkanes, up to those having 17

- 54 -

carbon atoms, are liquids at room temperature, while even higher alkanes are solids at room temperature.

- Melting and boiling points – Homologous alkanes show increases in their melting and boiling points with increased chain length, similar to the behavior of elements within the same group in the periodic table.
- Solubility – Alkanes, like all other organic chemicals, are insoluble in water. Instead, they are soluble in organic liquids. Alkanes are non-polar and are therefore soluble in other non-polar liquids, but they are not soluble in polar liquids, such as water.
- Combustion – Alkanes are flammable, and are easy to catch fire. Complete combustion of an alkane leads to carbon dioxide and water. During combustion, the supply of oxygen has to be sufficient: insufficient oxygen leads to the production of carbon monoxide, and the heat generated is less than when sufficient oxygen is available.
- Reactivity – Alkanes have saturated covalent bonds. Therefore, their reactivity with other chemicals is relatively low.
- Substitution reaction – In alkanes, substitution reactions are easily performed by the replacement of hydrogen atoms with more reactive atoms (e.g., chloride (Cl⁻)).

> **Review Video: Properties of Alkanes**
> *Visit **mometrix.com/academy** and enter **Code: 903333***

Methane
Chemical properties:
- Combustion – Methane burns in air with a blue flame. Methane produces a good amount of heat when it undergoes combustion, which is why it is used as a fuel.
- Reactivity – Methane is quite unreactive, except with fluorine, chlorine, etc. With these, it undergoes substitution reactions.

Uses:

- Because of its excellent burning capability, methane is used as a cooking gas.
- Methane is used to produce carbon dioxide gas.
- Methane is used to produce carbon black, which is used in rubber production.
- Methane is used as a starting material for other organic compounds, such as methyl chloride, methylene dichloride, chloroform, etc.

Alkenes

Hydrocarbons that contain two hydrogen atoms less than their corresponding alkanes are called alkenes, or olefins. They are called olefins because they react with chlorine to form oil-like derivatives (olefin means oil forming). Alkenes have at least one double bond, and are thus unsaturated carbon compounds. Their general formula is C_nH_{2n}, and their names are derived from the alkanes simply by changing the ending from "ane" into "ene" (e.g., propane → propene). The simplest of alkenes has two carbons connected by a double bond (1 sigma + 1 pi bond), called ethene (H–C=C–H). The table below gives the names and compositions of the first six alkenes.

Alkene	Number of C Atoms	Number of H Atoms	Molecular Formula
Ethene	2	4	C_2H_4
Propene	3	6	C_3H_6
Butene	4	8	C_4H_8
Pentene	5	10	C_5H_{10}
Hexene	6	12	C_6H_{12}
Heptene	7	14	C_7H_{14}

Ethene

A molecule of the simplest alkene, ethene, has five sigma bonds and one pi bond. The structural formula for ethene ($CH_2=CH_2$) is as follows:

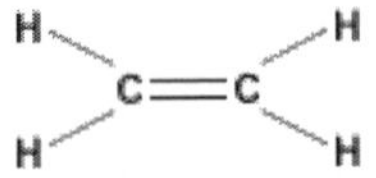

Ethylene
(Contains a double bond)

The next higher alkene is propene ($CH_3-CH=CH_2$). This has one double-bonded carbon atom.

The uses of ethene are as follows:
- Ethene is used for manufacturing organic compounds, such as ethanol and ethylene glycol. Ethylene glycol is used for making artificial fibers, like polyesters.
- Ethene is used for the manufacture of plastics. These plastics are made from the polymerization of ethene into polyethene. Polyethenes are used for making bags, electrical insulation, etc.
- Ethene is used for the artificial ripening of fruits, such as mangos, bananas, etc.

Benzene

Benzene consists of 6 carbon atoms linked together to form a hexagon. Each C atom is attached to two other C atoms and one hydrogen atom, and there are alternating double and single bonds between the C atoms. Experimentally, the C – C bonds in benzene are all the same length, and benzene is planar. We write resonance structures for benzene in which there are single bonds between each pair of C atoms and the 6 additional electrons are delocalized over the entire ring. This structure is depicted by a hexagon, representing benzene, with a circle contained within the hexagon that represents the delocalized electrons. Benzene belongs to a category of organic molecules that are called aromatic compounds (due to their odor). Aromatic compounds were being extracted from coal tar as early as the 1830s. As a result, many of these compounds were given common names that are still in use today. A few of these compounds are shown below.

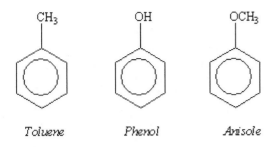

Toluene   Phenol   Anisole

Alkynes

Hydrocarbons that have at least two carbon atoms connected by an unsaturated triple bond are called alkynes. Their general formula is C_nH_{2n-2}, and their names are derived from the alkanes simply by changing the ending from "ane" into "yne" (e.g., propane → propyne). The simplest of alkynes has two carbon atoms connected by a triple bond (1 sigma + 2 pi bonds), called ethyne (H–C≡C–H). The table below gives the names and compositions of the first six alkynes (with 1 triple bond).

Alkyne	Number of C Atoms	Number of H Atoms	Molecular Formula
Ethyne	2	2	C_2H_2
Propyne	3	4	C_3H_4
Butyne	4	6	C_4H_6
Pentyne	5	8	C_5H_8
Hexyne	6	10	C_6H_{10}
Heptyne	7	12	C_7H_{12}

> ➤ **Review Video: Basics of Alkynes**
> *Visit **mometrix.com/academy** and enter **Code: 963837***

Reactions with hydrocarbons

Combustion of hydrocarbons

Alkanes, alkenes, and alkynes all undergo combustion reactions in the presence of O_2 and heat. Alkanes are less reactive than both alkenes and alkynes, which are generally highly exothermic. Alkanes burn with a blue flame, while both alkenes and alkynes burn with a yellow flame. All three give off carbon monoxide or soot if not burned in the presence of adequate amounts of O_2, and become increasingly difficult to ignite as their number of carbon atoms increase. The equation for complete combustion is as follows:

$C_nH_{2n+2} + (1.5n+0.5)O_2 →$ (n+1)H_2O +nCO_2

In the absence of sufficient O_2, the following equations may apply:

$C_nH_{2n+2} + (n+0.5)O_2 →$ (n+1)H_2O + nCO   (Carbon Monoxide)

$C_nH_{2n+2} + (0.5n+0.5)O_2 →$ (n+1)H_2O + nC   (Soot)

Nucleophilic aliphatic substitution

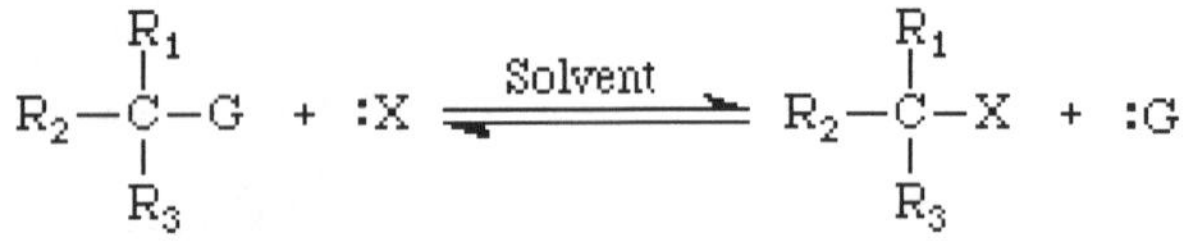

Where:

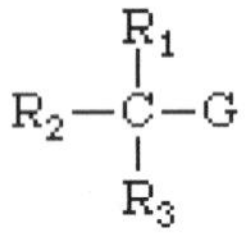

= The substrate.

R = The side group, generally an H, alkyl, or aryl.
:X = A nucleophilic reagent.
G = The leaving group.

Halogenation
Halogenation is the reaction of the carbon-carbon double bond in alkenes, such as ethene, with halogens, such as chlorine, bromine, and iodine. Reactions where the chlorine or bromine are in solution (e.g., "bromine water") are slightly more complicated, and are treated separately.

Polymerization
Polymerization is a process whereby long-chain molecules are formed from shorter chains. Alkenes, like ethene, undergo polymerization. Ethene is an unsaturated gas. For making a long-chain polymer, all of its pi bonds can be broken apart, and another ethene can be attached. Then, the pi bond of the second ethene molecule can be broken apart to add another ethene molecule. In this way, a very-long-chain molecule, or polymer, can be produced. When ethene gas is heated to a temperature $\geq 200°C$, and at a pressure ≥ 2000 atmospheres, it polymerizes to become a solid, called polyethene.
A large number of ethene molecules join together to make polythene (the "n" can be as large as 1000), and the molecular weight is very large.

Diels-Alder reaction
The Diels-Alder Reaction is a conjugate-addition reaction of a conjugated diene to an alkene (the dienophile) in order to produce a cyclohexene. Examples of the Diels-Alder reaction can be seen below.

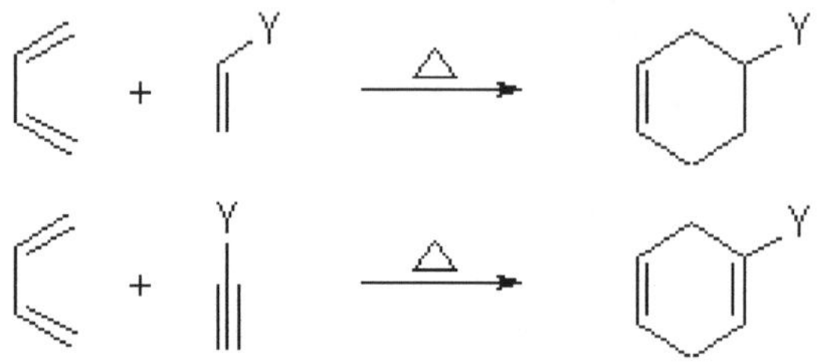

The [4+2]-cycloaddition of a conjugated diene and a dienophile (an alkene or alkyne) is an electro-cyclic reaction that involves the 4 π-electrons of the diene and 2 π-electrons of the dienophile. The driving force of the reaction is the formation of new σ-bonds, which are energetically more stable than the π-bonds. In the case of an alkynyl dienophile, the initial

- 58 -

adduct can still react as a dienophile if not too sterically hindered. In addition, either the diene or the dienophile can be substituted with cumulated double bonds, such as substituted allenes.

Substituents of aromatic rings

There are three ways in which a pair of substituents can be placed on an aromatic ring. In the ortho (o) isomer, the substituents are in adjacent positions on the ring. In the meta (m) isomer, they are separated by one carbon atom. And, in the para (p) isomer, they are on opposite ends of the ring. The three isomers of dimethylbenzene, or xylene, are shown below.

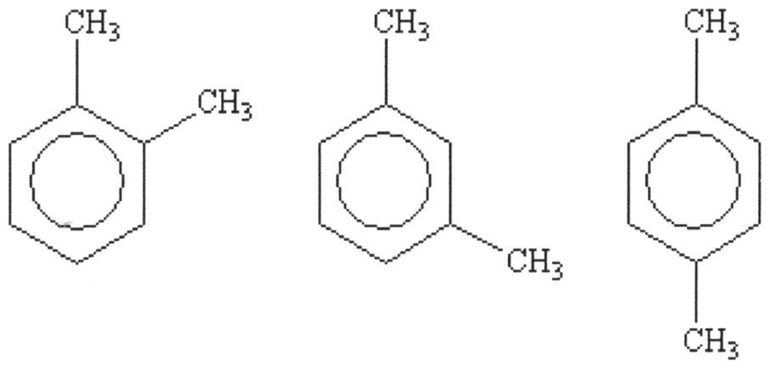

Ortho   *Meta*   *Para*

Alcohols

Organic compounds that have the hydroxyl group (–OH) attached to carbon atoms are known as alcohols. Methyl alcohol (CH_3OH) is the simplest of the alcohols. This is also known as methanol. The next higher alcohol is ethyl alcohol (C_2H_5OH), or ethanol. An alcohol is produced by replacing one hydrogen from an alkane with a hydroxyl group. The two equations below show how methanol and ethanol are made:

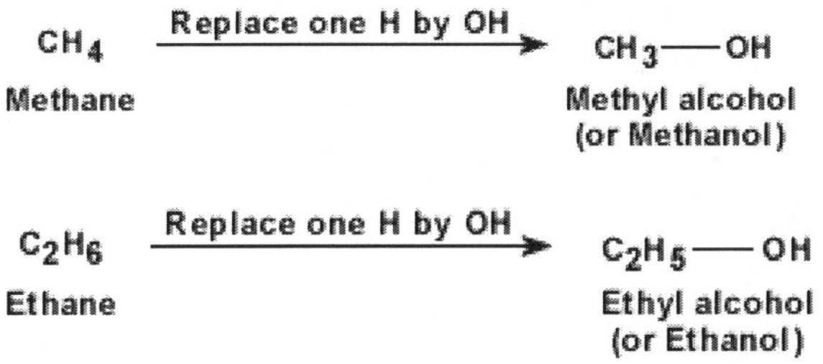

CH_4 $\xrightarrow{\text{Replace one H by OH}}$ CH_3——OH

Methane   Methyl alcohol
                                           (or Methanol)

C_2H_6 $\xrightarrow{\text{Replace one H by OH}}$ C_2H_5——OH

Ethane   Ethyl alcohol
                                           (or Ethanol)

In the IUPAC naming system, the names of alcohols are derived by the replacement of the terminal "e" of the hydrocarbon name with "ol" (e.g., propane → propanol). The IUPAC rules for naming alcohols are as follows:

- Find the alkane from which the alcohol is made, and name it similar to the nomenclature for straight-chain hydrocarbons. This is called the parent hydrocarbon.
- Find where the hydroxyl group is attached: in the branches or in the side chains.
- Number the carbon atoms in the straight chain so that the hydroxyl group of the side chain is attached to the smallest-numbered carbon atom.
- The position of the hydroxyl group gets the number of the carbon atom it is attached to.

> ➢ **Review Video: Basics of Alcohols**
> *Visit **mometrix.com/academy** and enter **Code:** **105795***

Phenols

Phenols are another class of alcohols in which an –OH group is attached to an aromatic ring, as shown in the figure below. Phenols are potent disinfectants. When antiseptic techniques were first introduced in the 1860s by Joseph Lister, it was phenol (or carbolic acid, as it was then known) that was used. Phenol derivatives, such as o-phenylphenol, are still used in commercial disinfectants, such as Lysol.

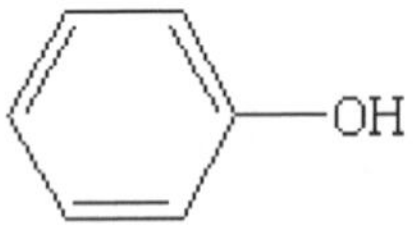

Phenol

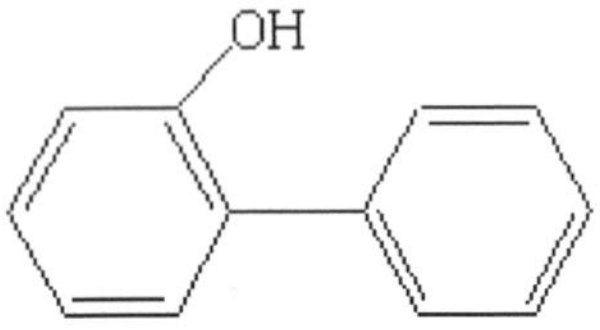

o-Phenylphenol

Physical properties of alcohols

The following are the physical properties of alcohols:

- Physical state – Alcohols are colorless liquids at ordinary room temperature.
- Odor – Lower members of the alcohol group have a characteristic fruity smell.
- Density – Alcohols are lighter than water.
- Solubility – Alcohols, such as methanol and ethanol, are completely soluble (miscible) in water. Longer-chain members of the alcohol group tend to be less soluble in water.
- Acidic nature – Alcohols are neutral liquids, and have no effect on litmus, or other acidity, tests.
- Conductivity – Alcohols are covalently bonded compounds, and are thus are non-ionic and non-conductors of electricity.

> ➢ **Review Video: Physical Properties of Alcohols**
> *Visit **mometrix.com/academy** and enter **Code:** **926662***

Properties of methanol

The following are the properties of methanol:

- Methanol is a colorless liquid at room temperature.
- Methanol has a slight fruity odor.
- The boiling point of methanol is 64.5°C.
- Methanol is completely miscible in water.
- The density of methanol is less than water.
- Methanol is a neutral solution, and shows negative results for all acidity tests.
- Methanol is poisonous, and can cause blindness if ingested.
- Methanol is very flammable, and burns with a pale blue flame. It forms carbon dioxide and water upon complete oxidation, or combustion.
- Methanol reacts with Na^+ to give off hydrogen gas.
- Methanol reacts with ethanoic acid to give methyl ethanoate, which is an ester.

Solubilities of alcohols

As a general rule, polar or ionic substances dissolve in polar solvents, while nonpolar substances dissolve in nonpolar solvents. As a result, hydrocarbons do not dissolve in water. They are often said to be immiscible (literally, "not mixable") in water. Alcohols, as might be expected, have properties between the extremes of hydrocarbons and water. When the hydrocarbon chain is short, the alcohol is soluble in water. There is no limit on the amount of methanol (CH_3OH) and ethanol (CH_3CH_2OH), for example, that can dissolve in a given quantity of water. As the hydrocarbon chain becomes longer, the alcohol becomes less soluble in water. One end of the alcohol molecules is so nonpolar in character that it is said to be hydrophobic (literally, "water hating"). The other end contains an –OH group that can form hydrogen bonds to neighboring water molecules, and is thus said to be hydrophilic (literally, "water loving"). As the hydrocarbon chain becomes longer, the hydrophobic character of the molecule increases, and the solubility of the alcohol in water gradually decreases until it becomes essentially insoluble in water.

Nucleophilic substitution reaction

Nucleophilic substitution (S_N1/S_N2) is the reaction of an electron-pair donor (the nucleophile, Nu) with an electron-pair acceptor (the electrophile). An sp^3-hybridized electrophile must have a leaving group (X) in order for the reaction to take place. An example of the nucleophilic substitution reaction can be seen below.

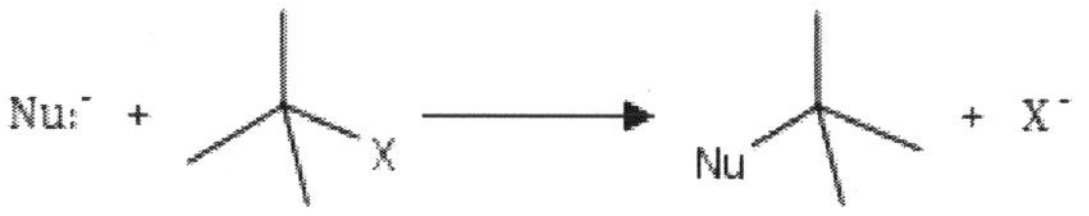

Combustion and oxidation of alcohols

The combustion of alcohols in air occurs very easily (e.g., methanol burns with a blue flame). Alcohols burn in air to give carbon dioxide and water. A large amount of heat is also generated during this chemical reaction. Oxidation differs from combustion in that the oxygen is supplied in a controlled fashion. Oxidation of alcohols gives rise to carbonic acids and water. The reaction of potassium dichloride and dilute sulphuric acid can provide atomic oxygen, or nascent oxygen, giving off methanoic acid and water as reaction products.

Pinacol rearrangement

The pinacol rearrangement reaction is a method of conversion of a 1,2-diol into a carbonyl under acidic conditions. In this reaction, one of the hydroxyl groups is protonated to form a carbocation, followed by the migration of an alkyl group from one of the adjacent carbons. The resultant oxonium ion has an increased relative stability, which serves as the driving force for the reaction.

Protection of alcohols

Since alcohol groups are subject to action by Grignard reagents, alcohol groups can be replaced by substituting groups that are later removed in order to maintain the presence and location of the alcohol group. For example, alcohols are easily sialated under mild conditions to form silyl ethers, which can later be reversed under mildly acidic conditions.

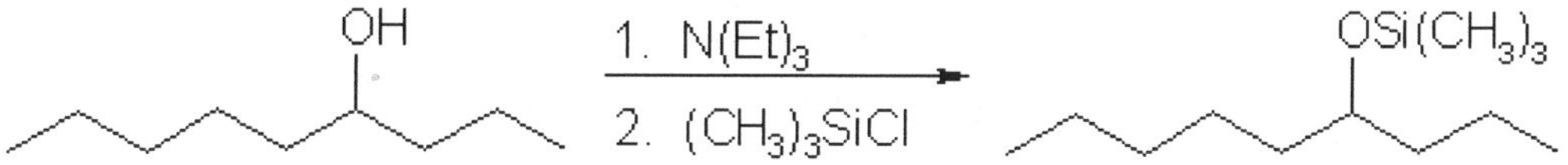

- 61 -

Tosylates

Alcohols can be converted into tosylates using tosyl chloride and a base to "mop-up" the HCl byproduct. Tosylates are good substrates for substitution reactions, used mostly for 1° and 2° ROH (S_N2 reaction). During these reactions, the –OH reacts first as a nucleophile, attacking the electrophilic center of the tosylate, displacing Cl^-, since tosylates have a much better leaving group: the conjugate base of tosic acid, pK_a = -2.8. The advantage of this method is that the substitution reactions are not under strongly acidic conditions. Tosylates react with nucleophiles in much the same way as alkyl halides. Alternatives to tosylates are mesylates (use CH_3SO_2Cl) and triflates (use CF_3SO_2Cl).

Reactions of alcohols with carboxylic acids

Carboxylic acids are organic acids. Alcohols react with carboxylic acids to form sweet-smelling organic compounds, called esters. The reaction of alcohols with carboxylic acids is called esterification. This is one of the major tests to see the presence of an alcoholic group in a sample of liquid mixtures. When methanol is heated with ethanoic acid in the presence of concentrated sulphuric acid, methyl ethanoate (an ester) and water are formed. The concentrated sulphuric acid acts as a catalyst for this reaction.

Alkanol reactions

The following are types of alkanol reactions:

- Dehydration (Elimination) – The products that are formed depend on the conditions used. For example, alkenes are formed in the presence of H_2SO_4 (H_3PO_4 is better since it does not produce as many by-products), and the correct temperature (hot for primary, warm for secondary, and cool for tertiary). Alcohols lose a water molecule.
- Oxidation – The products depend on the type of alcohol used: primary, secondary, or tertiary. For primary and secondary, a C=O bond replaces the C-OH, but this bond will either be at the end of the carbon chain (an aldehyde), or in the middle (a ketone). Aldehydes can be further oxidized to form carboxylic acids. Tertiary alcohols will not oxidise.
- Substitution – Not very important for the alcohols, except for halogenation using PCl_5, which may be used as an identifying test for the alcohol group.
- Reaction with active metals – Alcohols react with active metals, releasing hydrogen. This may also be used as an identifying test for alcohols.
- Esterification – This is the reaction between an alcohol and a carboxylic acid, which forms an ester link (-COO-), holding two carbon chains together. The conditions required for this reaction are concentrated H_2SO_4 and elevated temperatures.

> ➤ **Review Video: Alkanol Reactions**
> *Visit **mometrix.com/academy** and enter **Code: 788169***

Mitsunobu reaction

The Mitsunobu reaction allows for the conversion of primary and secondary alcohols to esters, amides, or thioethers. The nucleophile employed should be acidic, since one of the reagents (DEAD, diethylazodicarboxylate) must be protonated during the course of the reaction in order to prevent from side reactions. Examples of the Mitsunobu reaction can be seen below.

Preparation of aprotic solvents

Substances that cannot act as a source of a proton are said to be aprotic. Because ethers do not contain an –OH group, they are aprotic solvents. Ethers can be synthesized by splitting a molecule of water between two alcohols in the presence of heat and concentrated sulfuric acid.

$$2CH_3CH_2OH \xrightarrow{H^+} CH_3CH_2OCH_2CH_3$$

They can also be formed by reacting a primary alkyl halide with an alkoxide ion.

$$CH_3CH_2CH_2Br + CH_3O^- \longrightarrow CH_3CH_2CH_2OCH_3 + Br^-$$

Aldehydes and ketones

An aldehyde is an organic compound containing the formyl group, which is a carbonyl group bound to a terminal carbon, having the formula R-CHO. A ketone is an organic compound containing a carbonyl group bound to two carbon atoms, having the formula RC(=O)R′. An aldehyde differs from a ketone in that the carbonyl is located at the end of the compound rather than the middle. Both aldehydes and ketones are important in organic chemistry and industry. For example, many fragrances and fixatives are aldehydes, while many sugars and solvents are ketones. Aldehydes are generally named by replacing the suffix of the hydrocarbon with "-al", such as methane → methanal. In some special cases, non-conventional naming standards are used:

- If an aldehyde is added to a ring, then the suffix "–carbaldehyde" is used.
- If replacing the aldehyde group with a carboxyl (–COOH) group would yield a carboxylic acid with a trivial name, then the "–ic acid" ending can be replaced with "–oic acid" in the trivial name.
- If the compound is a natural product or carboxylic acid, then the prefix "n-oxo-" can be used to indicate the position of the aldehyde group, with "n" being the number of the carbon.

Ketones are named by replacing the suffix of the hydrocarbon with "-one", such as hexane → hexone. However, the most important ketones have generally retained trivial names, such as acetone and propriophenone.

Nucleophilic addition at the C=O bond

In aldehydes and ketones, nucleophiles react very readily at the carbonyl bond. During a nucleophile addition reaction, the carbonyl carbon converts from sp^2 to sp^3 hybridization, and the oxygen becomes protonated. If the nucleophile is an alcohol under acidic or basic conditions, then the product is a hemiacetal, which can be further reacted to produce an acetal and water under acidic conditions. If the nucleophile is an amine under acidic conditions, then the product is an imine-enamine tautomer (the imine form has a double-bonded nitrogen, while the enamine form has a single-bonded nitrogen).

Aldol addition/aldol reaction

'Aldol' is an abbreviation of aldehyde and alcohol. An aldol reaction is a reaction where the enolate of an aldehyde or a ketone reacts at the α-carbon with the carbonyl of another molecule, under basic or acidic conditions, in order to obtain β-hydroxy aldehyde or ketone. An example aldol addition/aldol reaction can be seen below.

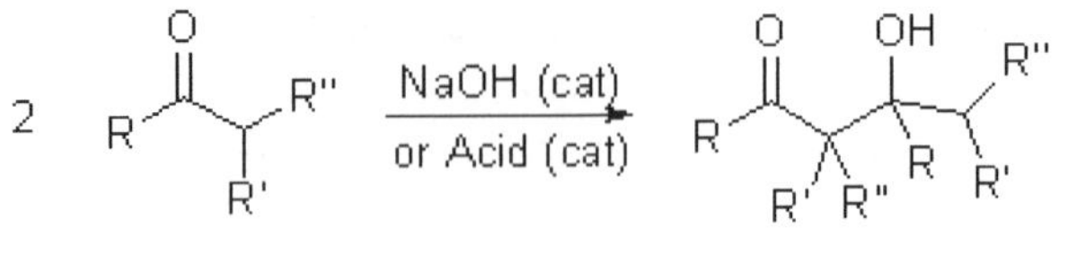

Aldol condensation reaction

In some cases, the adducts obtained from the aldol addition can easily be converted (*in situ*) to α,β-unsaturated carbonyl compounds, either thermally or under acidic or basic catalysis. The formation of the conjugated system is the driving force for this spontaneous dehydration. Under a variety of protocols, the condensation product can be obtained directly, without isolation of the aldol. An example aldol condensation reaction can be seen below.

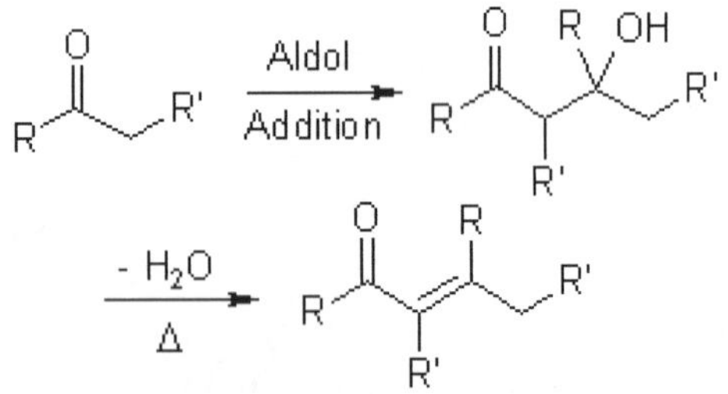

The aldol condensation is the second step of the Robinson annulation.

Keto enol tautomerism

Tautomerism refers to an equilibrium between two different structures of the same compound. Usually, the tautomers differ in the point of attachment of a hydrogen atom. One of the most common examples of a tautomeric system is the equilibrium between a ketone and its enol form, called keto enol tautomerism. An example of this reaction can be seen below.

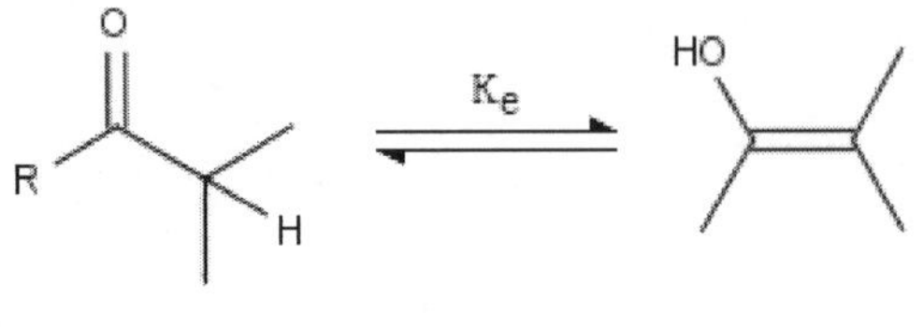

Wolff-Kishner reduction reaction

The Wolff-Kishner reduction reaction reduces aldehydes and ketones to alkanes. Condensation of the carbonyl compound with hydrazine forms the hydrazone, and treatment with base then induces the reduction of the carbon, coupled with oxidation of the

- 64 -

hydrazine to gaseous nitrogen, in order to yield the corresponding alkane. An example of the Wolff-Kishner reaction can be seen below.

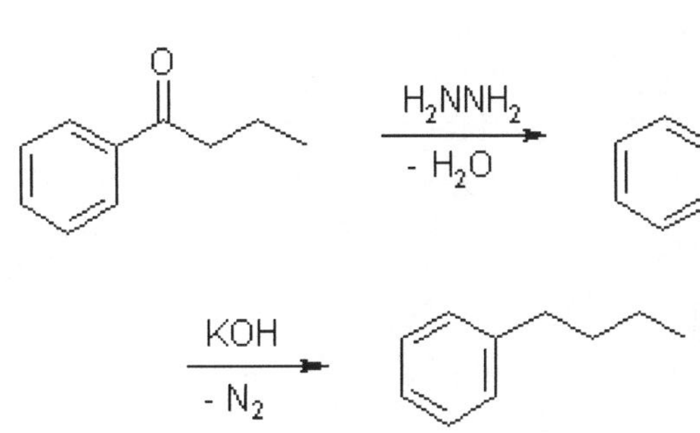

Grignard reagents

Grignard noted that alkyl halides react with magnesium metal in diethyl ether (Et_2O) to form compounds that contain a metal-carbon bond. Methyl bromide, for example, forms methyl-magnesium bromide.

$$CH_3Br + Mg \xrightarrow{Et_2O} CH_3MgBr$$

Because carbon is considerably more electronegative than magnesium, the metal-carbon bond in this compound has a significant amount of ionic character. Grignard reagents, such as CH_3MgBr, are best thought of as hybrids of ionic and covalent Lewis structures.

$$CH_3-Mg-Br \longleftrightarrow [CH_3^-][Mg^{2+}][Br^-]$$

Grignard reagents are our first source of carbanions (literally, "anions of carbon"). The Lewis structure of the CH_3^- ion suggests that carbanions can be Lewis bases, or electron-pair donors.

Perhaps the most important aspect of the chemistry of Grignard reagents is the ease with which this reaction allows us to couple alkyl chains. Isopropylmagnesium bromide, for example, can be used to graft an isopropyl group onto the hydrocarbon chain of an appropriate ketone, as shown in the figure below.

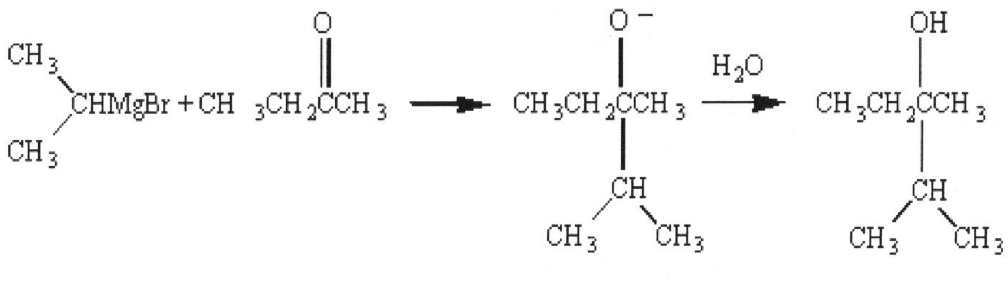

Organic acids

Organic compounds that have the carboxyl group (–COOH) behave like acids, and are thus known as carboxylic acids, or organic acids. The bonds in a carboxyl group are such that the C has a double bond to O, and a single bond to which the hydroxyl group –OH is attached. The simplest carboxylic acid is methanoic acid (HCOOH), commonly called formic acid. The

- 65 -

next acid with two carbon atoms is called ethanoic acid (CH_3COOH), or commonly called acetic acid. The carboxylic acids form a homologous series. Two hydrogen atoms of one of the carbon atoms in an alkane are replaced simultaneously by an oxygen atom and a hydroxyl group, to make a carboxylic acid. The oxygen atom is double bonded to the carbon atom. Thus, the general formula for carboxylic acid is R-COOH, where R is an alkyl group, like methyl (CH_3), ethyl (C_2H_5), propyl (C_3H_7), etc. In the case of the simplest of the acids, namely formic acid (H-COOH), the R is a hydrogen atom. The IUPAC names of organic acids are derived from the IUPAC names for their corresponding alkanes. The carboxyl group is given the "oic" suffix, which is then attached to the IUPAC name for the alkane, and the word acid is added to the end. The IUPAC rules for naming carboxylic acids are as follows:

- Find the alkane from which the alcohol is made, and name it similar to the nomenclature for straight-chain hydrocarbons. This is called the parent hydrocarbon.
- Add an "oic" suffix to the name for the alkane by removing the "e" from the alkane name.
- Find where the carboxyl group is attached: in the branches or in the side chains. The –COOH group is generally attached at the end of a branch.

> **Review Video: <u>The Basics of Organic Acids</u>**
> Visit *mometrix.com/academy* and enter *Code:* **238132**

Physical properties
The following are physical properties of organic acids:

- Physical state – The first three organic acids are colorless liquids at ordinary room temperatures. Organic acids having between 4 to 9 carbon atoms are colorless oily liquids at ordinary room temperatures. Carbonic acids with a higher number of carbon atoms are colorless wax-like substances at ordinary room temperatures.
- Odor – The first three members have a very pungent smell. Acids with between 4 to 9 carbon atoms smell pungent like goats butter. Still higher molecular weight organic acids are odorless.
- Solubility – The first four carbonic acids are soluble in water. As the molecular weight increases, their solubility in water decreases. Organic acids with 10 or more carbon atoms are insoluble in water. All organic acids are soluble in organic solvents, such as benzene, ethanol, ether, etc.
- Acidic nature – Organic acids are weak acids, as they can be only partially ionized in water to give H^+ ions. The acidic nature decreases as the homologous series increases. The lower members readily turn blue litmus paper to red.
- Fatty acids – Larger organic acids that have one –COOH group are also called monocarboxylic fatty acids. Most of these acids are produced by the hydrolysis of fats, and are therefore known as fatty acids. They have many industrial uses, especially in the soap and detergent industry.

> **Review Video: <u>Physical Properties of Organic Acids</u>**
> Visit *mometrix.com/academy* and enter *Code:* **342179**

Chemical properties
The following are chemical properties of organic acids:
- Action on litmus paper – Methanoic and ethanoic acids turn blue litmus paper to red quite easily. This indicates the acidic nature of the compounds. Larger organic acid molecules do not show this test result as readily.
- Reaction with sodium bicarbonate – Organic acid reacts with sodium bicarbonate to release water and carbon dioxide. If ethanol is reacted with sodium bicarbonate, sodium ethanoate, an ester, is formed along with water and carbon dioxide. The sodium bicarbonate test is a test for the presence of a carboxyl group (–COOH) in a compound because the reaction causes effervescence and the release of carbon dioxide.
- Reaction with alcohols – Esters are formed when alcohols are made to react with organic acids in the presence of concentrated sulphuric acid.

Uses
Uses of organic acids are as follows:
- Organic acids are used in some food items. For example, vinegar is dilute acetic acid. Vinegar is used in many preparations for pickles, salads, sauces, etc.
- Organic acids are used in the manufacture of soaps. Sodium salts of fatty acids are used in the soap and detergent industries.
- Organic acids find use in medicines. For example, acetic acid is used in the production of aspirin.
- Organic acids are used as industrial solvents.
- Organic acids are used in the preparation of perfumes and artificial essences that are used in food manufacturing.
- Acetic acid is used for making cellulose acetate, which is an important starting material for making artificial fibers.
- Acetic acid is also used for the coagulation of latex. This is needed when rubber is made from latex in a rubber manufacturing industry.

Preparation
Organic acids are prepared by oxidation of alcohols. Incomplete oxidation of alcohols leads to organic acids. Incomplete oxidation is achieved by providing nascent oxygen for the reaction. When air is made to pass over heated copper, oxygen from the air can break into atomic or nascent oxygen. This is made to react with an alcohol in order to give organic acid and water. In this manner, copper functions as a catalyst.

$$CH_3OH + O_2 \xrightarrow[\text{Heat}]{\text{Cu}} HCOOH + H_2O$$

Methanol or Methyl alcohol + Oxygen (From air) → Methanoic acid or Formic acid + Water

$$CH_3CH_2OH + O_2 \xrightarrow[\text{Heat}]{\text{Cu}} CH_3COOH + H_2O$$

Ethanol (Ethyl alcohol) + Oxygen (From air) → Ethanoic acid (Acetic acid) + Water

Nucleophilic attack and reduction
Because the α-carbon of carboxylic acids is extremely labile due to keto enol tautomerism, it is very prone to nucleophilic attack and can form a wide variety of compounds, such as

amines, halogenated variants, etc. Carboxylic acids can also be reduced to form aldehydes in the presence of the ester and diisobutylaluminum hydride (DIBAL).

Decarboxylation of organic acids
Decarboxylation is the loss of carbon dioxide. Simple carboxylic acids rarely undergo decarboxylation. Carboxylic acids with a carbonyl group at the 3- (or b-) position readily undergo thermal decarboxylation (e.g., derivatives of malonic acid). An example decarboxylation reaction can be seen below.

$$R-\overset{\overset{O}{\|}}{C}-OH \longrightarrow R-H \ + \ CO_2$$

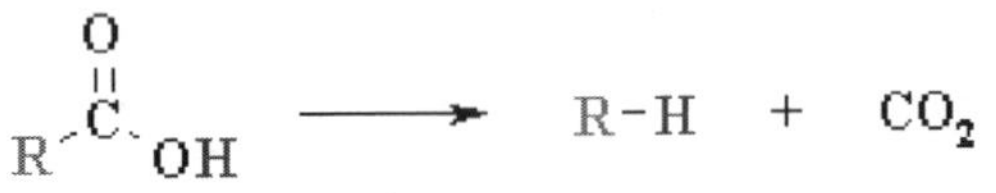

Esterification of organic acids
Esterification is a process where carboxylic acids react with alcohols to yield compounds called esters. Carboxylic acids react readily with alcohols in the presence of a catalytic amount of mineral acids. An example esterification reaction can be seen below.

$$RCOOH + R'OH \xleftrightarrow{\text{Mineral Acid}} RCOOR' + H_2O$$

Esters and acid derivatives

When the functional group is –COOR, where R is an alkyl group, the resultant compound is called an ester. The production of esters is accomplished through esterification, which produces an ester and water. Esterification is performed in the presence of concentrated sulphuric acid, which is a catalyst for the reaction. Ester tests are performed to identify whether an organic mixture has alcohol or an acid. Esters have a very sweet, fruity smell, and naturally occurring esters are found in fruits. The structure of a typical ester, namely ethyl ethanoate, is as follows:

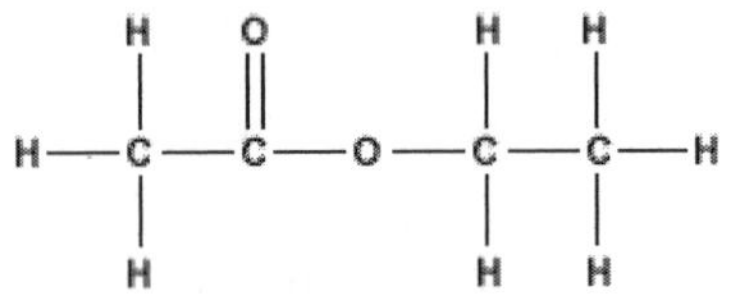

The common names of esters are derived from the organic acid and the alcohol from which they are derived. For example, when acetic acid reacts with ethyl alcohol, the ester that is formed is called ethyl acetate. However, the IPUAC name is different. Acetic acid is called ethanoic acid by the IUPAC rules. Thus, the ester formed is called ethyl ethanoate. The IUPAC names for esters are derived from the prefix of the alcohol and from the name of the acid.

Physical properties of esters
- Physical state – Lower molecular weight esters are colorless, volatile liquids. Higher esters are colorless, waxy solids.
- Odor – All esters have a strong fruity smell.
- Solubility – Lower members of the esters are soluble in water. The solubility decreases with increases in the molecular weight of the esters. Esters are also soluble in organic solvents. And, esters themselves are good organic solvents.

- Acidic nature – Esters are neutral to litmus tests.

Uses of esters
- Used as artificial perfumes or scents, as they emit a sweet smell.
- Used in making artificial food flavors that are added in many edible items, like ice creams, soft drinks, sweets, etc.
- Used as industrial solvents for making cellulose, fats, paints, and varnishes.
- Used as solvents in the pharmaceutical industries.
- Used as softeners in the plastic and molding industries.

Hofmann's rule
Hofmann's rule implies that steric effects have the greatest influence on the outcome of the Hofmann or similar eliminations. The loss of the β-hydrogen occurs preferably from the most unhindered (least substituted) position [$-CH_3$ > $-CH_2-R$ > $-CH(R_2)$]. The product alkene with the fewest substituents will predominate. Examples of the Hoffman rule can be seen below.

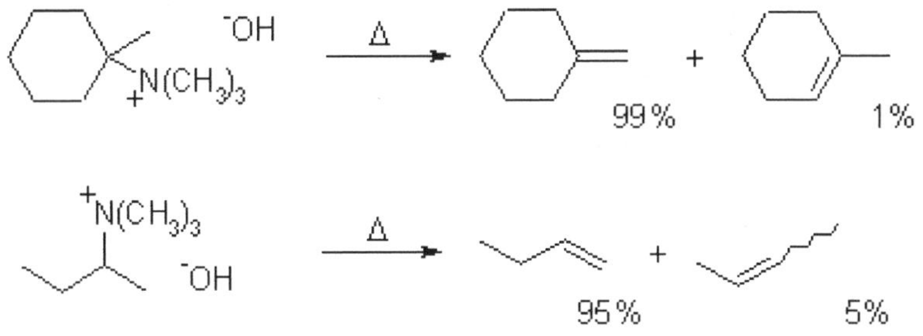

Hydrolysis of esters
Esters break down into the respective organic acids and alcohols from which they were formed. This process is called hydrolysis. When sodium hydroxide is added to an ester, for example to ethyl ethanoate, a salt is formed, sodium ethanoate, along with ethyl alcohol. This reaction is shown below.

$$CH_3COOC_2H_5 \quad + \quad NaOH \quad \xrightarrow{\text{Heat}} \quad CH_3COONa \quad + \quad C_2H_5OH$$

| Ethyl ethanoate or Ethyl acetate | Sodium hydroxide | | Sodium ethanoate or Sodium acetate | Ethanol or Ethyl alcohol |

The above reaction is a test for checking if esters are present in any solution. When a few drops of the indicator, phenolphthalein, are added to a solution of ester and NaOH, the solution will show a pink coloration. Heat the solution to speed up the reaction. When the ester has reacted completely, the pink color will disappear. Hydrolysis of an ester with an alkaline solution, such as sodium hydroxide, is known as saponification (soap making). This reaction is used in the preparation of soaps.

Saponification
Saponification is the hydrolysis of an ester under basic conditions to form an alcohol and the salt of the acid. Saponification is commonly used to refer to the reaction of a metallic alkali (base) with a fat or oil in order to produce soap.

<u>Acetoacetic ester synthesis process</u>

When α-keto acetic acid is treated with one mole of a base, the methylene group, which is more acidic, reacts with the base. And, the reaction with an alkylation reagent gives alkyl products attached to methylene. When this reaction is repeated in the next step, the other hydrogen can also react to a dialkyl product. The two alkylation agents may be the same or different (R', R''). β-keto esters tend to decarboxylate after hydrolysation to β-keto carboxylic acid and heating to give one or two alkyl-substituted ketones, respectively.

Metathesis reactions

Reactions in which none of the atoms undergo a change in oxidation number are called metathesis reactions. Consider the reaction between a carboxylic acid and an amine, for example.

$$CH_3CO_2H + CH_3NH_2 \longrightarrow CH_3CO_2^- + CH_3NH_3^+$$

Or, the reaction between an alcohol and hydrogen bromide.

$$CH_3CH_2OH + HBr \longrightarrow CH_3CH_2Br + H_2O$$

These are metathesis reactions because there is no change in the oxidation number of any atom in either reaction.

Willgerodt-Kindler reaction

The Willgerodt-Kindler reaction allows for the synthesis of amides from aryl ketones, under the influence of a secondary amine and a thiating agent. The mechanism involves the formation of an enamine, which undergoes thiation, and the carbonyl group migrates to the end of the chain via a cascade of thio-substituted iminium-aziridinium rearrangements. An example of the Willgerodt-Kindler reaction can be seen below.

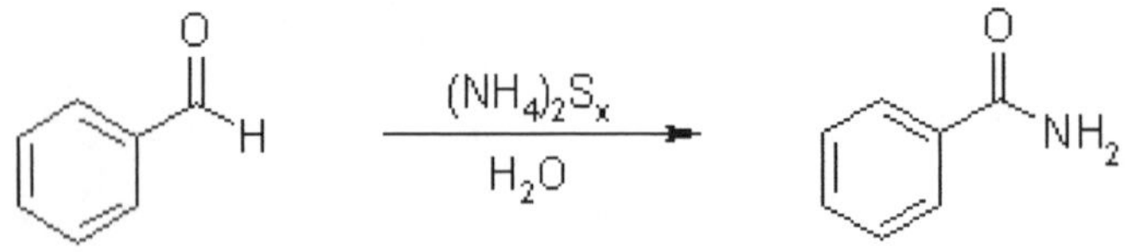

Chelating agents

Certain organic compounds are capable of forming coordinate bonds with metals through two or more atoms of the organic compound. Such organic compounds are called chelating agents. The compound that is formed by the reaction of the chelating agent and a metal is called a chelate. A chelating agent that has two coordinating atoms is called bidentate; one that has three, tridentate; and so on. EDTA, or ethylenediaminetetraacetate, is a common hexadentate chelating agent. Chlorophyll is a chelate that consists of a magnesium ion joined with a complex chelating agent. Heme, part of the hemoglobin in blood, is an iron chelate. Chelating agents are important in textile dyeing, water softening, enzyme deactivation, and as bacteriocides.

Amines

Amines are organic compounds that contain a nitrogen group with a lone pair of electrons. Amines are derivatives of ammonia with one or more hydrogen atoms replaced by alkyl or aryl groups. Amines are named either with either the prefix "amino–" or suffix "–amine" added to the root name of the compound.

Petasis reaction

The petasis reaction is a multicomponent reaction (MCR) that enables the preparation of amines and their derivatives, such as α-amino acids. This reaction is also referred to as the boronic acid Mannich reaction, since it proceeds via an imine, with the organic ligand of the boronic acid acting as the nucleophile, similar to the role of the enolizable ketone component in the original Mannich reaction. Examples of the Petasis reaction can be seen below.

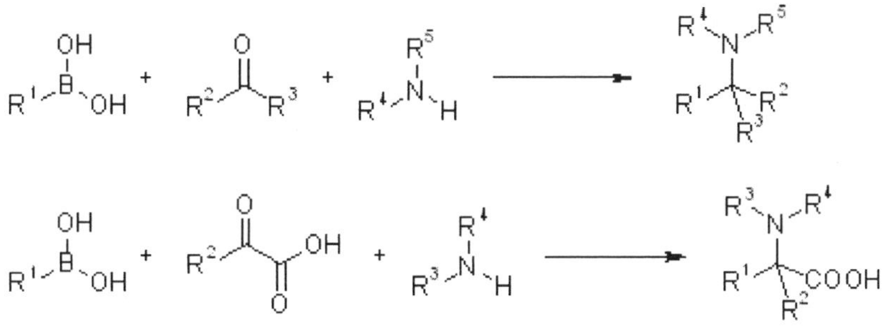

Sandmeyer reaction

The Sandmeyer reaction allows for the substitution of an aromatic amino group via preparation of its diazonium salt and subsequent displacement with a nucleophile (e.g., Cl⁻, I⁻, CN⁻, RS⁻, HO⁻, etc.). Many Sandmeyer reactions proceed under copper(I) catalysis, while the Sandmeyer-type reactions with thiols, water, and potassium iodide do not require catalysis. An example of a Sandmeyer reaction can be seen below.

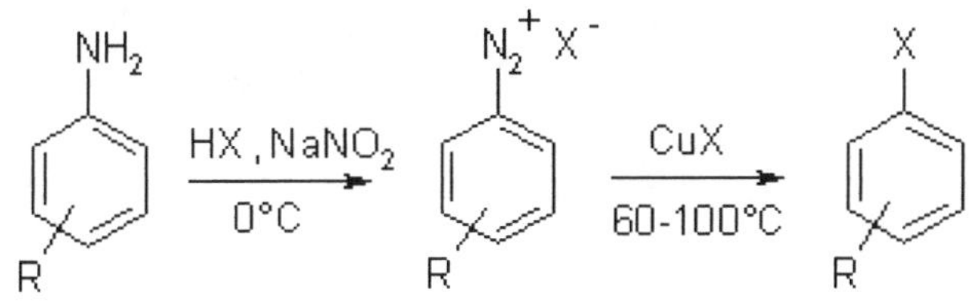

$X = CN, Br, Cl, SO_3H$

Hofmann elimination

Hofmann elimination is sometimes referred to as Hofmann degradation. This elimination reaction of alkyl trimethyl amines proceeds with anti-stereochemistry, and is generally suitable for producing alkenes with one or two substituents. The reaction follows Hofmann's rule. An example of a Hofmann elimination can be seen below.

NH₂   1. CH₃I
                →
      2. Ag₂O, H₂O, △

Biological Molecules

Carbohydrates

Carbohydrates are organic compounds that consist only of carbon, hydrogen, and oxygen. In general, the hydrogen to oxygen ratio in carbohydrates is 2:1, although carbohydrates are not technically hydrates of carbon; rather, they are more akin to polyhydroxy aldehydes and ketones. Carbohydrates are also referred to as saccharides, and are classified as either monosaccharides, disaccharides, oligosaccharides or polysaccharides. Mono- and disaccharides, which are composed of one and two carbohydrates, respectively, are referred to as sugars. Oligo- and polysaccharides are composed of longer, more complex chains of sugars (i.e., oligo = 2 to 10; poly = 11+), which are important for energy storage and the production of a wide variety of biological molecules.

Common carbohydrates are:
- Glucose (monosaccharide) – Blood sugar.
- Fructose (monosaccharide) – Fruit sugar.
- Sucrose (disaccharide) – Table sugar, composed of glucose and fructose.
- Lactose (disaccharide) – Milk sugar, composed of glucose and galactose.
- Oligofructose (oligosaccharide) – Short chain of fructose molecules naturally found in fruits.
- Oligogalactose (oligosaccharide) – Short chain of galactose molecules naturally found in milk; considered to be a prebiotic.
- 5. Starch (polysaccharide) – Polymer of glucose used to store energy in plants and fruits.
- Glycogen (polysaccharide) – Polymer of glucose used to store energy in animals.
- Cellulose (polysaccharide) – Polymer of hundreds to thousands of glucose subunits used for the structural composition of plants.
- Chitin (polysaccharide) – Polymer of *N*-acetylglucosamine that forms the cell walls of fungi and the exoskeletons of arthropods.

> ➤ **Review Video: <u>Carbohydrates</u>**
> *Visit **mometrix.com/academy** and enter **Code: 601714***

Structure
Originally, scientists considered any compound that conformed to the formula $C_m(H_2O)_n$ to be carbohydrates, including formaldehyde (CH_2O). However, today, carbohydrates are considered to be any compound that conforms to the formula $(CH_2O)_n$, where n is greater than or equal to three. Typically, carbohydrates have the structure H-$(CHOH)_x$(C=O)-$(CHOH)_y$-H, which is essentially an aldehyde or ketone with hydroxyl groups on each carbon atom that is not part of the aldehyde or ketone functional group. However, not all compounds that conform to this formula are considered to be carbohydrates (e.g., inositol

((CH$_2$O)$_6$)), and not all carbohydrates conform to this formula (e.g., fucose and deoxyribonucleic acid). In solutions, carbohydrates naturally exist in equilibrium between open- and closed-chain structures. For example, the open chain structure for glucose is as follows:

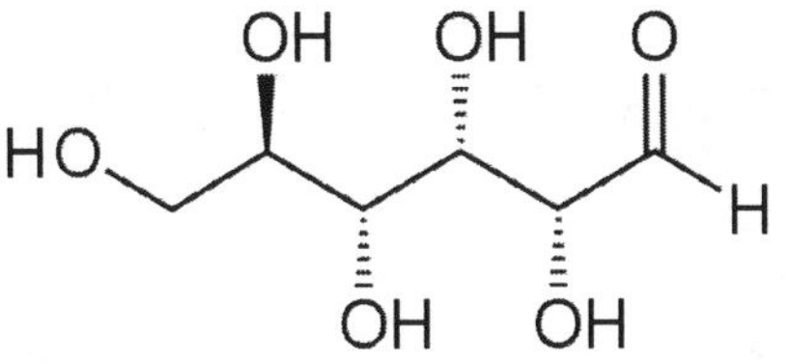

The open-chain structure of glucose forms four closed-chain, cyclic isomers by a nucleophilic addition reaction between the C-1 aldehyde group and either the C-4 or the C-5 carbon, yielding a hemiacetal group (i.e., -C(OH)H-O-). The four cyclic isomers of glucose are as follows:

α-D-Glucopyranose   β-D-Glucopyranose   α-D-Glucofuranose   β-D-Glucofuranose

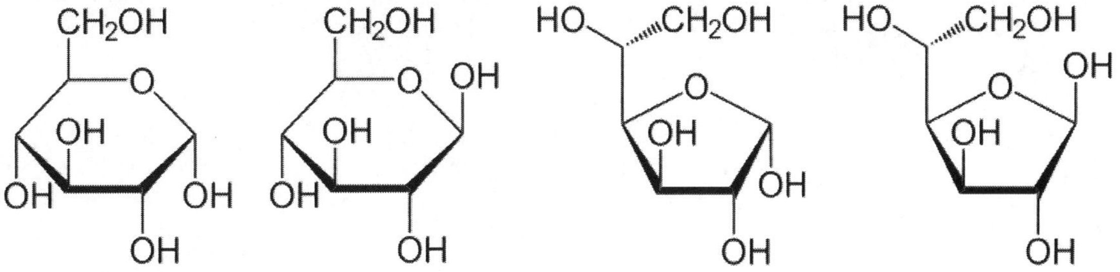

Note: The α- and β-cyclic isoforms of glucose differ by the final orientation of the hydroxyl group on the C-1 carbon. The hydroxyl group of the α-isoform is in the *trans* arrangement, meaning that it is opposite to the plane of the sugar molecule; while the hydroxyl group of the β-isoform is in the *cis* arrangement, meaning that it is on the same side as the plane of the sugar. Because of the different orientations of only the C-1 hydroxyl group of the glucose molecule, each of these isoforms are chiral, meaning that they have a mirror image that is non-superposable.

Glycosidic linkages
Chains of carbohydrates are formed by covalent bonds referred to as glycosidic linkages, which are formed by a dehydration reaction between two hydroxyl groups of the sugar molecules. This reaction yields two sugar molecules linked together by an oxygen atom and results in the release of a water molecule. Glycosidic bonds can still take place if the hydroxyl group is replaced by a thiol or amine group; however, instead of being referred to as O-glycosidic bonds, they are referred to as either S-glycosidic or N-glycosidic bonds, respectively. An example of a disaccharide, linked by an O-glycosidic bond can be seen below.

Glucose

Glucose ($C_6H_{12}O_6$) is a simple monosaccharide, and is an important source of energy in all biological systems. The name, glucose, is derived from the Greek word for sweet. All cells utilize glucose as their primary source of energy, and as a metabolic intermediate. Glucose is produced in plants as one of the primary products of photosynthesis, and is believed to be the most widely utilized monosaccharide in nature because of its stability and lower tendency to react with the amino groups of proteins. While there are many isomers of glucose, all of which can be divided into two stereoisomeric groups (i.e., dextrorotary (D, right handed) and levorotary (L, left handed), only the dextrorotary isoforms exist in nature. Because of this, glucose is sometimes referred to as dextrose, although this name is strongly discouraged due to confusion when discussing the levorotary isoforms.

Glycogen

Glycogen is a highly branched polymer of glucose in which most of the glucose residues are linked to each other by alpha-1,4-glycosidic bonds to form a linear backbone. Interspersed along the linear backbone, at intervals of 4-10 glucose residues, are branches created by alpha-1,6-glycosidic bonds. As a result of the extensive branching, the glycogen molecule has a frond-like and highly branched configuration with an open helical tertiary structure. The helix, in turn, is organized into spherical particles with a molecular weight of 10-15 million Daltons (60,000 glucose residues per particle), and the spherical particles, in turn, are organized into large granules. The granules range in size from 10-40 nm and are located in the cellular cytosol.

Structure of glycogen:

Ribose

Ribose ($C_5H_{10}O_5$) is a simple, five-carbon monosaccharide with all of the hydroxyl groups on the same side of the molecule in the Fisher projection. Ribose, along with its epimer arabinose, are derived from gum Arabic; and, similar to glucose, are only found as dextrorotary isoforms in nature. Ribose is a very important carbohydrate for biological systems, and serves as the backbone for a large number of important biological compounds, including the following:

- Ribonucleic acid (RNA) – Nucleic acids that are transcribed from DNA and then used for a variety of purposes, such as the template for ribosomes to produce proteins (messenger RNA), short sequences for silencing transcriptional activity (microRNAs), short sequences for triggering the degradation of mRNAs (silencing or short-hairpin RNAs), adapter molecules between mRNAs and amino acids (transfer RNAs), ribosomal structural molecules (ribosomal RNAs), etc. RNA is composed of chains of ribonucleotides, each consisting of a nucleobase, a ribose sugar, and a phosphate group.
- Deoxyribonucleic acid (DNA) – Nucleic acids that store long-term genetic information. DNA is composed similar to RNA, except with deoxyribose in the place of ribose, which is derived from the removal of an oxygen atom from ribose, and thymine in the place of uracil.
- Adenosine triphosphate (ATP) – Important for the storage and transmission of energy. Derived from the phosphorylation of the ribonucleoside, adenosine.
- Nicotinamide adenine dinucleotide (NADH) – A coenzyme used to carry electrons. Derived from two ribonucleosides linked by a pair of phosphate groups.
- Cyclic Adenosine Monophosphate (cAMP) and Cyclic Guanosine Monophosphate (cGMP) – Used as second messengers for many biological processes. Derived from ATP and GTP by the ester linkage of the first phosphate group to the C-3 hydroxyl group of the ribose molecule, catalyzed by phosphodiesterase.

Reactions of monosaccharides

Ring formation:

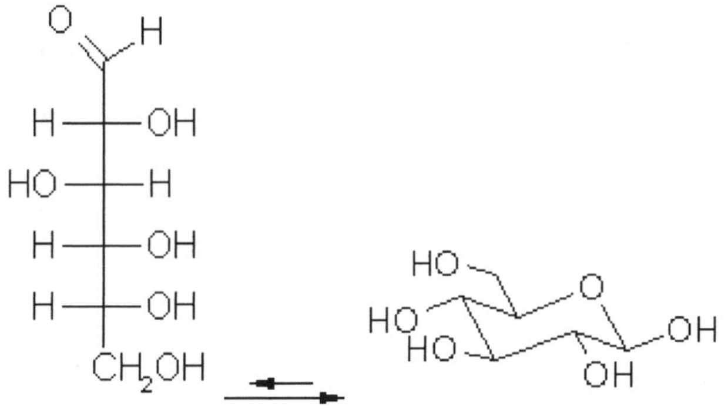

Oxidation reaction:

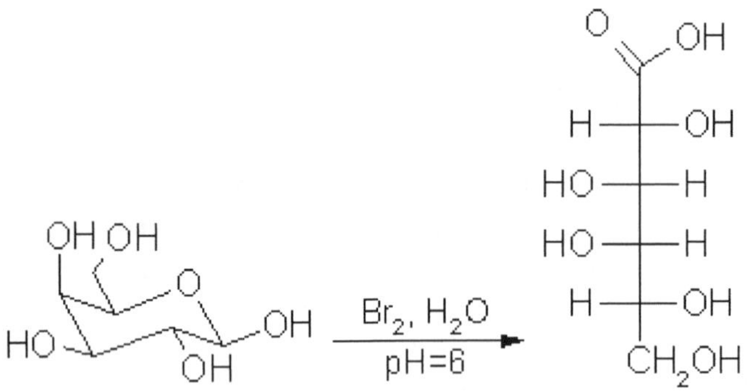

Mutarotation:

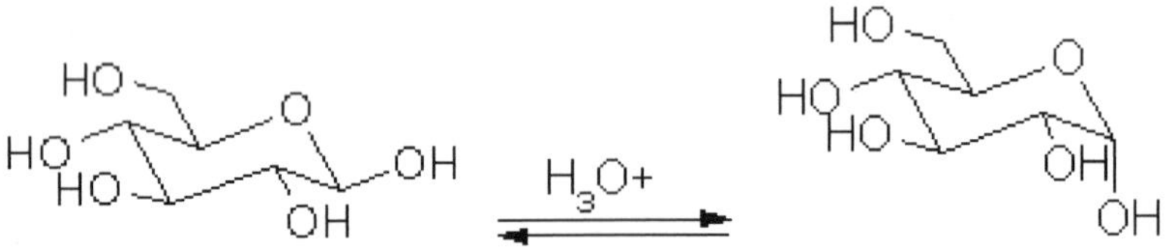

Ester formation:

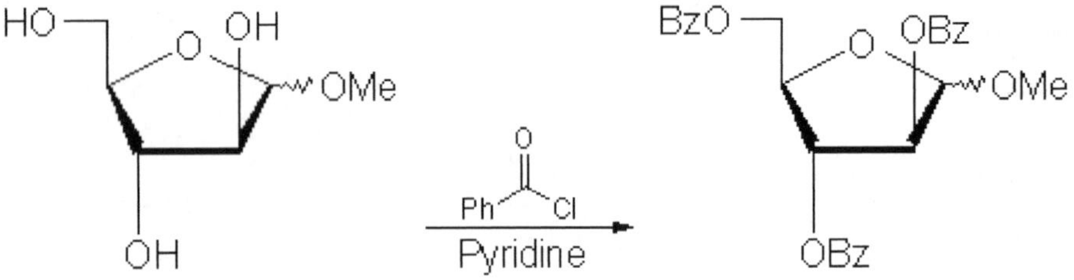

Amino acids and proteins

Amino acids are organic compounds that contain an amine group, a carboxylic acid group, and a side chain that is specific to each molecule. Amino acids are primarily composed of carbon, hydrogen, oxygen, and nitrogen, and generally conform to the formula $H_2NCHRCOOH$, where R represents the specific side chain of the amino acid. In most amino acids, the amine group is attached to the α-carbon, and they are thus referred to as α-amino acids; however, they can be also be found with the amine group bound to a different carbon, such as the γ-carbon in γ-amino acids. Amino acids are the building blocks of proteins, which are chains of amino acids. Each protein is composed of a specific sequence of amino acids. Since proteins are composed of 20 standard amino acids (as well as nonstandard amino acids on occasion) and vary in length from 20 amino acids to tens of thousands of amino acids, there are literally an infinite number of possible combinations. However, the proteins that are naturally produced within cells are limited to what is encoded by the genome, including alternative splice forms; and, are composed of domains and motifs of conserved amino acid sequences that confer specific functions to the proteins. Collectively, the proteins that are encoded by the genome control or participate in virtually every process within living cells.

➢ **Review Video: Amino Acids**
*Visit **mometrix.com/academy** and enter **Code:*** **190385**

Note: Amino acid chains of between 3-20 amino acids are called peptides, while amino acid chains of greater than 20 amino acids are called polypeptides.

Amino acid side chains

Nonpolar R-groups:

Glycine (G)

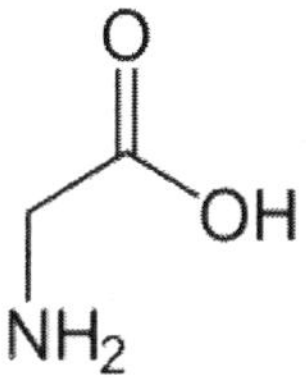

Alanine (A)

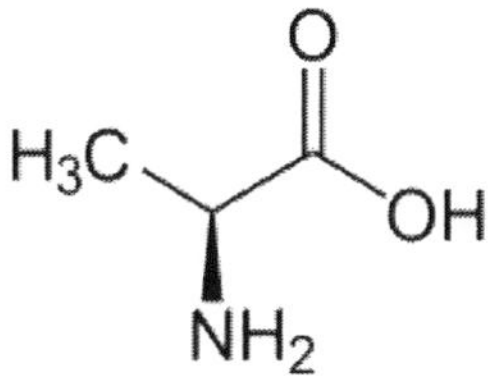

Valine (V)

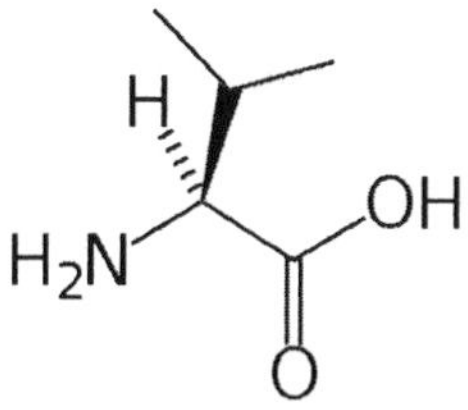

Leucine (L)

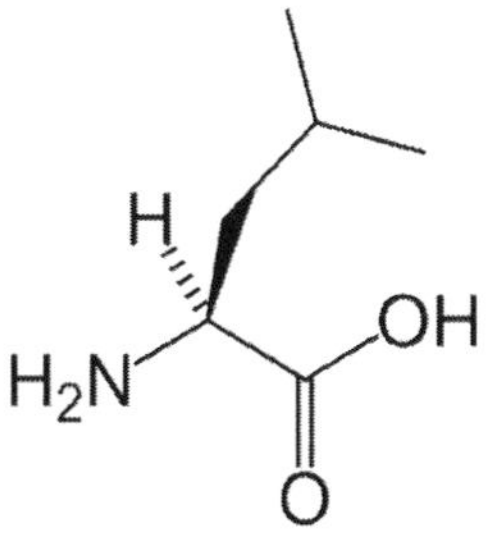

Isoleucine (I)

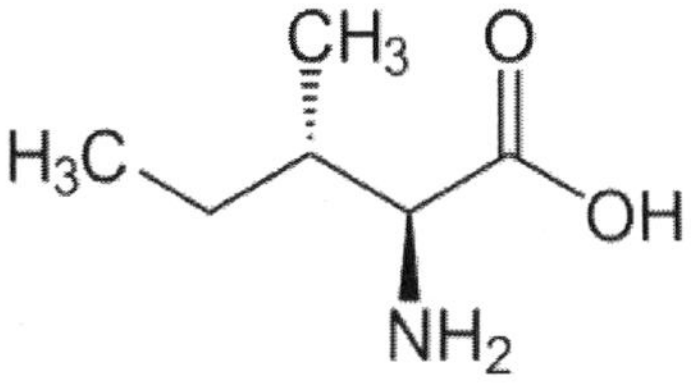

Proline (P)

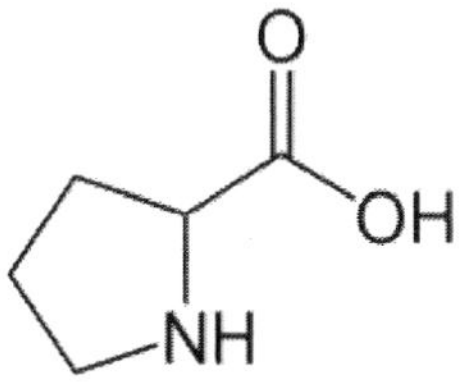

Polar, uncharged R-groups:

Serine (S)

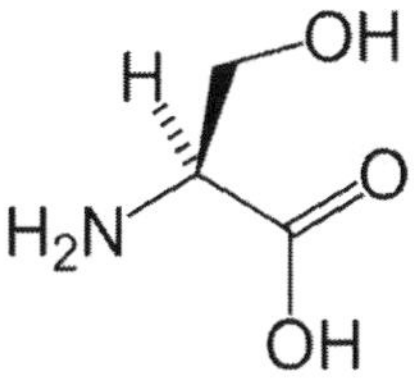

Threonine (T)

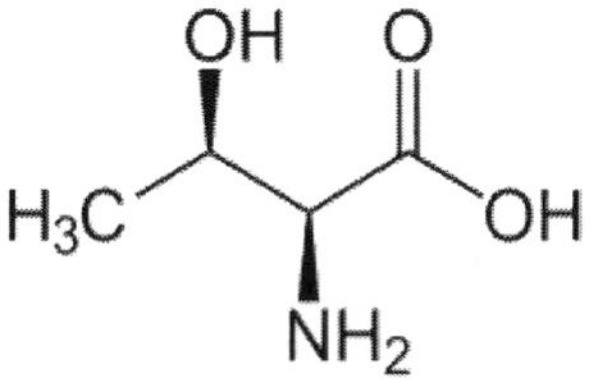

Cysteine (C)

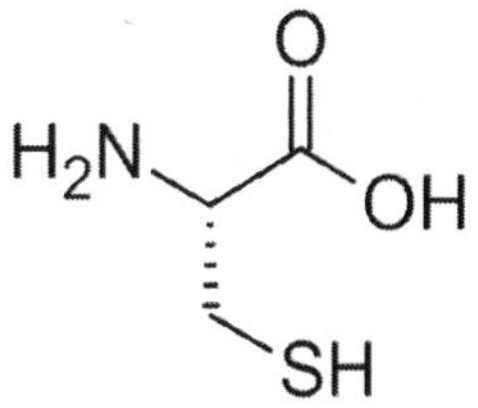

Methionine (M)

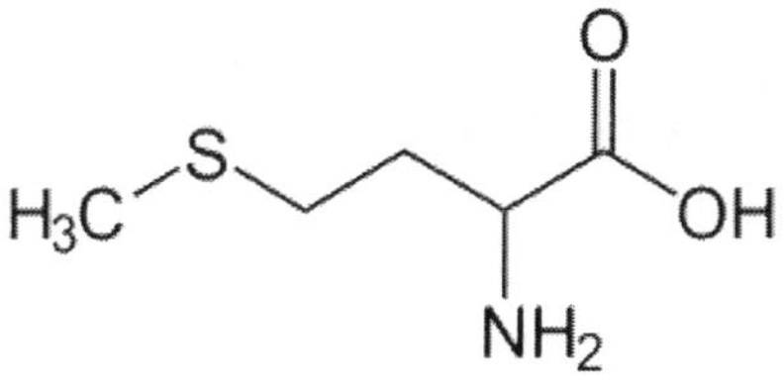

Asparagine (N)

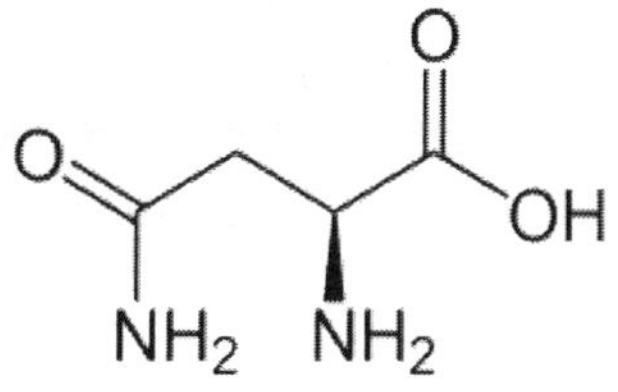

Glutamine (Q)

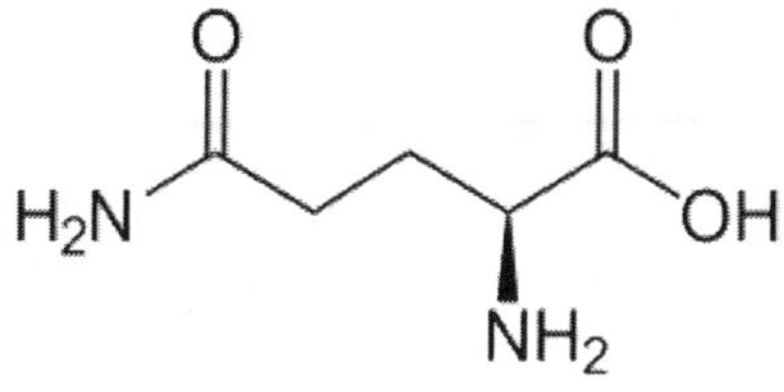

Positively charged R-groups:

Lysine (K)   Arginine (R)   Histidine (H)

Negatively charged R-groups:

Aspartate (D)   Glutamate (E)

Aromatic R-groups:

Phenylalanine (F)   Tyrosine (Y)   Tryptophan (W)

Peptide bond formation

Proteins are formed by the polymerization of amino acids. The polymerization of amino acids occurs through the formation of peptide bonds, where the amine group of one amino acid reacts with the carboxylic acid group of another amino acid to form an amide bond. In cells, this reaction occurs first by the ATP-dependent ester linkage of an amino acid to a specific tRNA by an aminoacyl tRNA synthetase, producing an aminoacyl tRNA. The aminoacyl tRNA then serves as a substrate for ribosomes, which catalyze the bond formation between the carboxylic acid group of the growing peptide chain and the ester bond of the aminoacyl tRNA. The result of this process is the formation of a peptide bond and the release of a water molecule. Because of the directionality of the peptide bond formation, proteins are synthesized from the N-terminus towards the C-terminus.

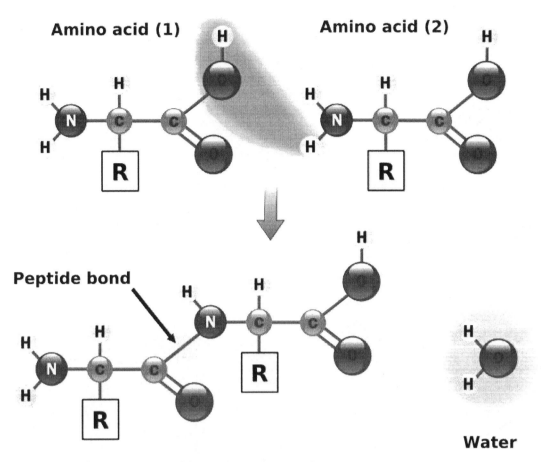

Amino acid (1)

Amino acid (2)

Peptide bond

Water

Dipeptide

Protein folding

As the growing peptide chain exits the ribosome, the linear sequence of amino acids is folded into secondary and tertiary structures based upon hydrophobicity, hydrogen bonding, van der Waal's forces, and disulfide bridges. The folding of proteins also requires chaperones:

- Chaperones (also called chaperonins) are needed every time a protein remains unfolded, or becomes unfolded to cross a membrane (or refolds on the other side). Two or more types of chaperones are involved in protein folding, and different ones are found in different parts of the cell.
- There are two major types (families) of chaperones: HSP60 or HSP70, depending on their molecular weight (60 kDa vs. 70 kDa), and mode of action.
- The major chaperone inside of the endoplasmic reticulum is a member of the HSP70 family, called binding immunoglobulin protein (BiP).

Primary and secondary structures

Primary structure refers to the linear number and order of the amino acids present in a peptide or protein. The convention for the designation of the order of amino acids is that the N-terminal end (i.e., the end bearing the residue with the free α-amino group) is to the left (and the number 1 amino acid), while the C-terminal end (i.e., the end with the residue containing a free α-carboxyl group) is to the right. The secondary structure is the ordered array of amino acids of a protein into regular conformational substructures, typically α-helices or β-strands, which are bound together by hydrogen bonding. Within a single protein, different regions of the polypeptide chain may assume different secondary conformations, and these conformations are determined by the primary amino acid sequence.

Tertiary and quanternary structures

The tertiary structure of a protein is the overall shape of the protein that is formed by salt bridges, hydrogen bonding, disulfide bonding, and posttranslational modifications between the secondary structures of a protein. The tertiary structure is what determines the overall functions of a protein, and denaturation of this structure will usually inactivate the protein. The quanternary structure of a protein is the structure of a macromolecular complex of proteins composed of more than one tertiary protein subunit. An example of a quanternary structure is the functional hemoglobin molecule, which is composed of multiple globular heme subunits held together by hydrogen bonding. While all proteins have tertiary structures, not all proteins have quanternary structures.

Hydrolysis of peptide bonds

Peptide bonds are metastable and can be broken spontaneously in the presence of water by a reaction, called amide hydrolysis. This reaction releases 8-16 kJ/mol, but occurs very slowly. In living organisms, this reaction is usually catalyzed by enzymes called peptidases.

Lipids

Lipids are hydrophobic or amphipathic molecules, including fats, sterols, monoglycerides, diglycerides, triglycerides, phospholipids, etc. The biological functions of lipids include energy storage, membrane structure formation, and cell signaling. Because of the amphipathic nature of phospholipids, cell membranes can be formed, where the hydrophilic regions are oriented towards the aqueous solutions both inside and outside of the membrane, and the hydrophobic regions are sandwiched together within the membrane, creating a barrier to entry/exit for the cells. The formation of a membrane allows for cellular and subcellular compartmentalization, which allows for the very creation of all living beings. Fatty acids are the basic building blocks of most lipids, and are composed of long hydrocarbon chains that terminate in a carboxylic acid group. Fatty acids that contain only single bonds are referred to as saturated, while fatty acids with one or more double bonds are referred to as unsaturated. Fatty acids can be synthesized by chain elongation using acetyl-CoA and malonyl- or meth-ylmalonyl-CoA groups in a process called fatty acid synthesis.

> ➤ **Review Video: Lipids**
> *Visit mometrix.com/academy and enter Code: 269746*

The following molecules are composed of fatty acids:
- Glycerolipids – Formed by the mono-, di-, and trisubstitution of fatty acids to a glycerol molecule. An example of an unsaturated triglyceride can be seen below.

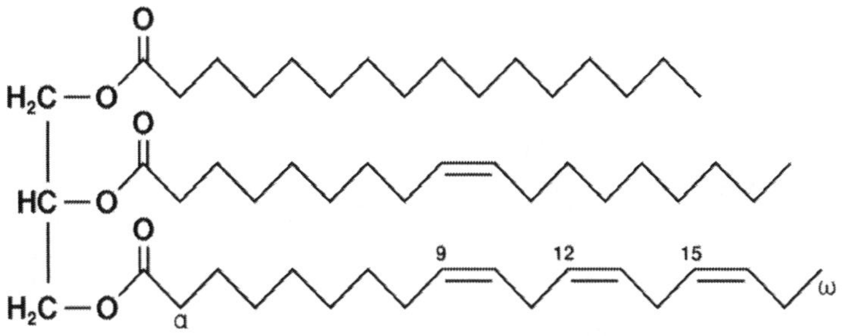

- Phospholipids – Formed by the di-substitution of fatty acids to a glycerol molecule containing one phosphate group. An example of a phospholipid, phosphatidylcholine, can be seen below.

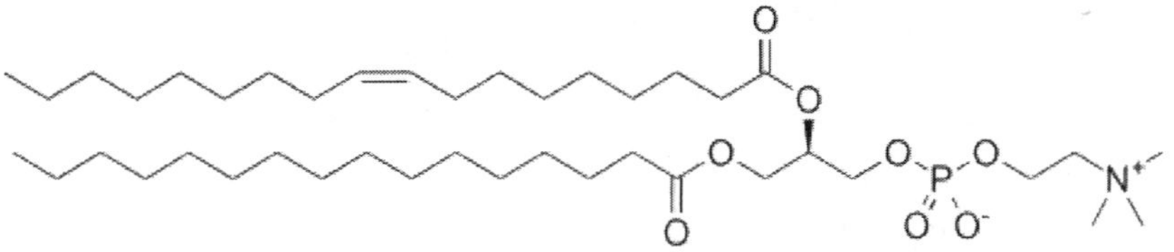

- Sphingolipids – A complicated family of lipids formed from a sphingoid base composed of a serine residue bound to a fatty acid residue. The sphingoid base is then converted into ceramides, phosphosphingolipids, glycosphingolipids, and other compounds. An example of a sphingolipid, sphingosine, can be seen below.

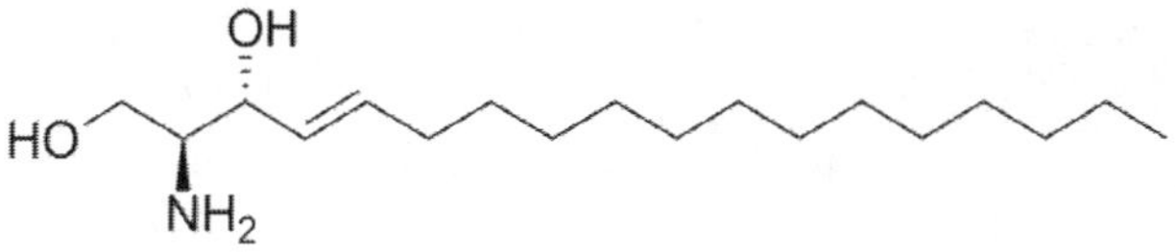

Common saturated fatty acids

Common Name	Chemical Structure	Carbon:Double Bond Ratio
Caprylic Acid	$CH_3(CH_2)_6COOH$	8:0
Capric Acid	$CH_3(CH_2)_8COOH$	10:0
Lauric Acid	$CH_3(CH_2)_{10}COOH$	12:0
Myristic Acid	$CH_3(CH_2)_{12}COOH$	14:0
Palmitic Acid	$CH_3(CH_2)_{14}COOH$	16:0
Stearic Acid	$CH_3(CH_2)_{16}COOH$	18:0
Arachidic Acid	$CH_3(CH_2)_{18}COOH$	20:0
Behenic Acid	$CH_3(CH_2)_{20}COOH$	22:0
Lignoceric Acid	$CH_3(CH_2)_{22}COOH$	24:0
Cerotic Acid	$CH_3(CH_2)_{24}COOH$	26:0

Common unsaturated fatty acids

Common Name	Chemical Structure	D^x	C:D	n-x
Myristoleic Acid	$CH_3(CH_2)_3CH=CH(CH_2)_7COOH$	cis-Δ^9	14:1	n-5
Palmitoleic Acid	$CH_3(CH_2)_5CH=CH(CH_2)_7COOH$	cis-Δ^9	16:1	n-7
Sapienic Acid	$CH_3(CH_2)_8CH=CH(CH_2)_4COOH$	cis-Δ^6	16:1	n-10
Oleic Acid	$CH_3(CH_2)_7CH=CH(CH_2)_7COOH$	cis-Δ^9	18:1	n-9
Elaidic Acid	$CH_3(CH_2)_7CH=CH(CH_2)_7COOH$	trans-Δ^9	18:1	n-9
Vaccenic Acid	$CH_3(CH_2)_5CH=CH(CH_2)_9COOH$	trans-Δ^{11}	18:1	n-7
Linoleic Acid	$CH_3(CH_2)_4CH=CHCH_2CH=CH(CH_2)_7COOH$	cis,cis-Δ^9,Δ^{12}	18:2	n-6
Linoelaidic Acid	$CH_3(CH_2)_4CH=CHCH_2CH=CH(CH_2)_7COOH$	trans,trans-Δ^9,Δ^{12}	18:2	n-6
α-Linolenic Acid	$CH_3CH_2CH=CHCH_2CH=CHCH_2CH=CH(CH_2)_7COOH$	cis,cis,cis-$\Delta^9,\Delta^{12},\Delta^{15}$	18:3	n-3
Arachidonic Acid	$CH_3(CH_2)_4CH=CHCH_2CH=CHCH_2CH=CHCH_2CH=CH(CH_2)_3COOH$	cis,cis,cis,cis-$\Delta^5,\Delta^8,\Delta^{11},\Delta^{14}$	20:4	n-6
Eicosapentaenoic Acid	$CH_3CH_2CH=CHCH_2CH=CHCH_2CH=CHCH_2CH=CHCH_2CH=CH(CH_2)_3COOH$	cis,cis,cis,cis,cis-$\Delta^5,\Delta^8,\Delta^{11},\Delta^{14},\Delta^{17}$	20:5	n-3
Erucic Acid	$CH_3(CH_2)_7CH=CH(CH_2)_{11}COOH$	cis-Δ^{13}	22:1	n-9
Docosahexaenoic Acid	$CH_3CH_2CH=CHCH_2CH=CHCH_2CH=CHCH_2CH=CHCH_2CH=CHCH_2CH=CH(CH_2)_2COOH$	cis,cis,cis,cis,cis,cis-$\Delta^4,\Delta^7,\Delta^{10},\Delta^{13},\Delta^{16},\Delta^{19}$	22:6	n-3

Terpenes

Terpenes are a diverse group of organic compounds that are produced in plants, primarily conifers, as well as some insects. Terpenes are the primary components of resins and essential oils, and are used commercially for both their aromatic and flavorful qualities. Structurally, terpenes and terpenoids consist of one or more units of isoprene, C_5H_8, and conform to the formula $(C_5H_8)_n$. Terpenes are also used as the building blocks for a wide variety of compounds in nearly every living creature, including steroids, which are derivatives of the triterpene, squalene. However, the products are not terpenes or terpenoids in the literal sense because they do not contain the characteristic number of carbon atoms.

Steroids

Steroids are a group of lipids that contains a characteristic arrangement of four cycloalkane rings joined to one another. The core structure of steroids consists of 20 carbon atoms joined together to create 3 cyclohexane rings and 1 cyclopentane ring. Steroids differ by the functional group that attaches to their core structure, as well as the oxidation states of the rings. Some examples of steroids include cholesterol, estradiol, testosterone, and dexamethasone.

Steroid core structure:

Cholesterol:

Cholesterol

Analysis of the structure of cholesterol indicates that its formula is $C_{27}H_{46}O$, which does not fit the pattern that is expected for a terpenoid. The most important property of this molecule is the fact that, with the exception of the –OH group on the lower left-hand corner of the molecule, there is nothing about its structure that would suggest that it is soluble in water.

Phosphorus compounds

Phosphorus is essential for life. Organophosphorus compounds contain carbon-phosphorus bonds, while organophosphate compounds contain phosphorus linked to carbon through an ester linkage ($-C-O-P(OH)_3$). In the form of phosphate, phosphorus is a critical component of DNA, RNA, ATP, cAMP, and phospholipids, among a wide variety of organophosphate compounds.

Phosphoric acids
The most basic phosphoric acid is H_3PO_4. When 1 or 2 hydrogens are removed from phosphoric acid, dihydrogen phosphate, $H_2PO_4^{1-}$ (1st conjugate base), and hydrogen phosphate, HPO_4^{2-} (2nd conjugate base), are formed. When all three hydrogen atoms are removed from phosphoric acid, the resulting compound is referred to as phosphate, PO_4^{3-} (3rd conjugate base). Phosphate is a very important functional group in organic chemistry and biochemistry, essential for most energy-dependent chemical reactions. Phosphoric acid monomers can be linked together to form polyphosphate-anhydride compounds through a condensation reaction that results in two phosphoric acid residues linked together by an ester linkage, along with the release of a water molecule. Common polyphosphate compounds are as follows:

- Pyrophosphate – Two phosphoric acid subunits.
- Tripolyphosphate – Three phosphoric acid subunits.
- Tetrapolyphosphate – Four phosphoric acid subunits.

- Trimetaphosphate – Three phosphoric acid subunits linked together into a cyclical ring.
- Phosphoric anhydride – Four phosphoric acid subunits linked together into a spherical complex.

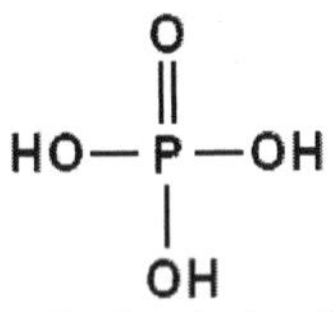

orthophosphoric acid 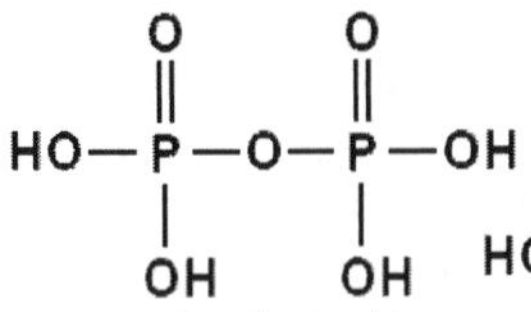   pyrophosphoric acid

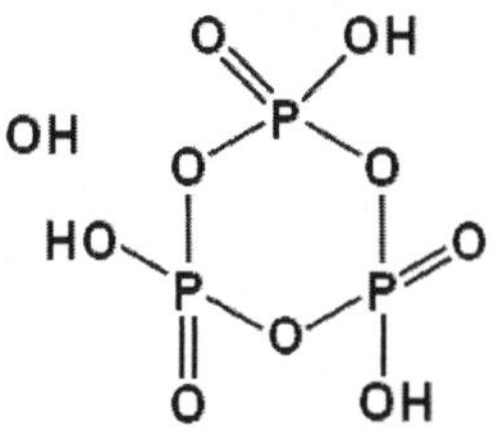

trimetaphosphoric acid

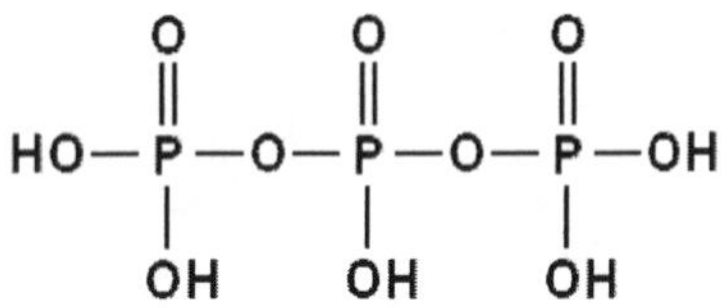

tripolyphosphoric acid

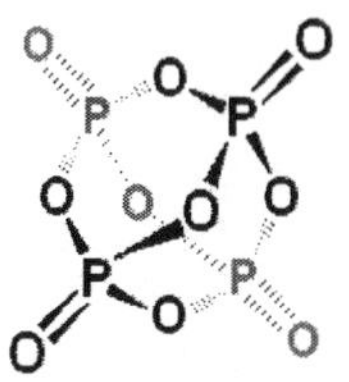

phosphoric anhydride (P$_4$O$_{10}$)

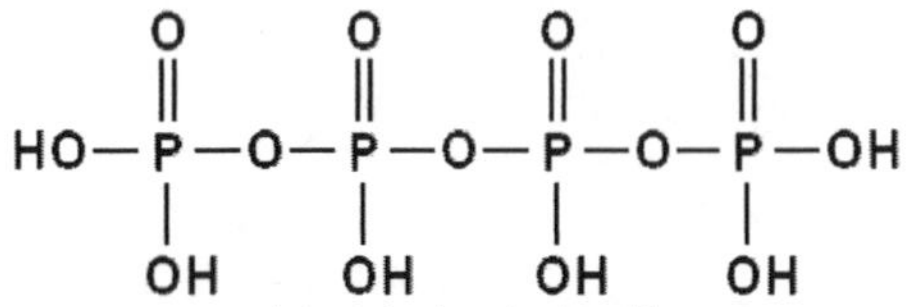

tetrapolyphosphoric acid

Phosphoester and phosphodiester linkages

Phosphates and polyphosphates can also be linked to other organic compounds, such as nucleotides or nucleic acids. In the case of nucleotides, the binding of one or more phosphates functions to store energy that can later be used for enzymatic reactions, due to the amount of energy that is stored in the phosphorester linkages. Given the repulsion of the phosphate groups to one another, when pyrophosphate or tripolyphosphate are linked to a nucleotide, forming ADP or ATP in the case of adenosine, the energy that is stored in the second and third bonds increases dramatically. Hydrolysis of these high-energy bonds by living systems allows such energy to be harnessed to power enzymatic processes. The amounts of energy that are released by hydrolysis of the third or second bonds of ATP, releasing inorganic phosphate (P$_i$) or pyrophosphate (PP$_i$), respectively, are as follows:

$$ATP + H_2O \rightarrow ADP + P_i \qquad \Delta G° = -30.5 \text{ kJ/mol}$$

$$ATP + H_2O \rightarrow AMP + PP_i \qquad \Delta G° = -45.6 \text{ kJ/mol}$$

As can be seen by the above reactions, the energy that is released by the second and third bonds is only 50% greater than the energy released by the third bond alone.

In the case of nucleic acids, phosphates are used to link nucleotides via phosphodiester linkages. Phosphodiester linkages are very strong covalent bonds that are formed between a phosphate group and two 5-carbon carbohydrate rings. In DNA, the carbohydrates are deoxyribose, while in RNA, the carbohydrates are ribose. Because phosphodiester linkages form the backbone of nucleic acids, they are essential to all known life.

Wittig reaction

The Wittig reaction allows for the preparation of an alkene by the reaction of an aldehyde or ketone with triphenol phosphonium ylide, also called Wittig reagent, which is generated from a phosphonium salt. The geometry of the resulting alkene depends upon the reactivity of the ylide. If R is Ph, then the ylide is stabilized, and is not as reactive as when R is an alkyl. Stabilized ylides give (E)-alkenes, whereas non-stabilized ylides lead to (Z)-alkenes. Examples of the Wittig reaction can be seen below.

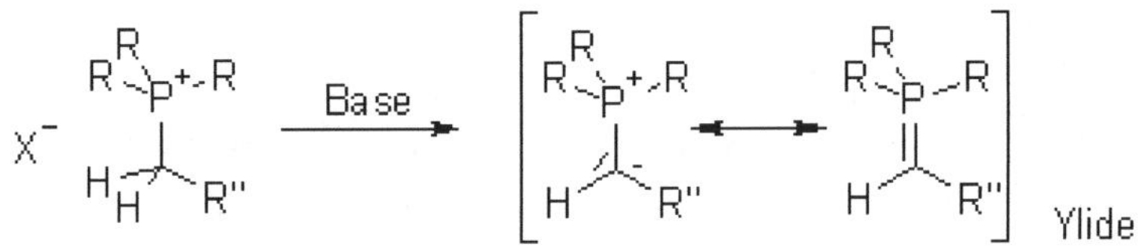

Physical Science

General Chemistry

Electronic Structure and the Periodic Table

Atomic number and mass number

The number of protons in an atom is known as the atomic number, Z, of the atom. Each element in the periodic table of elements has a different Z. For example, hydrogen (H) has 1 proton, and it's Z = 1. Calcium (Ca) has 20 protons, and it's Z = 20. Gold (Au) has 79 protons, and it's Z = 79. The number of neutrons in an atom is denoted by N. The mass number, A, is defined as the total number of protons and neutrons that are present in an atom. Thus, A = Z + N.

Electron capacity of an atomic shell

To determine the electron capacity of an atomic shell, the formula $2n^2$ is used when n = the shell number, or the principle quantum number. Electrons fill the orbitals and shells from the inside out, beginning with shell one. The valence shell is the outermost shell that is currently occupied, even if it only has one electron. Each shell, numbered from the one closest to the center of the nucleus outward (lowest to highest in energy), can hold up to a specific number of electrons due to its differing sublevel and orbital capacity:
- Shell 1: 2 electron capacity – s sublevel – 1 orbital
- Shell 2: 8 electron capacity – s and p sublevels – 4 orbitals
- Shell 3: 18 electron capacity – s, p, and d sublevels – 9 orbitals
- Shell 4: 32 electron capacity – s, p, d, and f sublevels – 16 orbitals

Octet rule

Because we know that s^2p^6 is the configuration of a noble gas, we assume that an atom is stable when surrounded by 8 electrons (4 electron pairs). This is known as the octet rule, and holds true for atoms of low atomic number (< 20).

Excited state and ground state

In quantum mechanics, an excited state of a system, such as an atom, molecule, or nucleus, is any configuration of the system that has a higher energy than the ground state. In other words, an excited state of a system involves any configuration where there is more energy than the absolute minimum. The lifetime of a system in an excited state is usually short: the spontaneous or induced emission of a quantum of energy, such as a photon or a phonon, usually occurs shortly after the system is promoted to the excited state, returning the system to a state with lower energy (either a less excited state or the ground state). A simple example of this concept involves the hydrogen atom: the ground state of the hydrogen atom corresponds to having the atom's single electron in the lowest possible orbit (that is, the spherically symmetric "1s" state, which has the lowest possible quantum numbers). By giving the atom additional energy (e.g., by the absorption of a photon of an appropriate energy), the electron is able to move into an excited state. If the photon has too much energy, then the electron will cease to be bound to the atom, and the atom will become ionized. Once the electron is in its excited state, we deem the hydrogen atom to be in its excited state.

Spectroscopy

Spectroscopy is the study of spectra, or the dependence of physical quantities on frequency. Spectroscopy is often used in physical and analytical chemistry for the identification of substances through the spectrum emitted or absorbed. A device for recording a spectrum is called a spectrometer. Spectroscopy can be classified according to the physical quantity that is measured or calculated, or the measurement process. The type of spectroscopy depends upon the physical quantity measured. Normally, the quantity that is measured is an amount or intensity of something.

Absorption and emission spectroscopy

Absorption spectroscopy uses the range of electromagnetic spectra in which a substance absorbs. In atomic absorption spectroscopy, the sample is atomized, and then light of a particular frequency is passed through the vapor. After calibration, the amount of absorption can be related to the concentrations of various metal ions using the Beer-Lambert law. Emission spectroscopy uses the range of electromagnetic spectra in which a substance radiates. The substance first absorbs energy, and then radiates this energy as light. This energy can be from a variety of sources, including collision (due either to high temperatures or otherwise), chemical reactions, and light. Absorption spectroscopy is utilized more commonly than emission spectroscopy.

Periodic table

The following is a diagram of a typical cell on the periodic table:

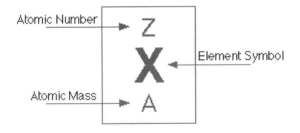

Periods of the periodic table

The periodic table consists of 7 horizontal periods. The lengths of the periods increase with the order of the period. And, elements within a period have consecutive atomic numbers. The 1st period is the shortest period. It consists of just two elements: H and He. The 2nd and 3rd periods have 8 elements each, and are called short periods. The 4th and 5th periods are longer periods, and have 18 elements each. The 6th period has 32 elements, including a 15 element series called the lanthanide series, which is separate from the table. The lanthanide series contains rare-earth elements that show similar properties. The 7th period contains all of the remaining elements, and is incomplete. This period also has a 15 element series called the actinide series, which is separate from the table. The actinide series has a separate identity, and contains uranium and most of the known transuranic elements.

Groups of the periodic table
The vertical columns of the periodic table are called groups. There are 18 groups in the periodic table, and the elements within each group do not have consecutive atomic numbers. The groups are further divided into two groups: A and B. Group 1A to VIII A has all the normal elements, while group 1B to VIII B holds all the transition metal elements. The two final groups are the lanthanide and the actinide series, also known as inner transition elements.

Note: The modern periodic table is approximately divided into metals and non-metals.

> **Review Video: <u>Periodic Table</u>**
*Visit **mometrix.com/academy** and enter **Code: 154828***

Alkali metals

The alkali metals are found in group 1 of the periodic table, formerly known as group IA. These metals are very reactive and do not occur freely in nature. Cesium and francium are the most reactive elements in this group. All of the alkali metals will explode if they are exposed to water. Alkali metals have only one electron in their outer shell, and are therefore ready to lose that one electron in ionic bonding with other elements. As with all other metals, the alkali metals are malleable, ductile, and are good conductors of heat and electricity. In addition, the alkali metals are softer than most other metals. The alkali metals are as follows:
- Lithium
- Sodium
- Potassium
- Rubidium
- Cesium
- Francium

Halogens

The halogens are five non-metallic elements that are found in group 7 of the periodic table. The term "halogen" means "salt-former", and compounds that contain halogens are called "salts". The halogens exist in all three states of matter at room temperature: solids (such as iodine and astatine), liquids (such as bromine), and gases (such as fluorine and chlorine). All halogens have 7 electrons in their outer shells, which gives them an oxidation number of -1. The halogens are as follows:
- Fluorine
- Chlorine
- Bromine
- Iodine
- Astatine

Noble gases

The six noble gases are found in group 18 of the periodic table. These elements were considered to be inert gases until the 1960's, because their oxidation number of 0 prevents them from readily forming compounds. All noble gases have the maximum number of electrons possible in their outer shell (2 for helium, 8 for all of the others), making them very stable. The noble gases are as follows:
- Helium
- Neon
- Argon
- Krypton
- Xenon
- Radon

> **Review Video: Noble Gases**
> Visit **mometrix.com/academy** *and enter* **Code: 122067**

Transition metals

The 38 elements in groups 3 through 12 of the periodic table are called "transition metals". As with all metals, the transition elements are both ductile and malleable, and conduct electricity and heat. The interesting thing about transition metals is that their valence electrons, or the electrons that they use to combine with other elements, are present in more than one shell. This is the reason why they often exhibit several common oxidation states. There are three noteworthy elements in the transition metals that are known to produce magnetic fields: iron, cobalt, and nickel.

Metalloids

Metalloids are the elements that are found along the stair-step line that distinguishes metals from non-metals. This line is drawn from between boron and aluminum to the border between polonium and astatine. The only exception to this is aluminum, which is classified under "other metals". Metalloids have properties of both metals and non-metals. Some of the metalloids, such as silicon and germanium, are semi-conductors. This means that they can carry an electrical charge under special conditions. This property makes metalloids useful in computers and calculators. The metalloids are as follows:
- Boron
- Silicon
- Germanium
- Arsenic
- Antimony
- Tellurium
- Polonium

Non-metals

The non-metals are the elements in groups 14-16 of the periodic table. Non-metals are not able to conduct electricity or heat very well. As opposed to metals, the non-metallic elements are very brittle, and cannot be rolled into wires, or pounded into sheets. The non-metals exist in two of the three states of matter at room temperature: solids (such as carbon) and gases (such as oxygen). The non-metals have no metallic luster, and do not reflect light. The non-metals have oxidation numbers of ±4, -3, or -2. The non-metal elements are as follows:

- Hydrogen
- Carbon
- Nitrogen
- Oxygen
- Phosphorus
- Sulfur
- Selenium

Other metals

The 7 elements that are classified as "other metals" are located in groups 13, 14, and 15. While these elements are ductile and malleable, they are not the same as the transition elements. Unlike the transition elements, these elements do not exhibit variable oxidation states, and their valence electrons are only present in their outer shell. All of these elements are solids, have a relatively high density, and are opaque. They have oxidation numbers of +3, ±4, or -3. The "other metals" are as follows:

- Aluminum
- Gallium
- Indium
- Tin
- Thallium
- Lead
- Bismuth

Physical properties of metals

The following are the physical properties of metals:
- Physical state – Metals are mostly solids at room temperature. Mercury (Hg) is the only exception: it is liquid at room temperature. The density of metals is high. Only sodium (Na) and potassium (K) have densities that are less than water. Therefore, all metals are hard materials except for sodium and potassium, which are soft metals. Lead is also considered to be a soft metal.
- Brittleness – Metals are not brittle, with the exception of zinc (Zn). Metals do not break easily because of their metallic bonds.
- Melting and boiling points – All metals, other than sodium (Na) and potassium (K), have high melting and boiling points. The melting points of sodium (Na) and potassium (K) are below 100°C, while the melting point of iron (Fe) is about 1540°C.
- Solubility – Pure metals are insoluble in solvents, such as water or any organic solvent. Metals can only be dissolved in acids.
- Sonorousness – Metals make a characteristic sound when hit with an object, and are thus sonorous. The sonorousness of metals depends upon the temperature and density.
- Malleability – Metals can be hammered or beaten into thin sheets without breaking. Malleable means that metallic bonds in the metals do not break easily. Gold (Au) and

silver (Ag) are highly malleable elements. Metals can be made into thin foil sheets because of malleability.

- Ductility – Metals can be melted and drawn into thin wires. Because of this property, metals are known as ductile. The ductility property follows from the malleability property. While being drawn into wires, metals are stretched. Because of the strong metallic bonds, the metal atoms do not separate easily. Copper (Cu), aluminum (Al), and Ag are very ductile, because very thin wires can be made out of these elements.
- Tensility – Due to their ductility and malleability properties, metals are very strong. Their bonds do not break easily, as their electrons are shared over an array of metal atoms. This gives metals a very high tensile strength, and therefore metals do not break easily.
- Conduction of heat and electricity – In metals, the bonds are formed by excess or free electrons moving around large arrays of atoms. These electrons are able to conduct electricity and heat. Ag, Cu, and Al are good conductors of heat and electricity, while lead (Pb) is a poor conductor of electricity.

Characteristics of elements in a period

The following are characteristics of elements in a period:
- The atomic numbers are consecutive.
- The number of valence electrons in the elements increases incrementally from left to right.
- The elements of the same period have different valencies.
- The atomic radii decrease while going from left to right in a period.
- Metallic character reduces while going from left to right in a period.
- Chemical reactivity is highest at the two extremes, and is the lowest in the center. The reactivity on the left extreme is the most electropositive, while the reactivity on the right extreme is the most electronegative.
- Oxides that are formed of elements on the left are basic in nature, while elements on the right are acidic in nature. Oxides of elements in the center are amphoteric.

Characteristics of elements in a group

The following are characteristics of elements in a group:
- The atomic numbers are not consecutive.
- The number of valence electrons in the elements is the same within a group.
- The elements of the same group have the same valencies.
- The atomic radii increase while going from top to bottom in a group.
- Metallic character increases while going from top to bottom in metallic groups. In non-metallic groups, the non-metallic nature decreases while going from top to bottom.
- Chemical reactivity increases while going from top to bottom in metallic groups. In non-metallic groups, the chemical reactivity decreases while going from top to bottom.

Valency

The tendency of atoms to donate or accept electrons in order to stabilize their outermost orbits is known as the valency of the element. Valency is the measure of reactivity of the element. Quite a lot of transition metals and non-metals show variable valency. A stable orbit may mean that there are no unpaired electrons left in the outermost orbit. Generally, it is observed that an atom tries to acquire the electronic configuration of its nearest noble gas atom. Amongst the transition metals, iron and nickel show variable valency. Amongst the non-metals, oxygen and nitrogen are good examples. These metals and non-metals combine to give various compounds that have different properties. For example, Fe_2O_3 is different from FeO. In Fe_2O_3, Fe shows a valency of +3, while O shows a valency of −2, and Fe_2O_3 is a magnetic compound. In FeO, Fe shows a valency of +2, and FeO is non-magnetic. Water (H_2O) and hydrogen peroxide (H_2O_2) are both compounds of hydrogen and oxygen. In H_2O, H shows a valence of +1, while O shows a valence of −2. However, in H_2O_2, H has a valency of +1, while O has a valency of −1. Water is a neutral compound, while H_2O_2 is a highly acidic compound.

Ionization energy

Ionization energy is the energy that is required to remove one mole of electrons from one mole of atoms in the gas phase. Ionization energy is a measure of how strongly an atom holds on to its electrons. The first ionization energy, I_1, is the amount of energy that is required to remove the first electron (i.e., to form the neutral atom). More energy is required to remove the second electron (I_2). The remaining electrons experience less

$e^- - e^-$ repulsion, and thus experience a greater effective nuclear charge. Therefore, ionization energy continues to increase as successive electrons are removed.

> ➢ **Review Video: Ionization Energy**
> *Visit **mometrix.com/academy** and enter **Code: 862908***

Electron affinity

The electron affinity of an element is the energy given off when a neutral atom in the gas phase gains an extra electron to form a negatively charged ion. A fluorine atom in the gas phase, for example, gives off energy when it gains an electron to form a fluoride ion:

$F(g) + e^- \rightarrow F^-(g) \quad \Delta H\,° = -328.0 \ \text{kJ/mol}$

Electron affinities are more difficult to measure than ionization energies, and are usually known to fewer significant figures. Electron affinities generally become smaller as we go down a column of the periodic table for two reasons: First, the electron being added to the atom is placed in larger orbitals, where it spends less time near the nucleus of the atom. And, second, the number of electrons on an atom increases as we go down a column, so the force of repulsion between the electron being added and the electrons already present on a neutral atom becomes larger. Electron affinity data are complicated by the fact that the repulsion between the electron being added to the atom and the electrons already present on the atom depends on the volume of the atom. Among the nonmetals in groups VIA and VIIA, this force of repulsion is largest for the very smallest atoms in these columns: oxygen and fluorine.

Electronegativity

Electronegativity is the affinity of an atom for electrons. The atoms of the various elements differ in their affinity for electrons. The Pauling scale is the most commonly used scale for electronegativity. Based upon the Pauling scale, fluorine, the most electronegative element, is assigned a value of 4.0, and values range down to cesium and francium, which are the least electronegative at 0.7.

Atom sizes

The atomic size is not easily defined since the electron orbitals only gradually go to zero as the distance from the nucleus increases. For atoms that can form solid crystals, the distance between adjacent nuclei can give an estimate of the atomic size. For atoms that do not form solid crystals, other techniques are used, including theoretical calculations. As an example, the size of a hydrogen atom is estimated to be approximately 1.2×10^{-10} m. Compare this to the size of the proton, the only particle in the nucleus of the hydrogen atom, which is approximately 0.87×10^{-15} m. Thus, the ratio between the sizes of the hydrogen atom to its nucleus is about 100,000 fold. Atoms of different elements do vary in size, but the sizes are roughly the same to within a factor of 2 or so. The reason for this is that elements with a large positive charge on the nucleus attract electrons to the center of the atom more strongly.

Bonding

Solid Bonds

- Bond strength – Energy required to break the bond.
- Covalent bond –The strongest bond.
  - Atoms share valence electrons.
  - Position is fixed – Makes the compound brittle.
- Ionic bond – Strong bond.
  - Attraction between + and – ions.
  - Lattice energy ($E = kQ_1Q_2/d$).
  - Position is fixed – Makes the compound brittle.
- Metallic bond – Variable bond strength.
  - Attraction between ions and valence electrons (electron–sea model).
  - Mobile electrons – Conductor.
  - Pliable metal ions – Malleable and ductile.
- Molecular bond – Weak bond.
  - Attraction between (+) and (−) regions.
  - Three levels – Strongest to weakest:
    - Hydrogen bond – N, O, and F (small with high electronegativity) bond to H (low electronegative); almost ionic.
    - Dipole force – Polar molecules.
    - London dispersion force – Temporary polarization of valence electrons (increases with increased atomic or molecular size).

Ionic bonds

Atomic bonds where electrons are transferred between the constituent atoms of a compound are known as ionic bonds (or electrovalent bonds). The compound formed is called an ionic or electrovalent compound. Generally, ionic bonds are formed between metallic atoms that have extra electrons to spare and non-metallic atoms which are electron deficient. Magnesium oxide (MgO), potassium chloride (KCl), and iron (II) oxide (FeO) are some examples of ionic compounds. Ionic compounds are crystalline in nature, and thus have high melting points. Also, because of the availability of ions, such compounds are good conductors of heat. They form electrolytes when molten or in solution. However, they are non-conductors of electricity when solid, as there are no free ions since they are all locked together in a crystal. When an ion loses an electron, it is called a positive ion, or a cation. When an ion gains an electron, it is called a negative ion, or an anion. In the examples above, Na^+, Mg^{2+}, K^+, and Fe^{2+} are cations, while Cl^-, and O^{2-} are anions.

> ➤ **Review Video: <u>Ionic Bonds</u>**
> *Visit **mometrix.com/academy** and enter **Code:** 116546*

Covalent bonds

In an oxygen (O) atom, the electronic configuration is 2 electrons in the K-shell, and 6 electrons in the L-shell. It would rather borrow two electrons from another atom in order to complete its last shell, rather than give up its six electrons. The hydrogen (H) atom has only one electron, and only needs to borrow one extra electron to complete its first shell. Two atoms of H and one atom of O can fulfill each other's needs by sharing electrons in their outermost orbits, forming a water molecule, H_2O. In an H_2O molecule, the electrons are not totally given up, as in the case of Na^+Cl^-, but are instead shared by each of the neighboring atoms. An atomic bond formed by the sharing of electrons is called a covalent bond. Compounds that are formed due to covalent bonding of atoms are called covalent compounds, and are generally formed between non-metals. Hydrogen gas (H_2), nitrogen gas (N_2), oxygen gas (O_2), and hydrochloric acid (HCl) are examples of covalently bonded compounds. If the neighboring atoms share a pair of electrons, then the covalent bond is a single covalent bond. On the other hand, if they share two or three pairs of electrons, then the covalent bond is double or triple covalent bond, respectively. Compared to ionic bonds, covalent bonds are shorter and more difficult to break.

There are two types of covalent bonds: sigma bonds and pi bonds. When the covalent bond is linear, or aligned along the plane containing the atoms, the bond is known as sigma (s) bond. Sigma bonds are strong and the electron sharing is at its maximum. Methane, CH_4, is a good example of sigma bonding, and it has four of them. When the covalent bond is parallel, formed by the overlap of two p-orbital lobes, the bond is known as a pi bond. Relative to sigma bonds, pi bonds are usually weaker because they have less orbital overlap due to their parallel orientation. Single bonds are composed solely of sigma bonds, while double and triple bonds are composed of one sigma bond and either one or two pi bonds, respectively.

> ➤ **Review Video: <u>Pi Bonds and Sigma Bonds</u>**
> *Visit **mometrix.com/academy** and enter **Code:** 316056*

VSEPR theory

The valence shell electron pair repulsion (VSEPR) theory is a model that is used to predict the shape of a molecule based on the assumption that all negatively charged valence electrons repel each other. This model is based on the simple idea, formulated by Lewis and others, that electrons tend to move as far away from one another as possible (like charges repel one another). Because electrons tend to pair with one another if they have opposite spins, we can modify the idea to say that pairs of electrons tend to adopt a geometry that minimizes repulsions. We have noted earlier that only the electrons in the valence shell are involved in bonding, so we only need to worry about those electrons.

Phases and Phase Equilibria

Gases

- Phase:
  - Molecules are free to fill an entire volume.
  - Molecules are far apart – Compressible.
- Pressure:
  - Force (weight)/Area.
  - Air pressure decreases with altitude.
  - Measuring tools:
    - Barometer – Measures absolute pressure.
    - Manometer – Measures pressure differences (gauge pressures).
      $$P_{gas} = P_{atmosphere} \pm \Delta H \text{ in mmHg}$$
- Kinetic Theory for Gases (ideal gas):
  - Molecules in constant random motion, which is proportional to the temperature:
    - $E = mu^2/2 = cT$
    - $u = (3RT/MM)^{1/2}$
    - Where: $R = 8.31$ kg·m^2/s^2·mol·K, and MM is in kg.
    - Temperature/velocity distribution curve.
  - Molecular volume is zero compared to the volume of the container.
  - Collisions produce pressure without loss of total kinetic energy.
  - Molecules do not interact.

Units of pressure

The height of a column of mercury, Hg, in millimeters is a standard way of measuring pressure (mmHg). At sea level, and at standard gravitational acceleration, the air pressure is defined as one atmosphere (atm):
- 1 atm = 760 mmHg.

There are also additional units of measuring pressure, including newtons (N)/m^2, pascals (Pa), bars, torr, and pounds per square inch (psi). In terms of atmospheres, the conversions for these units are as follows:
- 1 atm = 101,325 N/m^2
- 1 atm = 101,325 Pa (1 Pa = 1 N/m^2)

- 1 atm = 1.01325 bars
- 1 atm = 760 torr (1 torr = 1 mmHg)
- 1 atm = 14.7 psi

Gay-Lussac's law of combining gas volumes

The volumes of gases taking part in a chemical reaction show simple whole-number ratios to one another when those volumes are measured at the same temperature and pressure. For example, 1 liter of nitrogen gas (N_2) reacts with 3 liters of hydrogen gas (H_2) to produce 2 liters of ammonia gas (NH_3):
$$N_2(g) + 3H_2(g) \rightarrow 2NH_3(g)$$

Since all of the reactants and products are gases, the molar ratio of $N_2(g):H_2(g):NH_3(g)$ of 1:3:2 is also the ratio of the volumes of gases. Therefore, 10 mL of N_2 would react with 10 x 3 = 30 mL of H_2 to produce 10 x 2 = 20 mL NH_3.

Ideal gas law formula

The ideal gas law formula is pretty accurate for all gases, since we assume that the gas molecules are point masses, and the collisions of the molecules are totally elastic (a completely elastic collision means that the energy of the molecules before a collision equals the energy of the molecules after a collision). The formula becomes less accurate as the gas becomes very compressed and the temperature decreases. There are some correction factors for both of these factors for each gas in order to convert the ideal gas law formula into a real gas law formula, but the ideal gas law is a good estimation of the way that gases act. The ideal gas law formula is as follows:
$$PV = nRT$$
Where:
P = The absolute pressure of the gas in atm.
V = The volume of the gas in liters.
n = The moles of gas.
R = The universal gas constant, 0.0821 L·atm/mol·K.
T = The temperature in Kelvin.

Charles' law and Boyle's law

Charles' law gives the manner in which the volume of a gas changes with temperature. The law states that, for a constant pressure on a given mass of gas, the volume is directly proportional to the temperature:
$$V \propto T$$

Thus, the proportion, V/T, is constant (this constant of proportionality is not the same as that given by Boyle's law).

Robert Boyle made the following observations in the case of gases:
- At a constant temperature, the volume of a gas is inversely proportional to the pressure.
- At a constant temperature, the density of a gas is directly proportional to the pressure.

Boyle's law can be written mathematically as follows:

$PV = k$

Where:

P = The pressure of the system.

V = The volume of the system.

k = A constant representative of the pressure and volume of the system.

Note: Boyle's and Charles' laws only hold good for ideal gases.

> **Review Video: Charles' Law**
> Visit **mometrix.com/academy** and enter **Code: 537776**

> **Review Video: Boyle's Law**
> Visit **mometrix.com/academy** and enter **Code: 115757**

Kinetic theory

The kinetic theory is as follows:

- All matter is composed of atoms, which are the smallest units of each element. A particle of a gas could be an atom or a group of atoms.
- Atoms have an energy of motion that we perceive as temperature. The motion of atoms or molecules can be in the form of linear motion of translation, the vibration of atoms or molecules against one another or pulling against a bond, or the rotation of individual atoms or groups of atoms.
- There is a temperature to which we can extrapolate absolute zero, at which, theoretically, the motion of the atoms and molecules would stop.
- The pressure of a gas is due to the motion of the atoms or molecules of gas striking the object bearing that pressure. These collisions are elastic (without friction), when they are against the side of the container or other particles of gas.
- There is a very large distance between the particles of a gas, relative to the size of the particles, such that the size of the particle can be considered negligible.

Dalton's law of partial pressure

Dalton's law of partial pressure states that the pressure of a mixture of gases is equal to the sum of the "partial" pressures of all of the constituent gases alone. Mathematically, this can be represented as follows:

$Pressure_{Total} = Pressure_1 + Pressure_2 \ldots + Pressure_n$

> **Review Video: Dalton's Law of Partial Pressure**
> Visit **mometrix.com/academy** and enter **Code: 355830**

Hydrogen bonds

Hydrogen bonds occur between molecules that have a permanent net dipole, resulting from hydrogen being covalently bonded to either fluorine, oxygen, or nitrogen. For example, hydrogen bonds operate between molecules of water (H_2O), ammonia (NH_3), hydrogen fluoride (HF), hydrogen peroxide (H_2O_2), alkanols (alcohols) such as methanol (CH_3OH), alkanoic (carboxylic) acids such as ethanoic (acetic) acid (CH_3COOH), and organic amines such as methanamine (methyl amine, CH_3NH_2). Hydrogen bonding is a stronger intermolecular force than either dispersion forces or dipole-dipole interactions because the hydrogen nucleus is extremely small and positively charged, while fluorine, oxygen and nitrogen are very electronegative, so that the electron of the hydrogen atom is strongly attracted to them. This results in a highly positive charge localized on the hydrogen atom, and a highly negative charge localized on the fluorine, oxygen, or nitrogen atom. Therefore, the electrostatic attraction between these molecules will be greater than for the polar molecules that do not have hydrogen bonding.

Dipole-dipole interactions

Dipole-dipole interactions are as follows:
- Are stronger intermolecular forces than dispersion forces.
- Occur between molecules that have permanent net dipoles (polar molecules), such as SCl_2, PCl_3, and CH_3Cl.
- If the permanent net dipole within the polar molecules results from a covalent bond between a hydrogen atom and either fluorine, oxygen or nitrogen, then the resulting intermolecular force is referred to as a hydrogen bond.
- The partial positive charge on one molecule is electrostatically attracted to the partial negative charge on a neighboring molecule.

Metallic bonds

Metallic bonds are where the valence electrons of metal atoms are shared by more than one neighboring atom. This type of bond occurs in metals only. The metal atoms are held together by a "sea" of electrons floating around. Metals consist of a lattice of positive ions through which a cloud of electrons moves. The positive ions will tend to repel one another, but are held together by the negatively charged electron cloud. The mobile electrons can transfer thermal vibrations from one part of the structure to another (i.e., metals can conduct heat). They are also good conductors of electricity. Metals are malleable and ductile because the positive ions in a metal are not held together by rigid bonds. Instead, they are capable of sliding past one another if the metal is deformed.

> ➤ **Review Video: Metallic Bonds**
> *Visit **mometrix.com/academy** and enter **Code: 230855***

Van der Waal's bonds

Van der Waals forces are relatively weak electric forces that attract neutral molecules to one another in gases, in liquefied and solidified gases, and in almost all organic liquids and solids. Theses forces are named for the Dutch physicist, Johannes van der Waals, who first postulated these intermolecular forces in 1873 while developing a theory to account for the properties of real gases. Solids that are held together by van der Waals forces have characteristically lower melting points, and are softer than those that are held together by the stronger ionic, covalent, and metallic bonds. Van der Waals forces may arise from three sources: First, the molecules of some materials, although electrically neutral, may be permanent electric dipoles. Because of fixed distortion in the distribution of electric charge in the structure of some molecules, one side is always positive, while the other side is negative. The tendency of such permanent dipoles to align with each other results in a net attractive force. Second, the presence of molecules that are permanent dipoles temporarily distorts the electric charge in other nearby polar or nonpolar molecules, thereby inducing further polarization. An additional attractive force results from the interaction of a permanent dipole with a neighboring induced dipole. Third, even though no molecules of a material are permanent dipoles, a force of attraction exists between the molecules, accounting for condensing to the liquid state at sufficiently low temperatures.

Phase changes

A phase change occurs when a structural unit has sufficient energy (temperature) to break its solid bond.
- Pressure vs. Temperature Graph:
  - Triple point – Three-phase equilibrium.
  - Critical point – Permanent gas.
- Break Occurs in Two Stages – Triple point below atmospheric pressure:
  - Melting (solid → liquid):
    - Bond is weakened, but not altogether broken – Units can slide by each other.
    - Opposite is freezing.
  - Boiling (liquid → gas):
    - Bond is broken – Units are free of all cohesion.
    - Opposite is liquefaction.
- Break Occurs in One Stage – Triple point above atmospheric pressure: Sublimation (opposite is   deposition).
- Melting Temperature is Pressure Dependent – High pressure favors a denser phase.

The process of converting a solid into a liquid is known as melting. The temperature at which melting occurs is called the melting point. The inverse of melting is called freezing, or solidification. If solidification converts the solid into properly structured crystals, then the process is also known as a crystallization process. The process of converting a liquid into a gas is called vaporizing. The inverse of vaporizing is called condensation. The temperature at which the liquid turns into gas is called the boiling point of the substance. Some solids, like solid iodine, carbon dioxide, and naphthalene balls, convert directly into a gaseous state from their solid state. They skip the liquid phase. The process of going directly from a solid state to a gaseous state is known as sublimation. The inverse of sublimation is known as solid condensation, or deposition.

Colligative properties

The term "colligative properties" refers to macroscopic observable properties, such as thermodynamic variables (e.g., vapor pressure, boiling and melting temperatures, etc.).

Raoult's law

Raoult's law relates the vapor pressure of components to the composition of the solution. The law assumes ideal behavior. It gives a simple picture of the situation just as the ideal gas law does. The ideal gas law is very useful as a limiting law. As the interactive forces between molecules and the volume of the molecules approaches zero, the behavior of gases approach the behavior of the ideal gas. Raoult's law is similar in that it assumes that the physical properties of the components are identical. The more similar the components, the more their behavior approaches that described by Raoult's law. Using the example of a solution of two liquids, A and B, if no other gases are present, the total vapor pressure, P_{tot}, above the solution is equal to the sum of the vapor pressures of the two components, P_A and P_B.

$$P_{tot} = P_A + P_B$$

If the two components are very similar, or, in the limiting case, differ only in isotopic content, then the vapor pressure of each component will be equal to the vapor pressure of the pure substance, P_0, times the mole fraction in the solution. This is Raoult's law.

Boiling point elevation

A solution typically has a measurably higher boiling point than that of the pure solvent. For example, the boiling point of pure water is 100°C, while the boiling point of water can be elevated by the addition of a solute, such as a salt. This elevation of the boiling point is referred to as boiling point elevation. A treatment of boiling point elevation is given by Ebbing. The boiling point elevation, ΔT_b, is a colligative property of the solution, and for dilute solutions is found to be proportional to the molal concentration, c_m, of the solution:

$$\Delta T_b = K_b c_m$$

Where:
K_b = The boiling point elevation constant.

Freezing point depression

A solution typically has a measurably lower melting point than the pure solvent. For example, the freezing point of pure water is 0°C, but that freezing point can be depressed by the addition of a solute, such as a salt. This depression of the freezing point is known as freezing point depression. A practical example of freezing point depression is the use of ordinary salt (sodium chloride, NaCl) on icy roads in the winter to help melt the ice from the roads by lowering the freezing point of the ice. A 10% salt solution is said to lower the freezing point from 0°C to –6°C (20°F), and a 20% salt solution is said to lower it to –16°C (2°F). A more formal treatment of freezing point depression is given by Ebbing. The freezing point depression, ΔT_f, is a colligative property of the solution, and for dilute solutions is found to be proportional to the molal concentration, c_m, of the solution:

$$\Delta T_b = K_f c_m$$

Where:
K_f = The freezing point depression constant.

Osmotic pressure of a dilute solution

The osmotic pressure of a dilute solution is found to obey a relationship of the same form as the ideal gas law:

$$P_{osmotic} = \frac{nRT}{V}$$

In chemistry texts, it is usually expressed in terms of the molarity of the solution, and given the symbol Π.

$$\Pi = MR'\,T$$

In these relationships, $R = 8.3145$ J/k·mol is the normal gas constant, and $R' = 0.0821$ L·atm/K·mol is the gas constant expressed in terms of liters and atmospheres.

Osmolarity

Osmolarity is a measure of the osmotic pressure that is exerted by a solution across a perfect semi-permeable membrane (one that allows for the free passage of water, but completely prevents the movement of solutes), as compared to pure water. Osmolarity is dependent on the number of particles in solution, but independent of the nature of the particles. For example, 1 mole of glucose dissolved in 1 liter (L) of water has an osmolarity of 1 osmole (osm)/L. If 1 mole of another sugar, such as sucrose, were added to the same liter of water, then the osmolarity would become 2 osm/L. It does not matter that the solution contains 1 mole each of two different solutes: glucose and sucrose. If 1 mole of NaCl were dissolved in 1 L of water, it would produce a 1 mol/L NaCl solution with an osmolarity 2 osm/L, because NaCl dissociates into Na^+ and Cl^- (two particles) in solution. This is true of all compounds that dissociate in solution.

Properties of colloids

The properties of colloids are as follows:
- The particles of dispersant are between approximately 5-200 nm in diameter.
- The mixture does not separate upon standing in a standard gravity condition (i.e., one "g").
- The mixture does not separate by common fiber filter, but might be filterable by materials with a smaller mesh.
- The mixture is not necessarily completely homogeneous, but is usually close to being so.
- The mixture may appear cloudy or almost totally transparent; but, if you shine a light beam through it, the pathway of the light is visible from any angle. This scattering of light is called the Tyndall effect
- There usually is not a definite, sharp saturation point at which no more dispersant can be taken by the dispersing agent.
- The dispersant can be coagulated, or separated, by clumping the dispersant particles with heat, or by an increase in the concentration of ionic particles in solution into the mixture.
- There is usually only a small effect of any of the colligative properties due to the dispersant.

Henry's law

In chemistry, Henry's law states that the mass of a gas that dissolves in a definite volume of liquid is directly proportional to the pressure of the gas, provided that the gas does not react with the solvent. William Henry first formulated the law in 1801. The formula for Henry's law is as follows:

$$e^P = e^{kC}$$

Where:
P = The partial pressure of the gaseous solute above the solution.
C = The concentration of the gas in mol/L.
k = Henry's law constant, which has the units L·atm/mol.

Stoichiometry

Molecular weight

The unit of the molecular weight (MW), formula weight (FW), or atomic weight is "grams per mole", which provides a relationship between the mass in grams and moles of material. The formula to calculate this relationship is as follows:

$$MW = \frac{m}{n}$$

Where:
m = The mass of the material.
n = The number of moles of material.

Empirical formula and molecular formula

The empirical formula is the formula whose subscripts represent the simplest whole number ratio of atoms in a molecule, or the simplest whole number ratio of moles of each element in a mole of the compound. The simplest formula is usually determined by considering experimental data, hence the name "empirical", which means that it is based upon experimentation. The empirical formula speaks of relative numbers. For example, CH_2 says that there will be twice as many hydrogens as there are carbons in the compound that has this simplest formula. A molecular formula is a formula whose subscripts represent the exact numbers of atoms of each element per molecule of the compound, or the absolute number of moles of each element per mole of the compound. A molecular formula may be reducible to a simple formula if all of its subscripts are divisible by a common denominator. Some compounds have the same empirical and molecular formula. For example, carbon dioxide has, as its empirical and molecular formula, CO_2. The empirical and molecular formulas for sulfur dioxide are also the same: SO_2. There are many situations where two or more compounds have the same simplest formula, but differ by their molecular formulas.

Chemical formulas

Substances (either compounds or mixtures) can be written as a combination of the symbols for its constituent elements, but have to be written in correct proportion. The written representation of a molecule of a substance, using symbols of the constituent elements, is called the molecular or chemical formula. For example, a molecule of potassium permanganate is written as $KMnO_4$, which means that one molecule of potassium permanganate contains one atom of potassium (K), one atom of manganese (Mn), and four atoms of oxygen (O). A molecule of water is written as H_2O, which means that there are 2 atoms of hydrogen (H) and one atom of oxygen (O). In an ordinary molecule of table salt, or NaCl, there is one atom of sodium (Na) and one atom of chlorine (Cl).

Note: To be able to write a chemical formula, we must first know the chemical reaction that precedes the formation of the compound.

Molecular compounds

Molecular compounds are named differently than ionic compounds. For molecular compounds, a set of prefixes are used that identify the subscript in the formula. For example, in the case of PCl_3, there is one phosphorus atom (P^{3+}) and three chlorides ($3Cl^-$). In order to identify the subscript for chloride, we would use the prefix "tri-" to indicate that there are three chloride ions. Therefore, the molecular name for PCl_3 is Phosphorus Trichloride. Another example would be N_2O_4. In this case, we would use the prefix "di-" in front of the elemental name for nitrogen in order to indicate that there are 2 nitrogen atoms ($2N^{4+}$), and then we would use the prefix "tetra-" in front of the oxide ion to indicate that there are four oxides ($4O^{2-}$). Therefore, the molecular name for N_2O_4 is Dinitrogen Tetroxide.

Metric units

Length
1 centimeter (cm) = 10 millimeters (mm)
1 decimeter (dm) = 10 cm
1 meter (m) = 10 dm
1 decameter (dam) = 10 m

Volume
1 microliter (μL) = 10^{-6} liters (L)
1 milliliter (mL) = 10^{-3} L = 1000 μL
1 liter = 1000 mL
1 centiliter (cL) = 10 mL
1 deciliter (dL) = 10 cL
1 liter = 10 dL
1 cubic cm (cm^3) = 1000 mm^3
1 cubic dm (dm^3) = 1000 cm^3
1 cubic meter (m^3) = 1000 dm^3 = 1000 L

Weight
1 picogram (pg) = 10^{-12} grams (g)
1 nanogram (ng) = 10^{-9} g = 1000 pg
1 microgram (μg) = 10^{-6} g = 1000 ng
1 milligram (mg) = 10^{-3} g = 1000 μg
1 gram = 1000 mg
1 kilogram (kg) = 10^3 g = 1000 g
1 tonne = 1000 kg

Relationships
1 part per million (ppm) = 1 mg/kg = 1 μg/g
1 part per hundred (%) = 1 g/100 g = 1% w/w (weight to weight basis)

SI prefixes and their multiplying factors

yotta (Y) – 1,000,000,000,000,000,000,000,000 = 10^{24}
zetta (Z) – 1,000,000,000,000,000,000,000 = 10^{21}
exa (E) – 1,000,000,000,000,000,000 = 10^{18}
peta (P) – 1,000,000,000,000,000 = 10^{15}
tera (T) – 1,000,000,000,000 = 10^{12}
giga (G) – 1,000,000,000 = 10^9 = a billion
mega (M) – 1,000,000 = 10^6 = a million
kilo (k) – 1,000 = 10^3 = a thousand
hecto (h) – 100 = 10^2 = a hundred
deca (da) – 10 = ten
1
deci (d) – 0.1 = 10^{-1} = a tenth
centi (c) – 0.01 = 10^{-2} = a hundredth
milli (m) – 0.001 = 10^{-3} = a thousandth
micro (μ) – 0.000 001 = 10^{-6} = a millionth
nano (n) – 0.000 000 001 = 10^{-9} = a billionth
pico (p) – 0.000 000 000 001 = 10^{-12}
femto (f) – 0.000 000 000 000 001 = 10^{-15}
atto (a) – 0.000 000 000 000 000 001 = 10^{-18}
zepto (z) – 0.000 000 000 000 000 000 001 = 10^{-21}
yocto (y) – 0.000 000 000 000 000 000 000 001 = 10^{-24}

Gram atomic mass and moles

The amount of substance in grams equal to its atomic mass in grams is called the gram atomic mass. For example, since the atomic mass of Na is 23, the gram atomic mass of Na is 23 gm. Similarly, since the atomic mass of O is 16, the gram atomic mass of O is 16 gm. The gram atomic mass is also known as the gram atomic weight of a substance. It was discovered by Avogadro, that the gram atomic mass of substance contains 6.23×10^{23} atoms. This means that, if you take 23 gm of Na, there will be 6.23×10^{23} atoms of Na. Similarly, if you take 16 gm of O, you will have 6.23×10^{23} atoms of O. Since the sizes of atoms increases with the masses of the atoms, Avogadro's number remains constant for the different atomic masses. The mass of a substance that contains 6.23×10^{23} atoms is also known as the molar mass. Thus, 1 mole of Na will be 23 gm of Na, and 1 mole of O will be 16 gm of O. The amount of substance in grams equal to the molecular mass in grams is called the gram molecular mass. For example, the molecular mass of NaCl is 60. Thus, the gram molecular mass of NaCl is 60 gm. The molecular mass of O_2 is 32, and therefore the gram molecular mass of O_2 is 32 gm. Finally, since the molecular mass of water is 18, the gram molecular mass of water is 18 gm.

Density

The density of a substance determines whether it is in the solid, liquid, or gaseous state. Density is defined as follows:

$$\text{Density} = \frac{\text{Mass of Substance (in gm)}}{\text{Volume of Substance (in cubic cm)}}$$

Generally, if the density is high, then the substance is in solid form. If the density is low, then the substance is in liquid form. If the density is even lower, then the substance is in a gaseous state. It is imperative here that density is also a function of temperature. The density of iron is 7.86 gm/cc. The density of iron in liquid form (at a temperature of 1537°C) is approximately 7.23 gm/cc. Thus, it can be seen that the solid iron volume expands upon heating and becomes liquid. Other than ice, all substances become more dense when they solidify. Water is the only substance in nature whose volume expands upon solidification. The density of ice is 0.93 gm/cc, while the density of water is 1.0 gm/cc. This is the reason why ice floats on water.

Assigning oxidation numbers

The following are the ways in which oxidation numbers are assigned:
- The oxidation number for elements is always zero. For example, Na (s), O_2 (g), and C (s) all have zero oxidation numbers.
- The oxidation number of monoatomic ions is the same as their charge. This means that for Na^+ the oxidation number is +1, and for Cl^- the oxidation number is -1. Oxygen is assigned a -2 oxidation number in covalent compounds. This refers to compounds such as CO, CO_2, SO_2, and SO_3.
- There is an exception to the previous rule, and it involves peroxides, such as H_2O_2. Here, each O in the O_2^{2-} group has a -1 oxidation number.
- Hydrogen is assigned a +1 oxidation number in covalent compounds. This refers to compounds such as HCl, NH_3, and H_2O.
- In binary compounds, the element with the greatest attraction to electrons gets the negative oxidation number. In other words, the most electronegative of the pair gets the negative number.
- The sum of the oxidation numbers is zero for a neutral compound, and equal to the ionic charge for an ionic species. For example, in H_2O, a neutral species, H is +1, O is -2, and the sum of the two is 0. For CO_3^{2-}, each O is -2, C is +4, and the sum is -2.

Redox titrations

A redox titration (also called oxidation-reduction titration, or potentiometric titration) is a type of titration that is based upon a redox reaction between the analyte and titrant. A redox titration involves the use of a potentiometer. An analyte is the substance or chemical constituent that is being measured in an analytical procedure. For instance, in an immunoassay, the analyte may be the ligand, while in a blood glucose test, the analyte is glucose. A reagent of known concentration and volume, called the titrant, is used to react with a measured volume of reactant. Using a calibrated burette to add the titrant, it is possible to determine the exact amount that has been consumed when the endpoint is reached. The endpoint of a titration is when the pH of the reactant is just about equal to 7, and when the reactant stops reverting back to its original color.

Chemical reactions

The transformation of a substance into a new substance or substances is called a chemical reaction. For example, the chemical reaction for the production of water can be written as: $2H_2 + O_2 \rightarrow 2H_2O$. Hydrogen atoms exists as a diatomic gas, with 2 hydrogen atoms sticking together, written as H_2. The same is true for oxygen gas (O_2). This means that, for the reaction above, the two elements, hydrogen and oxygen in a diatomic gaseous form, combine in a reaction to produce water molecules. The numbers of atoms of each element have to be balanced before and after the reaction takes place. This is important due to the fact that atoms are neither created nor destroyed in a chemical reaction. The factors on the left-hand side of the equation are called the reactants, while the factors on the right-hand side are called the products. Chemical reactions are generally accompanied by heat changes. A reaction in which heat is evolved is called an exothermic chemical reaction. A reaction in which heat is absorbed is called an endothermic chemical reaction. Chemical reactions, whether exothermic or endothermic, are also categorized as reversible or irreversible reactions. A reaction that can proceed in either direction is called reversible, while a reaction that can proceed in only one direction is called irreversible. For example, if you burn sugar in air, you will get carbon and water. This reaction is irreversible because, if you take carbon and water and mix them together, you will never get the original sugar back!

> **Review Video: Chemical Reactions**
> *Visit **mometrix.com/academy** and enter **Code: 579876***

Writing chemical equations

The following are considerations for writing chemical equations:
- The number of atoms on the reactant side should be the same as the number of atoms on the product side: the reaction should be balanced.
- A horizontal arrow should indicate the direction in which the reaction is proceeding. Normally, the arrow is from left to right ($\rightarrow$). However, for a reversible reaction, the arrow can be shown from the right to left.
- In the case of precipitation of a compound after the reaction, a vertically downward arrow is indicated ($\downarrow$).
- In the case that a product is gaseous, a vertically upward arrow is indicated ($\uparrow$).
- The physical state of the reactants and products can be shown as follows: (s) = solid, (l) = liquid, and (aq) = aqueous (the compound is dissolved in water).
- The conditions under which the reaction takes place can also be indicated. For example, if heat is required to initiate the reaction (an endothermic reaction), it is written over the horizontal arrow, or on the left side of the equation. Alternatively, if heat is given out by the reaction (an exothermic reaction), it is written on the right side of the equation.
- If any catalyst is used for increasing the reaction rate, then it is written above the horizontal arrow.

Combination reactions

Combination reactions are the simplest type of chemical reaction. Here, two or more types of atoms, molecules, or compounds react or combine to produce products. The following are examples of combination reactions:

$2H_2 + O_2 \rightarrow 2H_2O$

$2Na + Cl_2 \rightarrow 2NaCl$

Decomposition reactions

A chemical reaction where a compound splits or decomposes into simpler substances is called a decomposition reaction. The following examples illustrate decomposition reactions:

$$2KClO_3 \xrightarrow{\text{Heat}} 2KCl + 3O_2$$

$$2H_2O \xrightarrow{\text{Electricity}} 2H_2 + O_2$$

Displacement reactions

A chemical reaction, where one element displaces another by virtue of it being more reactive, is called a displacement reaction. In order to determine which element is more reactive than the other, one has to consider the reactivity of the elements. Displacement reactions are primarily seen when one metallic salt solution reacts with another metal. If the second metal is more reactive than the first, then it replaces the first metal in the salt. The following example illustrates a typical displacement reaction:

$$CuSO_4 \text{ (aq)} + Zn(s) \rightarrow ZnSO_4 + Cu(s)$$

A blue copper sulphate solution reacting with solid zinc will give rise to a colorless zinc sulphate solution and solid copper. Thus, Zn displaces Cu in the salt form because Zn is more reactive than Cu.

Isomerization reactions

A chemical reaction where rearrangements of atoms occur within a substance without any change in the molecular formula is called an isomerization reaction. Compounds that have the same molecular formula, but different arrangements of atoms, are known as isomers (isomers are different from allotropes). Isomers occur mostly in organic chemistry. The following example illustrates an isomerization reaction:

$$H_4N-O-C\equiv N \xrightarrow{\text{heat}} H_2N-\underset{\underset{O}{\parallel}}{C}-NH_2$$

(ammonium cyanate) (urea)

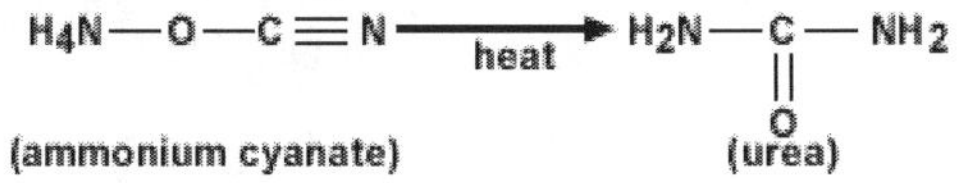

Even though ammonium cyanate and urea have the same chemical formula, their arrangements of atoms inside the molecules differ. They have different structures, and therefore widely differing physical and chemical properties.

Oxidation-reduction reactions

An oxidation reaction involves the addition of oxygen to a reactant, while a reduction reaction involves the addition of hydrogen to a reactant. In a broader perspective, an oxidation reaction is a reaction where an atom or ion loses electrons. Consider the following reaction:

$$CuSO_4 \text{ (aq)} + Zn \text{ (s)} \rightarrow ZnSO_4 + Cu \text{ (s)}$$

Here, the Zn atom donates two electrons. Since Zn is donating electrons, it is a reducing agent. Zn itself is getting oxidized:

$$Zn \rightarrow Zn^{2+} + 2e^-$$

Since Cu is accepting electrons, it is an oxidizing agent, and Cu is getting reduced.

$$CuSO_4 \rightarrow Cu^{2+} + SO_4{}^{2-}$$
$$Cu^{2+} + 2e^- \rightarrow Cu$$

Oxidation-reduction reactions are also known as redox reactions. A typical redox reaction is as follows:
$$CuO + H_2 \rightarrow Cu + H_2O$$

In the above reaction, the copper oxide loses an oxygen atom, so it is being reduced. The H_2 is gaining an extra oxygen; therefore, it is being oxidized. In this reaction, the CuO is functioning as an oxidizing agent, and the H_2 is functioning as a reducing agent. The term that is used to describe the degree of oxidation of an element is its oxidation number, or oxidation state.

Haber reaction

The Haber reaction involves the combination of nitrogen gas (N_2) and hydrogen gas (H_2) in order to make ammonia (NH_3):
$$N_2 + 3H_2 \rightarrow 2NH_3$$

The balanced equation requires one nitrogen molecule and three hydrogen molecules in order to make two ammonia molecules. This means that one nitrogen molecule reacts with three hydrogen molecules to make two ammonia molecules.

Thermodynamics and Thermochemistry

Enthalpy change

- The heat content of a chemical system is called the enthalpy (symbol: H).
- The enthalpy change (ΔH) is the amount of heat that is released or absorbed when a chemical reaction occurs at constant pressure.
- $\Delta H = H_{products} - H_{reactants}$
- ΔH is specified per mole of substance, as in the balanced chemical equation for the reaction.
- The units are usually given as kJ·mol^{-1} (kJ/mol), or sometimes as kcal·mol^{-1} (kcal/mol).
- 1 calorie (cal) = 4.184 joules (J)
- Energy changes are measured under standard laboratory conditions: 25°C (298 K) & 101.3 kPa (1 atmosphere).

Exothermic reactions

- Energy is released.
- Energy is a product of the reaction.
- The reaction vessel becomes warmer.
- The temperature inside of the reaction vessel increases.
- The energy of the reactants is greater than the energy of the products.
- $\Delta H = H_{(products)} - H_{(reactants)} = $ negative

For example:

$N_2(g) + 3H_2(g) \rightarrow 2NH_3(g) + 92.4$ kJ

$N_2(g) + 3H_2(g) \rightarrow 2NH_3(g) \quad \Delta H = -92.4$ kJ·mol^{-1}

Endothermic reactions

- Energy is absorbed.
- Energy is a reactant of the reaction.
- The reaction vessel becomes cooler.
- The temperature inside of the reaction vessel decreases.
- The energy of the reactants is less than the energy of the products.
- $\Delta H = H_{(products)} - H_{(reactants)}$ = positive

For example:

$2NH_3(g) + 92.4$ kJ $\rightarrow N_2(g) + 3H_2(g)$

$2NH_3(g) \rightarrow N_2(g) + 3H_2(g) \quad \Delta H = +92.4$ kJ·mol^{-1}

Hess's law

Hess's law states that the heat transferred in a reaction, or the change in enthalpy (ΔH), is the same regardless of whether the reaction occurs in a single step, or in several steps. The method for calculating the enthalpy of the reaction, developed by Hess, is called Hess's law of heat summation. According to this law, if a series of reactions are added together, the net change in the heat of the reaction is the sum of the enthalpy changes for each step. The rules for using Hess's law are as follows:

- If the reaction is multiplied (or divided) by some factor, then ΔH must also be multiplied (or divided) by that same factor.
- If the reaction is reversed (flipped), then the sign of ΔH must also be reversed.

> ➤ **Review Video: Hess's Law**
> *Visit **mometrix.com/academy** and enter **Code: 329059***

Missing mass and heat of combustion

Chemical reactions on a microscopic level are simply the breaking and forming of bonds between the reactant compounds involved in the reaction. It has been observed that a stable compound has less mass (or energy) than the sum of masses of each of the atoms that form the compound. The missing mass is called the binding energy of the compound, and goes to forming the bonds between the atoms. All chemical reactions proceed in the direction of attaining greater binding energy. The greater the binding energy, the more difficult it is to break the compound, and therefore it is more stable. If you plot the energy (or mass) scale vertically, you will see that a compound will be lower on the same scale. The lower down the compound is, the tighter the binding is. In Einstein's famous equation, $E = mc^2$, the missing mass becomes the binding energy of the compound or the molecule. The heat that is released upon completely burning 1 mole of a compound or substance in air (or oxygen) is known as the heat of combustion of the compound or substance. If the heat of combustion is high, then the compound or substance is a good material for burning.

Bond enthalpy and bond length

We know that multiple bonds are shorter than single bonds. We can also show that multiple bonds are stronger than single bonds, because atoms are held closer and more tightly together as the number of bonds between the atoms increases. Therefore, bond enthalpy increases as bond length decreases.

Calorimetric analysis

One method for determining the energy exchange between the reaction system and its environment is to conduct a calorimetric analysis. A calorimeter is a thermally insulated container where a reaction system can be performed, and the energy exchange between the system and its environment can be measured. The calorimeter and its contents are considered the environment, while the reaction system is a chemical or physical process that occurs within the confines of the calorimeter. The following equation applies:

$$Q_{surr} = Q_{cal} + Q_{contents}$$

The Q_{cal} can be determined if one knows the heat capacity of the calorimeter. This heat capacity can be experimentally determined, and is expressed in kJ/°C. In order to determine the Q_{cal}, you multiply the heat capacity of the calorimeter by the difference between the final and initial temperatures.

Thermal capacity

The thermal capacity of a substance is defined as the amount of heat that is required to raise (or lower) its temperature by 1°C.

Thermal Capacity = Mass × Specific Heat

The thermal capacity of water is very large. This is the reason why it is used as a coolant in many applications, such as in car radiators. It can store within its mass more heat energy before it starts to change its state to steam. Heat energy flows from a hotter body to a colder body when the two bodies are brought into contact. The heat will continue to flow until the temperatures are equalized. No heat flows from one body to the other when they are at equal temperatures. This is called thermal equilibrium.

Specific heat

Heat energy is measured in joules (J). But, more commonly, heat is measured in calories (cal) or in kilocalories (kcal). One kilocalorie is defined as the amount of heat that is needed to raise the temperature of 1 kg of water by 1°C. One calorie = 4.18 joules. The specific heat of a substance is defined as the amount of heat that is required to raise the temperature of 1 kg of the substance by 1°C. The specific heat is denoted by "s", and its unit of measurement is J/kg°C (joules per kilogram degree centigrade). The specific heat of water is 4180 J/kg°C. The quantity of heat, Q, that is taken in or given out by a body depends on the mass of the body, the specific heat of the body, and the change in temperature that occurs because of the heat taken in or given out. Thus,

$$Q = m \times s \times \Delta T$$

Where:

m = The mass of the substance.
s = The specific heat of the substance.
ΔT = The change in temperature

Gibbs free energy

The Gibbs free energy of a system, at any moment in time, is defined as the enthalpy of the system, minus the product of the temperature times the entropy of the system:
$G = H - TS$

The Gibbs free energy of a system is a state function, because it is defined in terms of thermodynamic properties that are state functions. The change in the Gibbs free energy of a system, which occurs during a reaction, is therefore equal to the change in the enthalpy of the system, minus the change in the product of the temperature times the entropy of the system:
$\Delta G = \Delta H - \Delta(TS)$

If the reaction is run at constant temperature, then this equation can be written as follows:
$G = \Delta H - \Delta TS$

There are 4 possible types of reactions with regard to the enthalpic and entropic contribution to the free energy change:
- ΔH = (-), $-T\Delta S$ = (-): Favorable enthalpic change (exothermic), and favorable entropic change (disorder increases).
- ΔH = (+), $-T\Delta S$ = (+): Unfavorable enthalpic change (endothermic), and unfavorable entropic change (disorder decreases).
- ΔH = (-), $-T\Delta S$ = (+): Favorable enthalpic change (exothermic), and unfavorable entropic change (disorder decreases).
- ΔH = (+), $-T\Delta S$ = (-): Unfavorable enthalpic change (endothermic), and favorable entropic change (disorder increases).

Spontaneous reactions often have the following characteristics:
- A negative enthalpy (release of heat energy, $\Delta H < 0$).
- An increase in entropy (increase in disorder, $\Delta S > 0$).

Zeroth law

According to the zeroth law, if two systems are in thermal equilibrium with a third system, then the two systems are also in thermal equilibrium. Two systems are said to be in thermal equilibrium if heat energy is not exchanged between two systems. The concept of temperature is made objective by this law, and is defined as the state of a thermodynamic system that determines the direction of the flow of heat.

Laws of thermodynamics

First law of thermodynamics
The conservation law, states that energy can neither be created nor destroyed. This law provides the basis for all quantitative accounts of energy, regardless of its form, and makes energy the most important concept in physics.

Second law of thermodynamics
Elements in a closed system tend to seek their most probable distribution. In a closed system, entropy always increases.

Third law of thermodynamics
The third law of thermodynamics, or the asymptotic law, states that all processes slow down as they operate closer to the thermodynamic equilibrium, making it difficult in practice to reach that equilibrium. This law suggests that the powerful and fast changes, which are typical of technology and characteristic of living forms of organization, are bound to occur only at levels that are far removed from thermodynamic equilibrium.

Every thermodynamic system possesses an interval energy, U, and has the capacity to do external work, W, which may be called the external energy. If heat energy is supplied (dQ) to a system, then according to the first law of thermodynamics, also known as the law of conservation of energy, it follows that the sum total of changes in the internal and external energy of the system must equal the heat energy supplied to the system:

$$dQ = dU + dW$$

Where:
1. dU is an exact differential that depends only on the initial and final states of the system, but not on the path that connects these states.
2. dQ and dW are inexact differentials, as they depend upon the path between the initial and final states.

> ➤ **Review Video: Laws of Thermodynamics**
> *Visit **mometrix.com/academy** and enter **Code: 253607***

Conversion between Fahrenheit and Celsius temperatures

To convert Fahrenheit temperatures into Celsius:
1. Subtract 32 from the Fahrenheit number.
2. Divide the answer by 9.
3. Multiply that answer by 5.

For example, to change 95° Fahrenheit to Celsius:
1. 95 – 32 = 63
2. 63 ÷ 9 = 7
3. 7 × 5 = 35°C

To convert Celsius temperatures into Fahrenheit:
1. Multiply the Celsius temperature by 9.
2. Divide the answer by 5.
3. Add 32 to the answer.

For example, to change 20° Celsius to Fahrenheit:
1. 20 × 9 = 180
2. 180 ÷ 5 = 36

3. $36 + 32 = 68°F$

Heat conduction

The law of heat conduction, also known as Fourier's law, states that the time rate of heat flow, Q, through an object is proportional to the gradient of the temperature difference:

$$Q = KA \frac{\Delta T}{\Delta x}$$

Where:
K = The conductivity constant, which is dependent upon the nature of the material and its temperature.
A = The transversal surface area.
ΔT = The temperature difference through which the heat is being transferred.
Δx = The thickness of the body of matter through which the heat is passing.

Note: This law forms the basis for the derivation of the heat equation.

Latent heat

The absorption (or release) of heat while changing states is known as the latent heat (L). The latent heat of a substance is the amount of heat that is absorbed (or released) by a unit of mass of a substance in order to change its state without any change in temperature. The MKS unit for latent heat is joules per kilogram, or J/kg. The latent heat for a solid to liquid transition is known as the latent heat of fusion, while the latent heat for a liquid to gas transition is known as the latent heat of vaporization. If L is the latent heat of a substance, and m is the mass of the substance, then the heat, Q (absorbed or released), that is required to change its state = $Q \times L$. It may be clear, now, that the latent heat of ice (to water) is different from the latent heat of water (to steam).

P-V diagrams

A P-V diagram is a graph that is used to evaluate the efficiency of a thermodynamic process by plotting the pressure, P, versus the volume, V, of the system. The product of pressure and volume represents a quantity of work, and this quantity is represented by the area beneath the P-V curve. Therefore, the area that is enclosed by the four boundaries of the P-V diagram represents the net work that is done by the process during one cycle.

Rate Processes in Chemical Reactions: Kinetics and Equilibrium

Nature of reactants

We have seen that some elements, because of the way that their electronic configuration occurs, are very reactive. For example, Na, K, and Rb readily give off their electrons, while F, Cl, and Br are elements which quickly accept electrons. On the other hand, noble gases like He, Ne, and Ar are completely chemically inert. Non-metals like C, N, and O also react, but not as vigorously as F, Cl, Br, etc. In most cases, the valence of the reactants will give you a rough estimate of the reaction rates. Reactions produce products by having the reacting molecules come into contact with one another. The more often that they collide, the more

likely the chance that product will form. If the reacting molecules move more rapidly, such as in the gaseous state, then the product will be more likely to form. This concept is part of an overriding theory that forms the foundation of all kinetics work, called the collisional theory of reaction rates. Reactions usually occur more rapidly when the reactants are in the gaseous state. The next most favorable reaction condition involves the reacting molecules dispersed in a solution. Reactions do occur in pure liquids or in solid form, but the rates tend to be a lot slower because the reacting molecules are very restricted in their movements among one another, and therefore do not come into contact as often. The relative reaction rates generally conform to the following order:
Gases > Solutions > Pure Liquids > Solids

Rate of change and the rate constant

The rate of change in the concentrations of the reactants and products can be used to characterize the rate of a chemical reaction. The rate of change in the concentration corresponds to the slope of the concentration-time plot. The rate constant, k, is a proportionality constant in the relationship between the rate and concentrations. This constant has a fixed value at any given temperature, but varies with temperature.

For a general reaction, $aA + bB \rightarrow cC + dD$, we would have the following rate law:
$$\text{Rate} = k[A]^m[B]^n$$

Catalysts

There are certain substances that, by their mere presence, enhance the rate of reaction. These substances are called catalysts. Catalysts themselves do not participate in the reaction, and remain unchanged. For a reversible and balanced reaction, a catalyst helps the reaction to be more favorable in one direction than the other. There are many examples of catalysts in chemical reactions. For example, if you heat $KClO_3$, it will start to decompose at a very high temperature. However, if a small quantity of MnO_2 is added, the decomposition of $KClO_3$ will occur faster, and at a lower temperature. The chlorophyll in plant leaves acts as a catalyst for the plants to convert energy from the sun into glucose. And, platinum is used as a catalyst for reactions where acids are manufactured.

Homogeneous catalysts

Homogeneous catalysts are catalysts that form a uniform distribution between themselves and the reactant molecules. These catalysts are in a solution together with the reactant molecules. Because they are dispersed within a solution, the surface area of the catalyst is maximized, and, usually, these types of catalysts tend to be more efficient in increasing product formation at a lower temperature. Examples of homogeneous catalysts include any protic acid. A protic acid is an acid that donates hydrogen ions (protons). Sulfuric acid, H_2SO_4, in water catalyzes the dehydration of alcohols (i.e., the loss of water), in order to produce double-bonded compounds, called alkenes. Phosphoric acid, H_3PO_4, can catalyze the formation of organic esters by combining alcohol and carboxylic acid molecules together, splitting out a water molecule. Aprotic acids, or Lewis acids, also serve as homogeneous catalysts. An aprotic acid is an acid that accepts electrons. Aprotic acids, such as $AlCl_3$, can catalyze substitution reactions in which a hydrogen atom on a benzene ring is replaced by a hydrocarbon group, such as a methyl group, $-CH_3$. This same aprotic acid is also useful in catalyzing the chlorination of an alkene in order to form a dichloroalkane.

Heterogeneous catalysts

Heterogeneous catalysts are sometimes called surface catalysts because they position the reactant molecules on their very surface. Many metals serve as heterogeneous catalysts, in which the reactant molecules have an interface between themselves and the catalyst surface. In the reaction, known as hydrogenation, double bonds between carbons accept two hydrogen atoms, and use the pi electrons between the two carbons in order to attach these hydrogen atoms to the carbon atom. The diatomic hydrogen molecule attaches itself to the surface of a metal catalyst, such as platinum, nickel, or palladium. The double-bonded organic molecule does the same. The single bond between the hydrogen atoms is broken, and so is the pi bond between the two carbons within the organic molecule. The hydrogen atoms then form a single bond between its single electron and one of the two pi electrons that previously constituted the pi bond between the two carbon atoms. Once the hydrogens have been attached, the product molecule disengages from the surface, only to have fresh reactant molecules take its place upon the surface of the metal. Heterogeneous catalysts are, as a rule, not as efficient as homogeneous catalysts.

> ➤ **Review Video: <u>Catalysts</u>**
> Visit ***mometrix.com/academy*** *and enter* **Code: 729053**

Reversible and irreversible processes

<u>Reversible process</u>
If a system is taken from one state to another, and can be brought back to the initial state, then the process is called a reversible process. The change from the initial to final state should obviously proceed through the infinitesimal changes, each being a quasistatic state of equilibrium. Some examples are changes in a gas through isochoric, isothermal, or adiabatic changes.

<u>Irreversible process</u>
If a system is taken from one state to another, but cannot be brought back to the initial state, then the process is called an irreversible process. Some examples are the free expansion of a gas, the dissipation of energy due to friction, or the mixing of two gases or liquids, etc.

Reversible chemical reactions

A chemical reaction in which substances react together to produce resultants, and the resultants in turn react with one another to produce the original substances, is known as a reversible chemical reaction. For example, if calcium oxide is kept in close contact with carbon dioxide, the two substances will slowly unite to make calcium carbonate.
$CaO + CO_2 \rightarrow CaCO_3$

If you heat $CaCO_3$, then you will get back CaO and CO_2.
The two equations can be combined as follows:
$CaCO_3 \Leftrightarrow CaO + CO_2 \uparrow$

The horizontal arrow shows that the reaction proceeds in both directions. The vertical arrow indicates that the carbon dioxide gas escapes. Each chemical reaction is characterized by a rate of reaction, which is the rate at which the reactants combine to produce the final product. The rate of a reaction depends on various factors, such as the temperature, the nature of the reacting substances, etc. In a reversible chemical reaction, if the rate of the forward reaction and the rate of backward reaction are the same, we say that the reaction has reached equilibrium.

Law of mass action

The law of mass action is universal, applicable under any circumstance. However, for reactions that are complete, the result may not be very useful. We introduce the mass action law by using a general chemical reaction equation in which reactants, A and B, react to give product, C and D:

$aA + bB \rightarrow cC + dD$

Where:

a, b, c, and d = The coefficients for a balanced chemical equation.

The law of mass action states that, if the system is at equilibrium at a given temperature, then the following ratio is a constant:

$$K_{eq} = \frac{[C]^c [D]^d}{[A]^a [B]^b}$$

The square brackets "[ ]" around the chemical species represent their concentrations. This is the ideal law of chemical equilibrium, otherwise known as the law of mass action.

Reaction quotients and the equilibrium constants

If the system is NOT at equilibrium, then the ratio is different from the equilibrium constant. In such cases, the ratio is called a reaction quotient which is designated as Q.

$$Q = \frac{[C]^c [D]^d}{[A]^a [B]^b}$$

A system that is not at equilibrium will tend toward equilibrium, and the requisite changes will alter the Q so that its value approaches the equilibrium constant, K_{eq}.

$Q \rightarrow K_{eq}$

K_{eq} is the ratio of products to reactants. Therefore, the larger K is, the more products will be present at equilibrium. Conversely, the smaller K is, the more reactants will be present at equilibrium. If K >> 1, then products dominate at equilibrium, and the equilibrium lies to the right. If K << 1, then the reactants dominate at equilibrium, and the equilibrium lies to the left.

Le Chatelier's principle

When a system at equilibrium is subjected to a disturbance, the composition of the system adjusts so as to minimize the effect of the disturbance. An increase in temperature favors an endothermic reaction. The heat absorbed tends to oppose the increase in temperature. A decrease in temperature favors an exothermic reaction. The heat released opposes the lowering of temperature. Changes in concentration will change the Q so that it no longer equals K, and leads to a shift to restore Q so that it is equal to K.

Reactions generally have the following characteristics:
- For an endothermic reaction heat can be considered as a reactant.
- For an exothermic reaction heat can be considered as a product.
- If $\Delta H > 0$, adding heat favors the forward reaction, while cooling favors the reverse reaction.
- If $\Delta H < 0$, adding heat favors the reverse reaction, while cooling favors the forward reaction.

Solution Chemistry

Radicals

Sometimes, in a chemical reaction of compounds, the constituent elements are not released, but there may be a group of atoms sticking together. These groups are called radicals. Thus, a radical is a component of a compound that consists of groups of atoms. Radicals can be positively or negatively charged. To simplify, ions are called simple radicals, and groups of atomic radicals are called compound radicals. For example, hydroxide (OH) is called a compound radical and is negatively charged. Thus, it is written as OH^-. Other common compound radicals are sulfate (SO_4^{2-}), nitrate (NO_3^-), etc.

Binary ionic compounds

Naming binary ionic compounds involves first naming the element that appears first in the formula, using the name of the element itself, and then naming the second part of the formula, which is usually the anion in an ionic compound, and typically ends in "-ide". If there is a multivalent element involved, such as iron, copper, lead, tin, or mercury, one will have to determine which valence is involved before the name can be established. For example, for $FeCl_3$, we know that Fe has two possible valences. We also know that the total positive charge plus the total negative charge will equal zero. Since we have one Fe, and we know that the halogens in binary compounds are -1, we can determine the valence, x, of Fe as follows:

$$1\,x_{Fe} + 3\,x_{Cl} = 0$$

Where:
x_{Fe} = Valence of Fe
x_{Cl} = Valence of Cl = -1

$$1(x_{Fe}) + 3(-1) = 0$$
$$x_{Fe} = +3$$

Therefore, the Fe atom is in the +3 state, and the name of the compound is: Iron (III) Chloride.

Ternary ionic compounds

Naming ternary ionic compounds uses the same procedure as binary ionic compounds. The one big difference is the ending of the name: it is seldom "ide", although in some cases it is. Other more common endings are "ate" and "ite".

What is the name of $Be(HSO_3)_2$?
First, identify the element name of Be^{2+}, which is Beryllium. Next, identify the HSO_3^- ion, which is Hydrogen Sulfite. Finally, add the two together to get the name: Beryllium Hydrogen Sulfite.

Standard solutions

There are two types of standard solutions: molar solutions and normal solutions. A molar solution (M) is a solution that contains 1 mole of solute for each liter of solution. One mole of a substance in grams is equivalent to the molecular weight (MW) of that substance (sometimes referred to as the 'gram molecular weight' (gMW)). Thus, a 1 M solution contains 1 gMW of solute per liter of solution. A normal solution (N) is a solution that contains 1 'gram equivalent weight' (gEW) of solute per liter of solution. The gEW is equivalent to the MW, expressed in grams, divided by the 'valency' of the solute.

Concentration units

- Mass Percent (%) – (g solute/total g) x 100.
- Mole Fraction (X) – Mole solute/total moles.
- Molality (m) – Mole solute/kg solvent.
- Molarity (M) – Mole solute/L solution.
- Conversion Between Concentration Units:
    - Assume an amount (denominator).
    - Calculate the mass/moles of solute and solvent.
    - Calculate the desired concentration.
- Dilution:
    - $M_1V_1 = M_2V_2$
    - Add sufficient solution to bring the final volume to the total.

Properties of solutions

The following are properties of solutions:
- The particles of solute are the size of individual small molecules, or individual small ions. One nanometer is about the maximum diameter for a solute particle.
- The mixture does not separate on standing. In a gravity environment, the solution will not come apart due to any difference in density of the materials in the solution.
- The mixture does not separate by common fiber filter. The entire solution will pass through the filter.
- Once it is completely mixed, the mixture is homogeneous. If you take a sample of the solution from any point in the solution, the proportions of the materials will be the same.
- The mixture appears clear rather than cloudy. It may have some color to it, but it seems to be transparent otherwise.

- The mixture shows no Tyndall effect: light is not scattered by the solution. If you shine a light into the solution, the pathway of the light through the solution is not revealed to an observer outside of the pathway.
- The solute is completely dissolved into the solvent up to a point that is characteristic of the solvent, solute, and temperature. At a saturation point, the solvent can no longer dissolve any more of the solute. If there is a saturation point, the point is distinct and characteristic of the type of materials, as well as the temperature of the solution.
- The solution of an ionic material into water will result in an electrolyte solution. The ions of solute will separate in water to permit the solution to carry an electric current.
- The solution shows an increase in osmotic pressure between it and a reference solution as the amount of solute is increased.
- The solution shows an increase in boiling point as the amount of solute is increased.
- The solution shows a decrease in melting point as the amount of solute is increased.
- A solution of a solid, non-volatile solute in a liquid solvent shows a decrease in vapor pressure above the solution as the amount of solute is increased.

Solubility of ionic compounds in water

- All compounds of the ammonium ion (NH_4^+), and of alkali metal (group IA) cations, are soluble.
- All nitrates and acetates (ethanoates) are soluble.
- All chlorides, bromides, and iodides are soluble EXCEPT for those of silver, lead, and mercury(I).
- All sulphates are soluble EXCEPT for those of silver, lead, mercury(I), barium, strontium, and calcium.
- All carbonates, sulfites, and phosphates are insoluble EXCEPT for those of ammonium and alkali metal cations.
- All hydroxides are insoluble EXCEPT for those of ammonium, barium, and alkali metal cations.
- All sulfides are insoluble EXCEPT for those of ammonium, alkali metal cations, and alkali earth metal (group II) cations.
- All oxides are insoluble EXCEPT for those of calcium, barium, and alkali metal cations. The soluble ones actually react with the water to form hydroxides (hydrolyse).

Homogenous and heterogeneous mixtures

Substances can also be made up of combinations of compounds, called mixtures. In a mixture, the individual constituents retain their original properties. For example, if you take brine (salt solution), it is a mixture of salt (sodium chloride) and water. If you boil brine, you will be able to separate the two compounds, and will get back pure water and pure salt. If you take lemon sherbet, you will be able to separate lemon juice, water, sugar, and salt from it. In a mixture, the constituents do not chemically combine to give a totally new substance, as happens during the formation of a compound. The example for brine is that of a homogenous mixture, where one compound is completely soluble in the other compound and the mixture displays the same property throughout its bulk. There are also cases where the mixtures consist of compounds that are not soluble with each other, called heterogeneous mixtures. An example of a heterogeneous mixture would be liquid mixtures of oil and water, mud and water, etc. Mixtures can be separated into their constituent parts by various processes such as evaporation, distillation, filtration, etc.

Separation of mixtures:
- Filtration – Particle size.
- Centrifugation – Density.
- Distillation – State.
- Fractional Distillation – Boiling point.
- Fractional Crystallization – Solubility vs. temperature.
- Chromatography – Solubility, size, and affinity.

Acids and Bases

Lewis and Bronsted-Lowry acids and bases

A Lewis acid is defined as an electron acceptor, while a Lewis base is defined as an electron donor. The Lewis theory of acids and bases is more general than the "one-sided" nature of the Bronsted-Lowry theory, which defines an acid as a proton donor and a base as a proton acceptor. Keep in mind that the Bronsted-Lowry theory REQUIRES the presence of a solvent, specifically a protic solvent, of which water is the usual example. Since almost all chemistry is performed in water, the fact that this limits the Bronsted-Lowry definition is of little practical consequence. The Lewis definition of an acid and base do not have the constraints that the Bronsted-Lowry theory does, and many more reactions are seen to be acidic or basic in nature when using the Lewis definition than when using the Bronsted-Lowry definition.

Dissociation of water

In pure water, the following equilibrium is established:

$$H_2O \; (l) \rightarrow H^+ \; (aq) + OH^- \; (aq)$$

At 25°C, the following is true:

$$K_w = [H_2O] = [H^+][OH^-] = 1.0 \times 10^{-14}$$

The above is called the autoionization of water. The H^+ (aq) ion is simply a proton with no electrons (elemental H has one proton, one electron, and no neutrons). In water, the H^+ (aq) ions form clusters. The simplest cluster is the hydronium ion, H_3O^+ (aq), while some examples of larger clusters are $H_5O_2^+$ and $H_9O_4^+$. $H_9O_4^+$, an H_3O^+ surrounded by three H-bonded water molecules, is currently accepted to be most important hydronium ion structure. Often, H_3O^+ is used to represent the hydronium ion, even though $H_9O_4^+$ is the more accurate formula for this species. Generally, we use H^+ (aq) and H_3O^+ (aq) interchangeably.

pH of solutions

To understand if a given solution is acidic or not, H^+ ion concentration is generally measured. The H^+ concentration is then converted to a logarithmic scale from 1-14, referred to as the pH of the solution. It has been found experimentally that the concentration of H^+ and OH^- in neutral water is 10^{-7} moles per liter. For an acidic solution, the concentration of H^+ ions is $> 10^{-7}$ moles per liter. And, for an alkaline solution, the OH^- concentration is $< 10^{-7}$ moles per liter. In the symbol, pH, p stands for potenz, which means strength (or power), while the H stands for H^+. Together, pH stands for the strength of the H^+ concentration in solution, expressed in moles per liter. The pH of a solution is defined as the negative logarithm of the exponent, or power, of 10 for the H^+ ion concentration. Thus, $[H^+] = 10^{-pH}$ (concentration is shown as a boxed bracket), and $-\log_{10}[H^+] = pH$. In a neutral solution, the pH is 7. In an acidic solution, the pH is between 1 and 7. And, in an alkaline solution, the pH is between 7 and 14.

Since the p "factor" is defined as the negative log of the molar concentration of whatever follows the letter p, it can also be combined with other components to be used as a measure of their concentration. Other possible derivatives include the following:
- $pCl = -\log[Cl^-]$
- $pK_a = -\log(K_a)$
- $pK_w = -\log(K_w)$
- $pAg = -\log[Ag^+]$
- $pOH = -\log[OH^-] = 14 - pH$

Conjugate acid-base pairs

Whatever is left of an acid after the proton is donated is called its conjugate base. Similarly, whatever remains of the base after it accepts a proton is called a conjugate acid. Consider the following reaction:

$$HA\ (aq) + H_2O\ (l) \rightarrow H_3O^+\ (aq) + A^-\ (aq)$$

After HA (acid) loses its proton, it is converted into A^- (base). Therefore, HA and A^- are conjugate acid-base pairs. After H_2O (base) gains a proton, it is converted into H_3O^+ (acid). Therefore, H_2O and H_3O^+ are also conjugate acid-base pairs. Conjugate acid-base pairs differ by only one proton: the acid has the extra proton, while the base has one less proton.

Examples:
- HSO_4^- is the conjugate base of H_2SO_4.
- HSO_4^- is the conjugate acid of SO_4^{2-}.
- SO_4^{2-} is not the conjugate base of H_2SO_4.

Strong Bronsted-Lowry acids and bases

Strong acids
- Are composed of H^+, combined with strongly ionic anions (e.g., Cl^-).
- The strong binary acids are HCl, HBr, and HI.
- Oxyanions are stronger anions than monatomic anions
- (i.e., $SO_4^{2-} > S^{2-}$).

- The more oxygens, the stronger the acid (i.e., $H_2SO_4 > H_2SO_3$).
- Half of the oxyanions of a particular element form strong acids, with the exception of B, C, and P (all of their oxyacids are weak).

Strong bases
- Hydroxides of group IA metals.
- Hydroxides of group IIA metals below Mg.

Dissociation of weak acids and the K_a value

The equation for the dissociation of a weak acid, HA, in solution is as follows:

$$HA + H_2O \Leftrightarrow H_3O^+ + A^-$$

And, the equation for determining its K_a value is as follows:

$$K_a = \frac{[H_3O^+][A^-]}{[HA]}$$

K_b value
For a weak base, B, the ionization is as follows:

$$B^- + H_2O \Leftrightarrow HB + OH^-$$

And, the equation for determining its K_b value is as follows:

$$K_b = \frac{[HB][OH^-]}{[B^-]}$$

Buffers

Balanced mixtures of conjugate weak acid-weak base pairs are called buffers. A buffer solution that contains an equal molar quantity of weak acid (HA) and its conjugate base (A⁻) has a pH of the pKa of the weak acid, HA. When OH⁻ is added to the buffer, the OH⁻ reacts with HA to produce A⁻ and water. But, the [HA]/[A⁻] ratio remains more or less constant, so the pH is not significantly changed. When H⁺ is added to the buffer, A⁻ is consumed to produce HA. Once again, the [HA]/[A⁻] ratio is more or less constant, so the pH does not change significantly. As long as the [weak base]/[weak acid] ratio stays within the range of 0.10 to 10.0 (a 100-fold change!), the pH does not change by more than 1.0 unit from the pH of the pKa of the weak acid. Strong acids and bases cannot exist in buffers. Reaction of weak base with an equal number of moles of strong acid results in the creation of an equal number of moles of weak acid, and complete destruction of original weak base. Reaction of weak acid with strong base has exactly the opposite effect.

Titration

Titration is a technique that is used to determine the amount or concentration of a given substance. A solution with a known volume and concentration is used to titrate, or react with, another solution with a known volume, but an unknown concentration. Some type of indicator is used to signal when all of the unknown substance has been reacted. This is commonly called the end point of the titration. The most common type of titration is one that involves an acid and a base reacting with one another. There are also other types of titrations.

> ➤ **Review Video:** <u>Titration</u>
> *Visit* **mometrix.com/academy** *and enter* **Code: 550131**

Indicators

Litmus paper turns red in acidic media, and blue in alkaline media. For this reason, litmus paper is known as an indicator. An indicator is a chemical that shows the acidity or alkalinity of a solution by means of sharp change in color. Many other indicators also change color when the acidity or alkalinity of the medium fluctuates. One such indicator is phenolphthalein. Phenolphthalein is deep pink in alkaline media, and the pinkness reduces as the alkalinity reduces. It is colorless in an acidic medium.

Neutralization and salts

If the concentration of H^+ and OH^- ions are equal in a solution, then that solution is called a neutral solution. Water, H_2O, is a neutral solution, since the number of H^+ and OH^- ions within H_2O are equal. When acids and bases react with each other, they nullify the effects of acidity and alkalinity within a solution, a process that is called neutralization. The byproducts of neutralization are salt and water. Salt, in chemistry, is a term that denotes all compounds whose positive radical is derived from a base, while its negative radical is derived from an acid. In addition to the salt, the H^+ ion from the acid and the OH^- radical (or ion) from the base form neutral, non-ionized water.

For example:
$NaOH \rightarrow Na^+ + OH^-$ (ionization)
$HCl \rightarrow H^+ + Cl^-$ (ionization)
$NaOH + HCl \rightarrow Na^+ + OH^- + H^+ + Cl^- \rightarrow NaCl + H_2O$ (neutralization)

Titration curves

The progress of a titration is usually monitored with an indicator. Frequently, during a titration, it is also useful to monitor the progress of the titration with a graph. This graph is known as a titration curve. Such a curve reflects the changes in pH that occur as material is added from a buret to the solution in the beaker below the buret. All curves start out with a very slow, or moderate, change in pH, while the base is being added to the acid. As the titration continues, and the endpoint is approached, the pH of the solution will start to change more dramatically. At the endpoint, the line changes most dramatically. Once the endpoint has been passed, the rate of pH change diminishes again, resembling the first part of the graph, except at a higher pH value. If the acid being titrated is weak, then the graph will not be nearly as vertical at the endpoint. The weaker the acid is, the more the graph deviates from being vertical.

Electrochemistry

Electrolysis and electrolytes

Electrolysis is a chemical process where a substance, in its molten state or in an aqueous solution, is decomposed by the passage of electric current. The complete setup for electrolysis is called an electrolytic cell. This cell consists of a vessel that contains the electrolyte, anode, cathode, battery, and wires. An electrolytic cell is also called a voltameter, since it generates voltage (or current) at its two terminals. Electrodes are the metallic strips that are inserted into the electrolytes for the conduction of electricity. A metal electrode that is connected to the positive terminal of a battery is called an anode (+), while a metal electrode that is connected to the negative terminal of a battery is called a cathode (-). An electrolyte is a compound that allows electric current to pass through itself when either in a molten state or in an aqueous solution. In an electrolysis experiment, solutions of sodium chloride, copper sulphate, dilute sulphuric acids, or acetic acid are common electrolytes. Strong electrolytes allow large electric currents to be passed through them, such as solutions of sodium chloride, copper sulphate, and dilute sulphuric acid. Weak electrolytes are compounds that are poor conductors of electricity when either in a molten state or in an aqueous solution. Non-electrolytes do not allow electric current to pass through themselves in any state, molten or aqueous.

Faraday's law of electrolysis

Faraday's law of electrolysis states that the mass of substance released at any electrode is directly proportional ($\propto$) to the electric charge that is passed through the electrolyte. Thus, if m is the mass of the substance released at the electrode, and Q is the amount of electric charge that is passed through the electrode, then according to Faraday's law of electrolysis:
$Q = I \times t$
Where:
I = Current in amperes.
t = Time in seconds.

m is therefore $\propto$ to I x t:
$m = Z \times I \times t$
Where:
Z = The constant of proportionality, known as the electromechanical equivalent.

The electromechanical equivalent, Z, of a substance is defined as the amount of substance in grams that are liberated at any electrode when one coulomb of charge is passed through an electrolyte.

Process of electrolysis

The following is the process of electrolysis:
- Electrolytes dissociate to form negatively charged anions and positively charged cations.
- The ions conduct electricity through the electrolyte.

- Cations are attracted toward the negative electrode. They take the excess electrons from the electrode and neutralize themselves.
- Anions are attracted towards the positive electrode. They give up the excess electrons from the electrode and neutralize themselves.
- The electrolyte dissociates, and the constituent elements of the salt are liberated at the electrodes.

The ions that will be released at the cathode or the anode will depend upon the following factors:
- The Relative Position of the Ion in the Electromechanical Series – The electromechanical series is a representation of how reactive the ion is. For example, in a solution that contains Na^+ and Hg^{2+} ions, the Na^+ ions will be preferentially released, as Na^+ accepts electrons more easily. However, this only happens if the concentration of Hg^{2+} ions is comparatively small. If the electrolyte is made up of NaCl in H_2O, then H^+ ions will be preferentially released, as H^+ is more reactive than Na^+.
- The Concentration of Ions in the Electrolyte – In the above example, if the concentration of Hg^{2+} ions is very large, then it will be preferentially released.
- The Nature of the Electrodes – Some electrode materials are non-corrosive, such as graphite or platinum, and are not affected by the ions surrounding it. However, some electrodes, such as copper, may enhance the release of ions, especially ions like Cu, Ag, Ni, etc.

Galvanic or voltaic cells

The redox reaction in a galvanic cell, or voltaic cell, is a spontaneous reaction. For this reason, galvanic cells are commonly used as batteries. Galvanic cell reactions supply energy that can be used to perform work. The energy is harnessed by situating the oxidation and reduction reactions in separate containers, which are joined by an apparatus that allows electrons to flow. A common galvanic cell is the Daniell cell. The overall chemical reaction of the galvanic cell is as follows:

$$Zn + Cu^{2+} \rightarrow Zn^{2+} + Cu$$

Electrical current in an electrolyte

In a conductor, electrical current flows through the material in its solid form. This is in contrast to an electrolyte, which can carry current in its molten state or in a solution form. Conductors are generally metals, while electrolytes are generally made from ionic compounds and noncovalent compounds (HCl and NH_3 are a few of the exceptions). When a current passes through a conductor, it may get heated up because of its inherent resistance. Other than this physical change, there are no other changes to the conductor. Once the current stops flowing, the conductor returns to its original state. In contrast to this, the cations and anions of an electrolyte go in opposite directions and get neutralized at the positive and negative electrodes, respectively. The chemical change thus produced is irreversible. After the current stops flowing, the electrolyte may change in strength relative to what it had started with. The current through a conductor is due to free electrons that flow and complete the circuit, while the current through an electrolytic cell is due to the flow of ions. For a given conductor or electrolytic cell, the current flowing through the circuit is constant. However, in an electrolytic cell, the current depends upon the strength of the electrolyte, which may change over time.

Appendix: Area, Volume, Surface Area Formulas

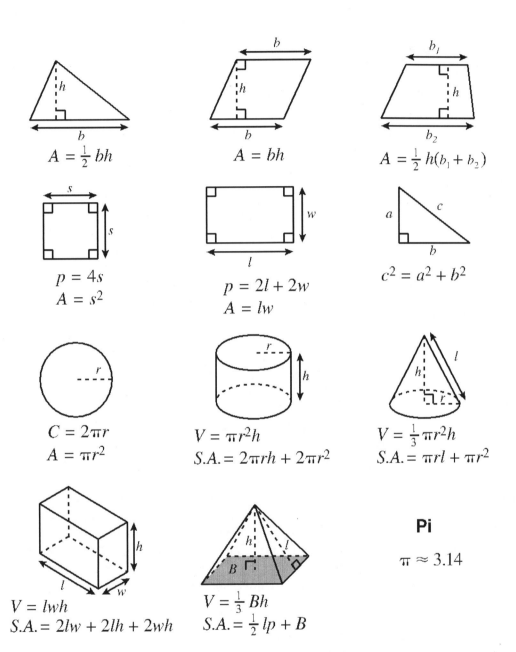

$A = \frac{1}{2}bh$

$A = bh$

$A = \frac{1}{2}h(b_1 + b_2)$

$p = 4s$
$A = s^2$

$p = 2l + 2w$
$A = lw$

$c^2 = a^2 + b^2$

$C = 2\pi r$
$A = \pi r^2$

$V = \pi r^2 h$
$S.A. = 2\pi rh + 2\pi r^2$

$V = \frac{1}{3}\pi r^2 h$
$S.A. = \pi rl + \pi r^2$

$V = lwh$
$S.A. = 2lw + 2lh + 2wh$

$V = \frac{1}{3}Bh$
$S.A. = \frac{1}{2}lp + B$

Pi

$\pi \approx 3.14$

Secret Key #1 – Time is Your Greatest Enemy

To succeed on the DAT, you must use your time wisely. Many students do not finish at least one section. The table below shows the time challenge you are faced with:

SECTION	Total amount of time allotted	Number of questions	Time to answer each question
Natural Sciences	90 min	100	.9 min
Perceptual Ability	60 min	90	.67 min
Reading Comprehension	60 min	50	1.2 min
Quantitative Reasoning	45 min	40	1.13 min

As you can see, the time constraints are brutal. To succeed, you must ration your time properly.

The Reading Comprehension section is separated into passages. The reason that time is so critical is that 1) every question counts the same toward your final score, and 2) the passages are not in order of difficulty. If you have to rush during the last passage, then you will miss out on answering easier questions correctly. It is natural to want to pause and figure out the hardest questions, but you must resist the temptation and move quickly.

Success Strategy #1

Pace Yourself

Wear a watch to the DAT Test. At the beginning of the test, check the time (or start a chronometer on your watch to count the minutes), and check the time after each passage or every few questions to make sure you are "on schedule."

If you find that you are falling behind time during the test, you must speed up. Even though a rushed answer is more likely to be incorrect, it is better to miss a couple of questions by being rushed, than to completely miss later questions by not having enough time. It is better to end with more time than you need than to run out of time. Once you catch back up, you can continue working each problem at your normal pace. If you have time at the end, go back then and finish the questions that you left behind.

If you are forced to speed up, do it efficiently. Usually one or more answer choices can be eliminated without too much difficulty. Above all, don't panic. Don't speed up and just begin guessing at random choices. By pacing yourself, and continually monitoring your progress against your watch, you will always know exactly how far ahead or behind you are with your available time. If you find that you are one minute behind on a section, don't skip one question without spending any time on it, just to catch back up. Spend perhaps 15 fewer seconds on the next four questions and you will have caught back up more gradually. Then you can continue working each problem at your normal pace.

Furthermore, don't dwell on the problems that you were rushed on. If a problem was taking up too much time and you made a hurried guess, it must be difficult. The difficult questions are the ones you are most likely to miss anyway, so it isn't a big loss. It is better to end with more time than you need than to run out of time. You can always go back and work the problems that you skipped. If you have time left over, as you review the skipped questions, start at the earliest skipped question, spend at most another minute, and then move on to the next skipped question.

Lastly, sometimes it is beneficial to slow down if you are constantly getting ahead of time. You are always more likely to catch a careless mistake by working more slowly than quickly, and among very high-scoring students (those who are likely to have lots of time left over), careless errors affect the score more than mastery of the material.

Estimation

For some math questions, estimate. Calculation takes time, and you should avoid it whenever possible. You can usually eliminate three obviously wrong choices quite easily. For example, suppose 48 mL of solution have been poured into a beaker in 11 seconds, and you are asked to find the rate of pour. You are given these choices:
250 mL/s
42 mL/s
4.4 mL/s
1.2 mL/s

You know that 48 divided by 11 will be a little over 4, so you can pick out C as the answer without ever doing the calculation.

Scanning

For passages, don't waste time reading, enjoying, and completely understanding the passage. Simply scan the passage to get a rough idea of what it is about. You will return to the passage for each question, so there is no need to memorize it. Only spend as much time scanning as is necessary to get a vague impression of its overall subject content.

Secret Key #2 – Guessing is not Guesswork

You probably know that guessing is a good idea on the DAT- unlike other standardized tests, there is no penalty for getting a wrong answer. Even if you have no idea about a question, you still have a 25% chance of getting it right.

Most students do not understand the impact that proper guessing can have on their score. Unless you score extremely high, guessing will significantly contribute to your final score.

Monkeys Take the DAT

What most students don't realize is that to insure that 25% chance, you have to guess randomly. If you put 20 monkeys in a room to take the DAT, assuming they answered once per question and behaved themselves, on average they would get 25% of the questions correct. Put 20 college students in the room, and the average will be much lower among guessed questions. Why?

DAT intentionally writes deceptive answer choices that "look" right. A student has no idea about a question, so picks the "best looking" answer, which is often wrong. The monkey has no idea what looks good and what doesn't, so will consistently be lucky about 25% of the time.

Students will eliminate answer choices from the guessing pool based on a hunch or intuition. Simple but correct answers often get excluded, leaving a 0% chance of being correct. The monkey has no clue, and often gets lucky with the best choice.

This is why the process of elimination endorsed by most test courses is flawed and detrimental to your performance- students don't guess, they make an ignorant stab in the dark that is usually worse than random.

Success Strategy #2

Let me introduce one of the most valuable ideas of this course- the $5 challenge:

You only mark your "best guess" if you are willing to bet $5 on it.
You only eliminate choices from guessing if you are willing to bet $5 on it.

Why $5? Five dollars is an amount of money that is small yet not insignificant, and can really add up fast (20 questions could cost you $100). Likewise, each answer choice on one question of the DAT will have a small impact on your overall score, but it can really add up to a lot of points in the end.

The process of elimination IS valuable. The following shows your chance of guessing it right:

If you eliminate this many choices:	0	1	2	3	4
Chance of getting it correct	20%	25%	33%	50%	100%

However, if you accidentally eliminate the right answer or go on a hunch for an incorrect answer, your chances drop dramatically: to 0%. By guessing among all the answer choices, you are GUARANTEED to have a shot at the right answer.

That's why the $5 test is so valuable- if you give up the advantage and safety of a pure guess, it had better be worth the risk.

What we still haven't covered is how to be sure that whatever guess you make is truly random. Here's the easiest way:

Always pick the first answer choice among those remaining.

Such a technique means that you have decided, **before you see a single test question**, exactly how you are going to guess- and since the order of choices tells you nothing about which one is correct, this guessing technique is perfectly random.

Let's try an example-

A student encounters the following problem on the Natural Sciences test. Part of the question has been removed in order to maintain a focus on the answer choices and guessing technique demonstrated:

In an experiment involving ... the amine will be?
neutralized
protonated
deprotonated
eliminated
dissolved

The student has a small idea about this question- he is pretty sure that the amine will be deprotonated, but he wouldn't bet $5 on it. He knows that the amine is either protonated or deprotoned, so he is willing to bet $5 on both choices A, D and E not being correct. Now he is down to B and C. At this point, he guesses B, since B is the first choice remaining.

The student is correct by choosing B, since the amine will be protonated. He only eliminated those choices he was willing to bet money on, AND he did not let his stale memories (often things not known definitely will get mixed up in the exact opposite arrangement in one's head) about protonation and deprotonation influence his guess. He blindly chose the first remaining choice, and was rewarded with the fruits of a random guess.

This section is not meant to scare you away from making educated guesses or eliminating choices- you just need to define when a choice is worth eliminating. The $5 test, along with a pre-defined random guessing strategy, is the best way to make sure you reap all of the benefits of guessing.

Specific Guessing Techniques

Slang

Scientific sounding answers are better than slang ones. In the answer choices below, choice B is much less scientific and is incorrect, while choice A is a scientific analytical choice and is correct.
Example:
    A.   To compare the outcomes of the two different kinds of treatment.

B. Because some subjects insisted on getting one or the other of the treatments.

Extreme Statements

Avoid wild answers that throw out highly controversial ideas that are proclaimed as established fact. Choice A is a radical idea and is incorrect. Choice B is a calm rational statement. Notice that Choice B does not make a definitive, uncompromising stance, using a hedge word "if" to provide wiggle room.
Example:
    A. Bypass surgery should be discontinued completely.
    B. Medication should be used instead of surgery for patients who have not had a heart attack if they suffer from mild chest pain and mild coronary artery blockage.

Similar Answer Choices

When you have two answer choices that are direct opposites, one of them is usually the correct answer.
Example:
    A. Paragraph 1 described the author's reasoning about the influence of his childhood on his adult life.
    B. Paragraph 2 described the author's reasoning about the influence of his childhood on his adult life.

These two answer choices are very similar and fall into the same family of answer choices. A family of answer choices is when two or three answer choices are very similar. Often two will be opposites and one may show an equality.
Example:
Operation I or Operation II can be conducted at equal cost
Operation I would be less expensive than Operation II
Operation II would be less expensive than Operation I
Neither Operation I nor Operation II would be effective at preventing the spread of cancer.

Note how the first three choices are all related. They all ask about a cost comparison. Beware of immediately recognizing choices B and C as opposites and choosing one of those two. Choice A is in the same family of questions and should be considered as well. However, choice D is not in the same family of questions. It has nothing to do with cost and can be discounted in most cases.

Hedging

When asked for a conclusion that may be drawn, look for critical "hedge" phrases, such as likely, may, can, will often, sometimes, etc, often, almost, mostly, usually, generally, rarely, sometimes. Question writers insert these hedge phrases to cover every possibility. Often an answer will be wrong simply because it leaves no room for exception. Avoid answer choices that have definitive words like "exactly," and "always".

Summary of Guessing Techniques

Eliminate as many choices as you can by using the $5 test. Use the common guessing strategies to help in the elimination process, but only eliminate choices that pass the $5 test. Among the remaining choices, only pick your "best guess" if it passes the $5 test. Otherwise, guess randomly by picking the first remaining choice that was not eliminated.

Secret Key #3 – Practice Smarter, Not Harder

Many students delay the test preparation process because they dread the awful amounts of practice time they think necessary to succeed on the test. We have refined an effective method that will take you only a fraction of the time.

There are a number of "obstacles" in your way on the DAT. Among these are answering questions, finishing in time, and mastering test-taking strategies. All must be executed on the day of the test at peak performance, or your score will suffer. The DAT is a mental marathon that has a large impact on your future.

Just like a marathon runner, it is important to work your way up to the full challenge. So first you just worry about questions, and then time, and finally strategy:

Success Strategy

1.   Find a good source for practice tests.
If you are willing to make a larger time investment, consider using more than one study guide- often the different approaches of multiple authors will help you "get" difficult concepts.
Take a practice test with no time constraints, with all study helps "open book." Take your time with questions and focus on applying strategies.
4. Take a practice test with time constraints, with all guides "open book."
5. Take a final practice test with no open material and time limits

If you have time to take more practice tests, just repeat step 5. By gradually exposing yourself to the full rigors of the test environment, you will condition your mind to the stress of test day and maximize your success.

Secret Key #4 - Prepare, Don't Procrastinate

Let me state an obvious fact: if you take the test three times, you will get three different scores. This is due to the way you feel on test day, the level of preparedness you have, and, despite the test writers' claims to the contrary, some tests WILL be easier for you than others.

Since your future depends so much on your score, you should maximize your chances of success. In order to maximize the likelihood of success, you've got to prepare in advance. This means taking practice tests and spending time learning the information and test taking strategies you will need to succeed.

Never take the test as a "practice" test, expecting that you can just take it again if you need to. Feel free to take sample tests on your own, but when you go to take the official test, be prepared, be focused, and do your best the first time!

Secret Key #5 - Test Yourself

Everyone knows that time is money. There is no need to spend too much of your time or too little of your time preparing for the test. You should only spend as much of your precious time preparing as is necessary for you to get the score you need.

Once you have taken a practice test under real conditions of time constraints, then you will know if you are ready for the test or not.

If you have scored extremely high the first time that you take the practice test, then there is not much point in spending countless hours studying. You are already there.

Benchmark your abilities by retaking practice tests and seeing how much you have improved. Once you score high enough to guarantee success, then you are ready.

If you have scored well below where you need, then knuckle down and begin studying in earnest. Check your improvement regularly through the use of practice tests under real conditions. Above all, don't worry, panic, or give up. The key is perseverance!

Then, when you go to take the test, remain confident and remember how well you did on the practice tests. If you can score high enough on a practice test, then you can do the same on the real thing.

General Strategies

The most important thing you can do is to ignore your fears and jump into the test immediately- do not be overwhelmed by any strange-sounding terms. You have to jump into the test like jumping into a pool- all at once is the easiest way.

Make Predictions

As you read and understand the question, try to guess what the answer will be. Remember that several of the answer choices are wrong, and once you begin reading them, your mind will immediately become cluttered with answer choices designed to throw you off. Your mind is typically the most focused immediately after you have read the question and digested its contents. If you can, try to predict what the correct answer will be. You may be surprised at what you can predict.

Quickly scan the choices and see if your prediction is in the listed answer choices. If it is, then you can be quite confident that you have the right answer. It still won't hurt to check the other answer choices, but most of the time, you've got it!

Answer the Question

It may seem obvious to only pick answer choices that answer the question, but the test writers can create some excellent answer choices that are wrong. Don't pick an answer just because it sounds right, or you believe it to be true. It MUST answer the question. Once you've made your selection, always go back and check it against the question and make sure that you didn't misread the question, and the answer choice does answer the question posed.

Benchmark

After you read the first answer choice, decide if you think it sounds correct or not. If it doesn't, move on to the next answer choice. If it does, mentally mark that answer choice. This doesn't mean that you've definitely selected it as your answer choice, it just means that it's the best you've seen thus far. Go ahead and read the next choice. If the next choice is worse than the one you've already selected, keep going to the next answer choice. If the next choice is better than the choice you've already selected, mentally mark the new answer choice as your best guess.

The first answer choice that you select becomes your standard. Every other answer choice must be benchmarked against that standard. That choice is correct until proven otherwise by another answer choice beating it out. Once you've decided that no other answer choice seems as good, do one final check to ensure that your answer choice answers the question posed.

Valid Information

Don't discount any of the information provided in the question. Every piece of information may be necessary to determine the correct answer. None of the information in the question is there to throw you off (while the answer choices will certainly have information to throw you off). If two seemingly unrelated topics are discussed, don't ignore either. You can be confident there is a relationship, or it wouldn't be included in the question, and you are probably going to have to determine what is that relationship to find the answer.

Avoid "Fact Traps"

Don't get distracted by a choice that is factually true. Your search is for the answer that answers the question. Stay focused and don't fall for an answer that is true but incorrect. Always go back to the question and make sure you're choosing an answer that actually answers the question and is not just a true statement. An answer can be factually correct, but it MUST answer the question asked. Additionally, two answers can both be seemingly correct, so be sure to read all of the answer choices, and make sure that you get the one that BEST answers the question.

Milk the Question

Some of the questions may throw you completely off. They might deal with a subject you have not been exposed to, or one that you haven't reviewed in years. While your lack of knowledge about the subject will be a hindrance, the question itself can give you many clues that will help you find the correct answer. Read the question carefully and look for clues. Watch particularly for adjectives and nouns describing difficult terms or words that you don't recognize. Regardless of if you completely understand a word or not, replacing it with a synonym either provided or one you more familiar with may help you to understand what the questions are asking. Rather than wracking your mind about specific detailed information concerning a difficult term or word, try to use mental substitutes that are easier to understand.

The Trap of Familiarity

Don't just choose a word because you recognize it. On difficult questions, you may not recognize a number of words in the answer choices. The test writers don't put "make-believe" words on the test; so don't think that just because you only recognize all the words in one answer choice means that answer choice must be correct. If you only recognize words in one answer choice, then focus on that one. Is it correct? Try your best to determine if it is correct. If it is, that is great, but if it doesn't, eliminate it. Each word and answer choice you eliminate increases your chances of getting the question correct, even if you then have to guess among the unfamiliar choices.

Eliminate Answers

Eliminate choices as soon as you realize they are wrong. But be careful! Make sure you consider all of the possible answer choices. Just because one appears right, doesn't mean that the next one won't be even better! The test writers will usually put more than one good answer choice for every question, so read all of them. Don't worry if you are stuck between two that seem right. By getting down to just two remaining possible choices, your odds are now 50/50. Rather than wasting too much time, play the odds. You are guessing, but guessing wisely, because you've been able to knock out some of the answer choices that you know are wrong. If you are eliminating choices and realize that the last answer choice you are left with is also obviously wrong, don't panic. Start over and consider each choice again. There may easily be something that you missed the first time and will realize on the second pass.

Tough Questions

If you are stumped on a problem or it appears too hard or too difficult, don't waste time. Move on! Remember though, if you can quickly check for obviously incorrect answer choices, your chances of guessing correctly are greatly improved. Before you completely give up, at least try to knock out a couple of possible answers. Eliminate what you can and then guess at the remaining answer choices before moving on.

Brainstorm

If you get stuck on a difficult question, spend a few seconds quickly brainstorming. Run through the complete list of possible answer choices. Look at each choice and ask yourself, "Could this answer the question satisfactorily?" Go through each answer choice and consider it independently of the other. By systematically going through all possibilities, you may find something that you would otherwise overlook. Remember that when you get stuck, it's important to try to keep moving.

Read Carefully

Understand the problem. Read the question and answer choices carefully. Don't miss the question because you misread the terms. You have plenty of time to read each question thoroughly and make sure you understand what is being asked. Yet a happy medium must be attained, so don't waste too much time. You must read carefully, but efficiently.

Face Value

When in doubt, use common sense. Always accept the situation in the problem at face value. Don't read too much into it. These problems will not require you to make huge leaps of logic. The test writers aren't trying to throw you off with a cheap trick. If you have to go beyond creativity and make a leap of logic in order to have an answer choice answer the question, then you should look at the other answer choices. Don't overcomplicate the problem by creating theoretical relationships or explanations that will warp time or space. These are normal problems rooted in reality. It's just that the applicable relationship or explanation may not be readily apparent and you have to figure things out. Use your common sense to interpret anything that isn't clear.

Prefixes

If you're having trouble with a word in the question or answer choices, try dissecting it. Take advantage of every clue that the word might include. Prefixes and suffixes can be a huge help. Usually they allow you to determine a basic meaning. Pre- means before, post- means after, pro - is positive, de- is negative. From these prefixes and suffixes, you can get an idea of the general meaning of the word and try to put it into context. Beware though of any traps. Just because con is the opposite of pro, doesn't necessarily mean congress is the opposite of progress!

Hedge Phrases

Watch out for critical "hedge" phrases, such as likely, may, can, will often, sometimes, often, almost, mostly, usually, generally, rarely, sometimes. Question writers insert these hedge phrases to cover every possibility. Often an answer choice will be wrong simply because it leaves no room for exception. Avoid answer choices that have definitive words like "exactly," and "always".

Switchback Words

Stay alert for "switchbacks". These are the words and phrases frequently used to alert you to shifts in thought. The most common switchback word is "but". Others include although, however, nevertheless, on the other hand, even though, while, in spite of, despite, regardless of.

New Information

Correct answer choices will rarely have completely new information included. Answer choices typically are straightforward reflections of the material asked about and will directly relate to the question. If a new piece of information is included in an answer choice that doesn't even seem to relate to the topic being asked about, then that answer choice is likely incorrect. All of the information needed to answer the question is usually provided for you, and so you should not have to make guesses that are unsupported or choose answer choices that require unknown information that cannot be reasoned on its own.

Time Management

On technical questions, don't get lost on the technical terms. Don't spend too much time on any one question. If you don't know what a term means, then since you don't have a dictionary, odds are you aren't going to get much further. You should immediately recognize terms as whether or not you know them. If you don't, work with the other clues that you have, the other answer choices and terms provided, but don't waste too much time trying to figure out a difficult term.

Contextual Clues

Look for contextual clues. An answer can be right but not correct. The contextual clues will help you find the answer that is most right and is correct. Understand the context in which a phrase or statement is made. This will help you make important distinctions.

Don't Panic

Panicking will not answer any questions for you. Therefore, it isn't helpful. When you first see the question, if your mind goes blank, take a deep breath. Force yourself to mechanically go through the steps of solving the problem and using the strategies you've learned.

Pace Yourself

Don't get clock fever. It's easy to be overwhelmed when you're looking at a page full of questions, your mind is full of random thoughts and feeling confused, and the clock is ticking down faster than you would like. Calm down and maintain the pace that you have set for yourself. As long as you are on track by monitoring your pace, you are guaranteed to have enough time for yourself. When you get to the last few minutes of the test, it may seem like you won't have enough time left, but if you only have as many questions as you should have left at that point, then you're right on track!

Answer Selection

The best way to pick an answer choice is to eliminate all of those that are wrong, until only one is left and confirm that is the correct answer. Sometimes though, an answer choice may immediately look right. Be careful! Take a second to make sure that the other choices are not equally obvious. Don't make a hasty mistake. There are only two times that you should stop before checking other answers. First is when you are positive that the answer choice you have selected is correct. Second is when time is almost out and you have to make a quick guess!

Check Your Work

Since you will probably not know every term listed and the answer to every question, it is important that you get credit for the ones that you do know. Don't miss any questions through careless mistakes. If at all possible, try to take a second to look back over your answer selection and make sure you've selected the correct answer choice and haven't made a costly careless mistake (such as marking an answer choice that you didn't mean to mark). This quick double check should more than pay for itself in caught mistakes for the time it costs.

Beware of Directly Quoted Answers

Sometimes an answer choice will repeat word for word a portion of the question or reference section. However, beware of such exact duplication – it may be a trap! More than likely, the correct choice will paraphrase or summarize a point, rather than being exactly the same wording.

Slang

Scientific sounding answers are better than slang ones. An answer choice that begins "To compare the outcomes…" is much more likely to be correct than one that begins "Because some people insisted…"

Extreme Statements

Avoid wild answers that throw out highly controversial ideas that are proclaimed as established fact. An answer choice that states the "process should used in certain situations, if…" is much more likely to be correct than one that states the "process should be discontinued completely." The first is a calm rational statement and doesn't even make a definitive, uncompromising stance, using a hedge word "if" to provide wiggle room, whereas the second choice is a radical idea and far more extreme.

Answer Choice Families

When you have two or more answer choices that are direct opposites or parallels, one of them is usually the correct answer. For instance, if one answer choice states "x increases" and another answer choice states "x decreases" or "y increases," then those two or three answer choices are very similar in construction and fall into the same family of answer choices. A family of answer choices is when two or three answer choices are very similar in construction, and yet often have a directly opposite meaning. Usually the correct answer choice will be in that family of answer choices. The "odd man out" or answer choice that doesn't seem to fit the parallel construction of the other answer choices is more likely to be incorrect.

Special Report: Retaking the Test: What Are Your Chances at Improving Your Score?

After going through the experience of taking a major test, many test takers feel that once is enough. The test usually comes during a period of transition in the test taker's life, and taking the test is only one of a series of important events. With so many distractions and conflicting recommendations, it may be difficult for a test taker to rationally determine whether or not he should retake the test after viewing his scores.

The importance of the test usually only adds to the burden of the retake decision. However, don't be swayed by emotion. There a few simple questions that you can ask yourself to guide you as you try to determine whether a retake would improve your score:

1. What went wrong? Why wasn't your score what you expected?

Can you point to a single factor or problem that you feel caused the low score? Were you sick on test day? Was there an emotional upheaval in your life that caused a distraction? Were you late for the test or not able to use the full time allotment? If you can point to any of these specific, individual problems, then a retake should definitely be considered.

2. Is there enough time to improve?

Many problems that may show up in your score report may take a lot of time for improvement. A deficiency in a particular math skill may require weeks or months of tutoring and studying to improve. If you have enough time to improve an identified weakness, then a retake should definitely be considered.

3. How will additional scores be used? Will a score average, highest score, or most recent score be used?

Different test scores may be handled completely differently. If you've taken the test multiple times, sometimes your highest score is used, sometimes your average score is computed and used, and sometimes your most recent score is used. Make sure you understand what method will be used to evaluate your scores, and use that to help you determine whether a retake should be considered.

4. Are my practice test scores significantly higher than my actual test score?

If you have taken a lot of practice tests and are consistently scoring at a much higher level than your actual test score, then you should consider a retake. However, if you've taken five practice tests and only one of your scores was higher than your actual test score, or if your practice test scores were only slightly higher than your actual test score, then it is unlikely that you will significantly increase your score.

5. Do I need perfect scores or will I be able to live with this score? Will this score still allow me to follow my dreams?

What kind of score is acceptable to you? Is your current score "good enough?" Do you have to have a certain score in order to pursue the future of your dreams? If you won't be happy with your current score, and there's no way that you could live with it, then you should consider a retake. However, don't get your hopes up. If you are looking for significant improvement, that may or may not be possible. But if you won't be happy otherwise, it is at least worth the effort.

Remember that there are other considerations. To achieve your dream, it is likely that your grades may also be taken into account. A great test score is usually not the only thing necessary to succeed. Make sure that you aren't overemphasizing the importance of a high test score.

Furthermore, a retake does not always result in a higher score. Some test takers will score lower on a retake, rather than higher. One study shows that one-fourth of test takers will achieve a significant improvement in test score, while one-sixth of test takers will actually show a decrease. While this shows that most test takers will improve, the majority will only improve their scores a little and a retake may not be worth the test taker's effort.

Finally, if a test is taken only once and is considered in the added context of good grades on the part of a test taker, the person reviewing the grades and scores may be tempted to assume that the test taker just had a bad day while taking the test, and may discount the low test score in favor of the high grades. But if the test is retaken and the scores are approximately the same, then the validity of the low scores are only confirmed. Therefore, a retake could actually hurt a test taker by definitely bracketing a test taker's score ability to a limited range.

Special Report: How to Overcome Test Anxiety

The very nature of tests caters to some level of anxiety, nervousness or tension, just as we feel for any important event that occurs in our lives. A little bit of anxiety or nervousness can be a good thing. It helps us with motivation, and makes achievement just that much sweeter. However, too much anxiety can be a problem; especially if it hinders our ability to function and perform.

"Test anxiety," is the term that refers to the emotional reactions that some test-takers experience when faced with a test or exam. Having a fear of testing and exams is based upon a rational fear, since the test-taker's performance can shape the course of an academic career. Nevertheless, experiencing excessive fear of examinations will only interfere with the test-takers ability to perform, and his/her chances to be successful.

There are a large variety of causes that can contribute to the development and sensation of test anxiety. These include, but are not limited to lack of performance and worrying about issues surrounding the test.

Lack of Preparation

Lack of preparation can be identified by the following behaviors or situations:

Not scheduling enough time to study, and therefore cramming the night before the test or exam
Managing time poorly, to create the sensation that there is not enough time to do everything
Failing to organize the text information in advance, so that the study material consists of the entire text and not simply the pertinent information
Poor overall studying habits

Worrying, on the other hand, can be related to both the test taker, or many other factors around him/her that will be affected by the results of the test. These include worrying about:

Previous performances on similar exams, or exams in general
How friends and other students are achieving
The negative consequences that will result from a poor grade or failure

There are three primary elements to test anxiety. Physical components, which involve the same typical bodily reactions as those to acute anxiety (to be discussed below). Emotional factors have to do with fear or panic. Mental or cognitive issues concerning attention spans and memory abilities.

Physical Signals

There are many different symptoms of test anxiety, and these are not limited to mental and emotional strain. Frequently there are a range of physical signals that will let a test taker know that he/she is suffering from test anxiety. These bodily changes can include the following:

Perspiring
Sweaty palms
Wet, trembling hands
Nausea
Dry mouth
A knot in the stomach
Headache
Faintness
Muscle tension
Aching shoulders, back and neck
Rapid heart beat
Feeling too hot/cold

To recognize the sensation of test anxiety, a test-taker should monitor him/herself for the following sensations:

The physical distress symptoms as listed above
Emotional sensitivity, expressing emotional feelings such as the need to cry or laugh too much, or a sensation of anger or helplessness
A decreased ability to think, causing the test-taker to blank out or have racing thoughts that are hard to organize or control.

Though most students will feel some level of anxiety when faced with a test or exam, the majority can cope with that anxiety and maintain it at a manageable level. However, those who cannot are faced with a very real and very serious condition, which can and should be controlled for the immeasurable benefit of this sufferer.

Naturally, these sensations lead to negative results for the testing experience. The most common effects of test anxiety have to do with nervousness and mental blocking.

Nervousness

Nervousness can appear in several different levels:

The test-taker's difficulty, or even inability to read and understand the questions on the test
The difficulty or inability to organize thoughts to a coherent form
The difficulty or inability to recall key words and concepts relating to the testing questions (especially essays)
The receipt of poor grades on a test, though the test material was well known by the test taker

Conversely, a person may also experience mental blocking, which involves:

Blanking out on test questions
Only remembering the correct answers to the questions when the test has already finished.

Fortunately for test anxiety sufferers, beating these feelings, to a large degree, has to do with proper preparation. When a test taker has a feeling of preparedness, then anxiety will be dramatically lessened.

The first step to resolving anxiety issues is to distinguish which of the two types of anxiety are being suffered. If the anxiety is a direct result of a lack of preparation, this should be considered a normal reaction, and the anxiety level (as opposed to the test results) shouldn't be anything to worry about. However, if, when adequately prepared, the test-taker still panics, blanks out, or seems to overreact, this is not a fully rational reaction. While this can be considered normal too, there are many ways to combat and overcome these effects.

Remember that anxiety cannot be entirely eliminated, however, there are ways to minimize it, to make the anxiety easier to manage. Preparation is one of the best ways to minimize test anxiety. Therefore the following techniques are wise in order to best fight off any anxiety that may want to build.

To begin with, try to avoid cramming before a test, whenever it is possible. By trying to memorize an entire term's worth of information in one day, you'll be shocking your system, and not giving yourself a very good chance to absorb the information. This is an easy path to anxiety, so for those who suffer from test anxiety, cramming should not even be considered an option.

Instead of cramming, work throughout the semester to combine all of the material which is presented throughout the semester, and work on it gradually as the course goes by, making sure to master the main concepts first, leaving minor details for a week or so before the test.

To study for the upcoming exam, be sure to pose questions that may be on the examination, to gauge the ability to answer them by integrating the ideas from your texts, notes and lectures, as well as any supplementary readings.

If it is truly impossible to cover all of the information that was covered in that particular term, concentrate on the most important portions, that can be covered very well. Learn these concepts as best as possible, so that when the test comes, a goal can be made to use these concepts as presentations of your knowledge.

In addition to study habits, changes in attitude are critical to beating a struggle with test anxiety. In fact, an improvement of the perspective over the entire test-taking experience can actually help a test taker to enjoy studying and therefore improve the overall experience. Be certain not to overemphasize the significance of the grade - know that the result of the test is neither a reflection of self worth, nor is it a measure of intelligence; one grade will not predict a person's future success.

To improve an overall testing outlook, the following steps should be tried:

Keeping in mind that the most reasonable expectation for taking a test is to expect to try to demonstrate as much of what you know as you possibly can.

Reminding ourselves that a test is only one test; this is not the only one, and there will be others.

The thought of thinking of oneself in an irrational, all-or-nothing term should be avoided at all costs.

A reward should be designated for after the test, so there's something to look forward to. Whether it be going to a movie, going out to eat, or simply visiting friends, schedule it in advance, and do it no matter what result is expected on the exam.

Test-takers should also keep in mind that the basics are some of the most important things, even beyond anti-anxiety techniques and studying. Never neglect the basic social, emotional and biological needs, in order to try to absorb information. In order to best achieve, these three factors must be held as just as important as the studying itself.

Study Steps

Remember the following important steps for studying:

Maintain healthy nutrition and exercise habits. Continue both your recreational activities and social pass times. These both contribute to your physical and emotional well being. Be certain to get a good amount of sleep, especially the night before the test, because when you're overtired you are not able to perform to the best of your best ability.

Keep the studying pace to a moderate level by taking breaks when they are needed, and varying the work whenever possible, to keep the mind fresh instead of getting bored.

When enough studying has been done that all the material that can be learned has been learned, and the test taker is prepared for the test, stop studying and do something relaxing such as listening to music, watching a movie, or taking a warm bubble bath.

There are also many other techniques to minimize the uneasiness or apprehension that is experienced along with test anxiety before, during, or even after the examination. In fact, there are a great deal of things that can be done to stop anxiety from interfering with lifestyle and performance. Again, remember that anxiety will not be eliminated entirely, and it shouldn't be. Otherwise that "up" feeling for exams would not exist, and most of us depend on that sensation to perform better than usual. However, this anxiety has to be at a level that is manageable.

Of course, as we have just discussed, being prepared for the exam is half the battle right away. Attending all classes, finding out what knowledge will be expected on the exam, and knowing the exam schedules are easy steps to lowering anxiety. Keeping up with work will remove the need to cram, and efficient study habits will eliminate wasted time. Studying should be done in an ideal location for concentration, so that it is simple to become interested in the material and give it complete attention. A method such as SQ3R (Survey, Question, Read, Recite, Review) is a wonderful key to follow to make sure that the study habits are as effective as possible, especially in the case of learning from a textbook. Flashcards are great techniques for memorization. Learning to take good notes will mean that notes will be full of useful information, so that less sifting will need to be done to seek out what is pertinent for studying. Reviewing notes after class and then again on occasion will keep the information fresh in the mind. From notes that have been taken summary sheets and outlines can be made for simpler reviewing.

A study group can also be a very motivational and helpful place to study, as there will be a sharing of ideas, all of the minds can work together, to make sure that everyone understands, and the studying will be made more interesting because it will be a social occasion.

Basically, though, as long as the test-taker remains organized and self confident, with efficient study habits, less time will need to be spent studying, and higher grades will be achieved.

To become self confident, there are many useful steps. The first of these is "self talk." It has been shown through extensive research, that self-talk for students who suffer from test anxiety, should be well monitored, in order to make sure that it contributes to self confidence as opposed to sinking the student. Frequently the self talk of test-anxious students is negative or self-defeating, thinking that everyone else is smarter and faster, that they always mess up, and that if they don't do well, they'll fail the entire course. It is important to decreasing anxiety that awareness is made of self talk. Try writing any negative self thoughts and then disputing them with a positive statement instead. Begin self-encouragement as though it was a friend speaking. Repeat positive statements to help reprogram the mind to believing in successes instead of failures.

Helpful Techniques

Other extremely helpful techniques include:

Self-visualization of doing well and reaching goals
While aiming for an "A" level of understanding, don't try to "overprotect" by setting your expectations lower. This will only convince the mind to stop studying in order to meet the lower expectations.
Don't make comparisons with the results or habits of other students. These are individual factors, and different things work for different people, causing different results.
Strive to become an expert in learning what works well, and what can be done in order to improve. Consider collecting this data in a journal.
Create rewards for after studying instead of doing things before studying that will only turn into avoidance behaviors.
Make a practice of relaxing - by using methods such as progressive relaxation, self-hypnosis, guided imagery, etc - in order to make relaxation an automatic sensation.
Work on creating a state of relaxed concentration so that concentrating will take on the focus of the mind, so that none will be wasted on worrying.
Take good care of the physical self by eating well and getting enough sleep.
Plan in time for exercise and stick to this plan.

Beyond these techniques, there are other methods to be used before, during and after the test that will help the test-taker perform well in addition to overcoming anxiety.

Before the exam comes the academic preparation. This involves establishing a study schedule and beginning at least one week before the actual date of the test. By doing this, the anxiety of not having enough time to study for the test will be automatically eliminated. Moreover, this will make the studying a much more effective experience, ensuring that the learning will be an easier process. This relieves much undue pressure on the test-taker.

Summary sheets, note cards, and flash cards with the main concepts and examples of these main concepts should be prepared in advance of the actual studying time. A topic should never be eliminated from this process. By omitting a topic because it isn't expected to be on the test is only setting up the test-taker for anxiety should it actually appear on the exam. Utilize the course syllabus for laying out the topics that should be studied. Carefully go over the notes that were made in class, paying special attention to any of the issues that the professor took special care to emphasize while lecturing in class. In the textbooks, use the chapter review, or if possible, the chapter tests, to begin your review.

It may even be possible to ask the instructor what information will be covered on the exam, or what the format of the exam will be (for example, multiple choice, essay, free form, true-false). Additionally, see if it is possible to find out how many questions will be on the test. If a review sheet or sample test has been offered by the professor, make good use of it, above anything else, for the preparation for the test. Another great resource for getting to know the examination is reviewing tests from previous semesters. Use these tests to review, and aim to achieve a 100% score on each of the possible topics. With a few exceptions, the goal that you set for yourself is the highest one that you will reach.

Take all of the questions that were assigned as homework, and rework them to any other possible course material. The more problems reworked, the more skill and confidence will form as a result. When forming the solution to a problem, write out each of the steps. Don't simply do head work. By doing as many steps on paper as possible, much clarification and therefore confidence will be formed. Do this with as many homework problems as possible, before checking the answers. By checking the answer after each problem, a reinforcement will exist, that will not be on the exam. Study situations should be as exam-like as possible, to prime the test-taker's system for the experience. By waiting to check the answers at the end, a psychological advantage will be formed, to decrease the stress factor.

Another fantastic reason for not cramming is the avoidance of confusion in concepts, especially when it comes to mathematics. 8-10 hours of study will become one hundred percent more effective if it is spread out over a week or at least several days, instead of doing it all in one sitting. Recognize that the human brain requires time in order to assimilate new material, so frequent breaks and a span of study time over several days will be much more beneficial.

Additionally, don't study right up until the point of the exam. Studying should stop a minimum of one hour before the exam begins. This allows the brain to rest and put things in their proper order. This will also provide the time to become as relaxed as possible when going into the examination room. The test-taker will also have time to eat well and eat sensibly. Know that the brain needs food as much as the rest of the body. With enough food and enough sleep, as well as a relaxed attitude, the body and the mind are primed for success.

Avoid any anxious classmates who are talking about the exam. These students only spread anxiety, and are not worth sharing the anxious sentimentalities.

Before the test also involves creating a positive attitude, so mental preparation should also be a point of concentration. There are many keys to creating a positive attitude. Should fears become rushing in, make a visualization of taking the exam, doing well, and seeing an A written on the paper. Write out a list of affirmations that will bring a feeling of confidence, such as "I am doing well in my English class," "I studied well and know my material," "I enjoy this class." Even if the affirmations aren't believed at first, it sends a positive message to the subconscious which will result in an alteration of the overall belief system, which is the system that creates reality.

If a sensation of panic begins, work with the fear and imagine the very worst! Work through the entire scenario of not passing the test, failing the entire course, and dropping out of school, followed by not getting a job, and pushing a shopping cart through the dark alley where you'll live. This will place things into perspective! Then, practice deep breathing and create a visualization of the opposite situation - achieving an "A" on the exam, passing the entire course, receiving the degree at a graduation ceremony.

On the day of the test, there are many things to be done to ensure the best results, as well as the most calm outlook. The following stages are suggested in order to maximize test-taking potential:

Begin the examination day with a moderate breakfast, and avoid any coffee or beverages with caffeine if the test taker is prone to jitters. Even people who are used to managing caffeine can feel jittery or light-headed when it is taken on a test day.
Attempt to do something that is relaxing before the examination begins. As last minute cramming clouds the mastering of overall concepts, it is better to use this time to create a calming outlook.
Be certain to arrive at the test location well in advance, in order to provide time to select a location that is away from doors, windows and other distractions, as well as giving enough time to relax before the test begins.
Keep away from anxiety generating classmates who will upset the sensation of stability and relaxation that is being attempted before the exam.
Should the waiting period before the exam begins cause anxiety, create a self-distraction by reading a light magazine or something else that is relaxing and simple.

During the exam itself, read the entire exam from beginning to end, and find out how much time should be allotted to each individual problem. Once writing the exam, should more time be taken for a problem, it should be abandoned, in order to begin another problem. If there is time at the end, the unfinished problem can always be returned to and completed.

Read the instructions very carefully - twice - so that unpleasant surprises won't follow during or after the exam has ended.

When writing the exam, pretend that the situation is actually simply the completion of homework within a library, or at home. This will assist in forming a relaxed atmosphere, and will allow the brain extra focus for the complex thinking function.

Begin the exam with all of the questions with which the most confidence is felt. This will build the confidence level regarding the entire exam and will begin a quality momentum. This will also create encouragement for trying the problems where uncertainty resides.

Going with the "gut instinct" is always the way to go when solving a problem. Second guessing should be avoided at all costs. Have confidence in the ability to do well.

For essay questions, create an outline in advance that will keep the mind organized and make certain that all of the points are remembered. For multiple choice, read every answer, even if the correct one has been spotted - a better one may exist.

Continue at a pace that is reasonable and not rushed, in order to be able to work carefully. Provide enough time to go over the answers at the end, to check for small errors that can be corrected.

Should a feeling of panic begin, breathe deeply, and think of the feeling of the body releasing sand through its pores. Visualize a calm, peaceful place, and include all of the sights, sounds and sensations of this image. Continue the deep breathing, and take a few minutes to continue this with closed eyes. When all is well again, return to the test.

If a "blanking" occurs for a certain question, skip it and move on to the next question. There will be time to return to the other question later. Get everything done that can be done, first, to guarantee all the grades that can be compiled, and to build all of the confidence possible. Then return to the weaker questions to build the marks from there.

Remember, one's own reality can be created, so as long as the belief is there, success will follow. And remember: anxiety can happen later, right now, there's an exam to be written!

After the examination is complete, whether there is a feeling for a good grade or a bad grade, don't dwell on the exam, and be certain to follow through on the reward that was promised...and enjoy it! Don't dwell on any mistakes that have been made, as there is nothing that can be done at this point anyway.

Additionally, don't begin to study for the next test right away. Do something relaxing for a while, and let the mind relax and prepare itself to begin absorbing information again.

From the results of the exam - both the grade and the entire experience, be certain to learn from what has gone on. Perfect studying habits and work some more on confidence in order to make the next examination experience even better than the last one.

Learn to avoid places where openings occurred for laziness, procrastination and day dreaming.

Use the time between this exam and the next one to better learn to relax, even learning to relax on cue, so that any anxiety can be controlled during the next exam. Learn how to relax the body. Slouch in your chair if that helps. Tighten and then relax all of the different muscle groups, one group at a time, beginning with the feet and then working all the way up to the neck and face. This will ultimately relax the muscles more than they were to begin with. Learn how to breathe deeply and comfortably, and focus on this breathing going in and out as a relaxing thought. With every exhale, repeat the word "relax."

As common as test anxiety is, it is very possible to overcome it. Make yourself one of the test-takers who overcome this frustrating hindrance.

Special Report: How to Overcome Your Fear of Math

If this article started by saying "Math," many of us would feel a shiver crawl up our spines, just by reading that simple word. Images of torturous years in those crippling desks of the math classes can become so vivid to our consciousness that we can almost smell those musty textbooks, and see the smudges of the #2 pencils on our fingers.

If you are still a student, feeling the impact of these sometimes overwhelming classroom sensations, you are not alone if you get anxious at just the thought of taking that compulsory math course. Does your heart beat just that much faster when you have to split the bill for lunch among your friends with a group of your friends? Do you truly believe that you simply don't have the brain for math? Certainly you're good at other things, but math just simply isn't one of them? Have you ever avoided activities, or other school courses because they appear to involve mathematics, with which you're simply not comfortable?

If any one or more of these "symptoms" can be applied to you, you could very well be suffering from a very real condition called "Math Anxiety."

It's not at all uncommon for people to think that they have some sort of math disability or allergy, when in actuality, their block is a direct result of the way in which they were taught math!

In the late 1950's with the dawning of the space age, New Math - a new "fuzzy math" reform that focuses on higher-order thinking, conceptual understanding and solving problems - took the country by storm. It's now becoming ever more clear that teachers were not supplied with the correct, practical and effective way in which they should be teaching new math so that students will understand the methods comfortably. So is it any wonder that so many students struggled so deeply, when their teachers were required to change their entire math systems without the foundation of proper training? Even if you have not been personally, directly affected by that precise event, its impact is still as rampant as ever.

Basically, the math teachers of today are either the teachers who began teaching the new math in the first place (without proper training) or they are the students of the math teachers who taught new math without proper training. Therefore, unless they had a unique, exceptional teacher, their primary, consistent examples of teaching math have been teachers using methods that are not conducive to the general understanding of the entire class. This explains why your discomfort (or fear) of math is not at all rare.

It is very clear why being called up to the chalk board to solve a math problem is such a common example of a terrifying situation for students - and it has very little to do with a fear of being in front of the class. Most of us have had a minimum of one humiliating experience while standing with chalk dusted fingers, with the eyes of every math student piercing through us. These are the images that haunt us all the way through adulthood. But it does not mean that we cannot learn math. It just means that we could be developing a solid case of math anxiety.

But what exactly is math anxiety? It's an very strong emotional sensation of anxiety, panic, or fear that people feel when they think about or must apply their ability to understand mathematics. Sufferers of math anxiety frequently believe that they are incapable of doing activities or taking classes that involve math skills. In fact, some people with math anxiety have developed such a fear that it has become a phobia; aptly named math phobia.

The incidence of math anxiety, especially among college students, but also among high school students, has risen considerably over the last 10 years, and currently this increase shows no signs of slowing down. Frequently students will even chose their college majors and programs based specifically on how little math will be compulsory for the completion of the degree.

The prevalence of math anxiety has become so dramatic on college campuses that many of these schools have special counseling programs that are designed to assist math anxious students to deal with their discomfort and their math problems.

Math anxiety itself is not an intellectual problem, as many people have been lead to believe; it is, in fact, an emotional problem that stems from improper math teaching techniques that have slowly built and reinforced these feelings. However, math anxiety can result in an intellectual problem when its symptoms interfere with a person's ability to learn and understand math.

The fear of math can cause a sort of "glitch" in the brain that can cause an otherwise clever person to stumble over even the simplest of math problems. A study by Dr. Mark H. Ashcraft of Cleveland State University in Ohio showed that college students who usually perform well, but who suffer from math anxiety, will suffer from fleeting lapses in their working memory when they are asked to perform even the most basic mental arithmetic. These same issues regarding memory were not present in the same students when they were required to answer questions that did not involve numbers. This very clearly demonstrated that the memory phenomenon is quite specific to only math.

So what exactly is it that causes this inhibiting math anxiety? Unfortunately it is not as simple as one answer, since math anxiety doesn't have one specific cause. Frequently math anxiety can result of a student's either negative experience or embarrassment with math or a math teacher in previous years.

These circumstances can prompt the student to believe that he or she is somehow deficient in his or her math abilities. This belief will consistently lead to a poor performance in math tests and courses in general, leading only to confirm the beliefs of the student's inability. This particular phenomenon is referred to as the "self-fulfilling prophecy" by the psychological community. Math anxiety will result in poor performance, rather than it being the other way around.

Dr. Ashcraft stated that math anxiety is a "It's a learned, almost phobic, reaction to math," and that it is not only people prone to anxiety, fear, or panic who can develop math anxiety. The image alone of doing math problems can send the blood pressure and heart rate to race, even in the calmest person.

The study by Dr. Ashcraft and his colleague Elizabeth P. Kirk, discovered that students who suffered from math anxiety were frequently stumped by issues of even the most basic math rules, such as "carrying over" a number, when performing a sum, or "borrowing" from a number when doing a subtraction. Lapses such as this occurred only on working memory questions involving numbers.

To explain the problem with memory, Ashcraft states that when math anxiety begins to take its effect, the sufferer experiences a rush of thoughts, leaving little room for the focus required to perform even the simplest of math problems. He stated that "you're draining away the energy you need for solving the problem by worrying about it."

The outcome is a "vicious cycle," for students who are sufferers of math anxiety. As math anxiety is developed, the fear it promotes stands in the way of learning, leading to a decrease in self-confidence in the ability to perform even simple arithmetic.

A large portion of the problem lies in the ways in which math is taught to students today. In the US, students are frequently taught the rules of math, but rarely will they learn why a specific approach to a math problems work. Should students be provided with a foundation of "deeper understanding" of math, it may prevent the development of phobias.

Another study that was published in the Journal of Experimental Psychology by Dr. Jamie Campbell and Dr. Qilin Xue of the University of Saskatchewan in Saskatoon, Canada, reflected the same concepts. The researchers in this study looked at university students who were educated in Canada and China, discovering that the Chinese students could generally outperform the Canadian-educated students when it came to solving complex math problems involving procedural knowledge - the ability to know how to solve a math problem, instead of simply having ideas memorized.

A portion of this result seemed to be due to the use of calculators within both elementary and secondary schools; while Canadians frequently used them, the Chinese students did not.

However, calculators were not the only issue. Since Chinese-educated students also outperformed Canadian-educated students in complex math, it is suggested that cultural factors may also have an impact. However, the short-cut of using the calculator may hinder the development of the problem solving skills that are key to performing well in math.

Though it is critical that students develop such fine math skills, it is easier said than done. It would involve an overhaul of the training among all elementary and secondary educators, changing the education major in every college.

Math Myths

One problem that contributes to the progression of math anxiety, is the belief of many math myths. These erroneous math beliefs include the following:

Men are better in math than women - however, research has failed to demonstrate that there is any difference in math ability between the sexes.

There is a single best way to solve a math problem - however, the majority of math problems can be solved in a number of different ways. By saying that there is only one way to solve a math problem, the thinking and creative skills of the student are held back.

Some people have a math mind, and others do not - in truth, the majority of people have much more potential for their math capabilities than they believe of themselves.

It is a bad thing to count by using your fingers - counting by using fingers has actually shown that an understanding of arithmetic has been established.
People who are skilled in math can do problems quickly in their heads - in actuality, even math professors will review their example problems before they teach them in their classes.

The anxieties formed by these myths can frequently be perpetuated by a range of mind games that students seem to play with themselves. These math mind games include the following beliefs:

I don't perform math fast enough - actually everyone has a different rate at which he or she can learn. The speed of the solving of math problems is not important as long as the student can solve it.

I don't have the mind for math - this belief can inhibit a student's belief in him or herself, and will therefore interfere with the student's real ability to learn math.

I got the correct answer, but it was done the wrong way - there is no single best way to complete a math problem. By believing this, a student's creativity and overall understanding of math is hindered.

If I can get the correct answer, then it is too simple - students who suffer from math anxiety frequently belittle their own abilities when it comes to their math capabilities.

Math is unrelated to my "real" life - by freeing themselves of the fear of math, math anxiety sufferers are only limiting their choices and freedoms for the rest of their life.

Fortunately, there are many ways to help those who suffer from math anxiety. Since math anxiety is a learned, psychological response to doing or thinking about math, that interferes with the sufferer's ability to understand and perform math, it is not at all a reflection of the sufferer's true math sills and abilities.

Helpful Strategies

Many strategies and therapies have been developed to help students to overcome their math anxious responses. Some of these helpful strategies include the following:

Reviewing and learning basic arithmetic principles, techniques and methods. Frequently math anxiety is a result of the experience of many students with early negative situations, and these students have never truly developed a strong base in basic arithmetic, especially in the case of multiplication and fractions. Since math is a discipline that is built on an accumulative foundation, where the concepts are built upon gradually from simpler concepts, a student who has not achieved a solid basis in arithmetic will experience difficulty in learning higher order math. Taking a remedial math course, or a short math course that focuses on arithmetic can often make a considerable difference in reducing the anxious response that math anxiety sufferers have with math.

Becoming aware of any thoughts, actions and feelings that are related to math and responses to math. Math anxiety has a different effect on different students. Therefore it is very important to become familiar with any reactions that the math anxiety sufferer may have about him/herself and the situation when math has been encountered. If the sufferer becomes aware of any irrational or unrealistic thoughts, it's possible to better concentrate on replacing these thoughts with more positive and realistic ones.

Find help! Math anxiety, as we've mentioned, is a learned response, that is reinforced repeatedly over a period of time, and is therefore not something that can be eliminated instantaneously. Students can more effectively reduce their anxious responses with the help of many different services that are readily available. Seeking the assistance of a psychologist or counselor, especially one with a specialty in math anxiety, can assist the sufferer in performing an analysis of his/her psychological response to math, as well as learning anxiety management skills, and developing effective coping strategies. Other great tools are tutors, classes that teach better abilities to take better notes in math class, and other math learning aids.

Learning the mathematic vocabulary will instantly provide a better chance for understanding new concepts. One major issue among students is the lack of understanding of the terms and vocabulary that are common jargon within math classes. Typically math classes will utilize words in a completely different way from the way in which they are utilized in all other subjects. Students easily mistake their lack of understanding the math terms with their mathematical abilities.

Learning anxiety reducing techniques and methods for anxiety management. Anxiety greatly interferes with a student's ability to concentrate, think clearly, pay attention, and remember new concepts. When these same students can learn to relax, using anxiety management techniques, the student can regain his or her ability to control his or her emotional and physical symptoms of anxiety that interfere with the capabilities of mental processing.

Working on creating a positive overall attitude about mathematics. Looking at math with a positive attitude will reduce anxiety through the building of a positive attitude.

Learning to self-talk in a positive way. Pep talking oneself through a positive self talk can greatly assist in overcoming beliefs in math myths or the mind games that may be played. Positive self-talking is an effective way to replace the negative thoughts - the ones that create the anxiety. Even if the sufferer doesn't believe the statements at first, it plants a positive seed in the subconscious, and allows a positive outlook to grow.

Beyond this, students should learn effective math class, note taking and studying techniques. Typically, the math anxious students will avoid asking questions to save themselves from embarrassment. They will sit in the back of classrooms, and refrain from seeking assistance from the professor. Moreover, they will put off studying for math until the very last moment, since it causes them such substantial discomfort. Alone, or a combination of these negative behaviors work only to reduce the anxiety of the students, but in reality, they are actually building a substantially more intense anxiety.

There are many different positive behaviors that can be adopted by math anxious students, so that they can learn to better perform within their math classes.

Sit near the front of the class. This way, there will be fewer distractions, and there will be more of a sensation of being a part of the topic of discussion.
If any questions arise, ASK! If one student has a question, then there are certain to be others who have the same question but are too nervous to ask - perhaps because they have not yet learned how to deal with their own math anxiety.

Seek extra help from the professor after class or during office hours.

Prepare, prepare, prepare - read textbook material before the class, do the homework and work out any problems available within the textbook. Math skills are developed through practice and repetition, so the more practice and repetition, the better the math skills.

Review the material once again after class, to repeat it another time, and to reinforce the new concepts that were learned.

Beyond these tactics that can be taken by the students themselves, teachers and parents need to know that they can also have a large impact on the reduction of math anxiety within students.

As parents and teachers, there is a natural desire to help students to learn and understand how they will one day utilize different math techniques within their everyday lives. But when the student or teacher displays the symptoms of a person who has had nightmarish memories regarding math, where hesitations then develop in the instruction of students, these fears are automatically picked up by the students and commonly adopted as their own.

However, it is possible for teachers and parents to move beyond their own fears to better educate students by overcoming their own hesitations and learning to enjoy math.

Begin by adopting the outlook that math is a beautiful, imaginative or living thing. Of course, we normally think of mathematics as numbers that can be added or subtracted, multiplied or divided, but that is simply the beginning of it.

By thinking of math as something fun and imaginative, parents and teachers can teach children different ways to manipulate numbers, for example in balancing a checkbook. Parents rarely tell their children that math is everywhere around us; in nature, art, and even architecture. Usually, this is because they were never shown these relatively simple connections. But that pattern can break very simply through the participation of parents and teachers.

The beauty and hidden wonders of mathematics can easily be emphasized through a focus that can open the eyes of students to the incredible mathematical patterns that arise everywhere within the natural world. Observations and discussions can be made into things as fascinating as spider webs, leaf patterns, sunflowers and even coastlines. This makes math not only beautiful, but also inspiring and (dare we say) fun!

Pappas Method

For parents and teachers to assist their students in discovering the true wonders of mathematics, the techniques of Theoni Pappas can easily be applied, as per her popular and celebrated book "Fractals, Googols and Other Mathematical Tales." Pappas used to be a math phobia sufferer and created a fascinating step-by-step program for parents and teachers to use in order to teach students the joy of math.

Her simple, constructive step-by-step program goes as follows:

Don't let your fear of math come across to your kids - Parents must be careful not to perpetuate the mathematical myth - that math is only for specially talented "math types." Strive not to make comments like; "they don't like math" or "I have never been good at math." When children overhear comments like these from their primary role models they begin to dread math before even considering a chance of experiencing its wonders. It is important to encourage your children to read and explore the rich world of mathematics, and to practice mathematics without imparting negative biases.

Don't immediately associate math with computation (counting) - It is very important to realize that math is not just numbers and computations, but a realm of exciting ideas that touch every part of our lives -from making a telephone call to how the hair grows on someone's head. Take your children outside and point out real objects that display math concepts. For example, show them the symmetry of a leaf or angles on a building. Take a close look at the spirals in a spider web or intricate patterns of a snowflake.

Help your child understand why math is important - Math improves problem solving, increases competency and should be applied in different ways. It's the same as reading. You can learn the basics of reading without ever enjoying a novel. But, where's the excitement in that? With math, you could stop with the basics. But why when there is so much more to be gained by a fuller Understanding? Life is so much more enriching when we go beyond the basics. Stretch your children's minds to become involved in mathematics in ways that will not only be practical but also enhance their lives.

Make math as "hands on" as possible - Mathematicians participate in mathematics. To really experience math encourage your child to dig in and tackle problems in creative ways. Help them learn how to manipulate numbers using concrete references they understand as well as things they can see or touch. Look for patterns everywhere, explore shapes and symmetries. How many octagons do you see each day on the way to the grocery store? Play math puzzles and games and then encourage your child to try to invent their own. And, whenever possible, help your child realize a mathematical conclusion with real and tangible results. For example, measure out a full glass of juice with a measuring cup and then ask your child to drink half. Measure what is left. Does it measure half of a cup?

Read books that make math exciting:

Fractals, Googols and Other Mathematical Tales introduces an animated cat who explains fractals, tangrams and other mathematical concepts you've probably never heard of to children in terms they can understand. This book can double as a great text book by using one story per lesson.

A Wrinkle in Time is a well-loved classic, combining fantasy and science.

The Joy of Mathematics helps adults explore the beauty of mathematics that is all around.

The Math Curse is an amusing book for 4-8 year olds.

The Gnarly Gnews is a free, humorous bi-monthly newsletter on mathematics.

The Phantom Tollbooth is an Alice in Wonderland-style adventure into the worlds of words and numbers.

Use the internet to help your child explore the fascinating world of mathematics.

Web Math provides a powerful set of math-solvers that gives you instant answers to the stickiest problems.

Math League has challenging math materials and contests for fourth grade and above.

Silver Burdett Ginn Mathematics offers Internet-based math activities for grades K-6.

The Gallery of Interactive Geometry is full of fascinating, interactive geometry activities.

Math is very much like a language of its own. And like any second language, it will get rusty if it is not practiced enough. For that reason, students should always be looking into new ways to keep understanding and brushing up on their math skills, to be certain that foundations do not crumble, inhibiting the learning of new levels of math.

There are many different books, services and websites that have been developed to take the fear out of math, and to help even the most uncertain student develop self confidence in his or her math capabilities.

There is no reason for math or math classes to be a frightening experience, nor should it drive a student crazy, making them believe that they simply don't have the "math brain" that is needed to solve certain problems.

There are friendly ways to tackle such problems and it's all a matter of dispelling myths and creating a solid math foundation.

Concentrate on re-learning the basics and feeling better about yourself in math, and you'll find that the math brain you've always wanted, was there all along.

Practice Tests and Additional Bonus Material

Due to our efforts to try to keep this book to a manageable length, we've created a link that will give you access to all of your additional bonus material.

Please visit http://www.mometrix.com/bonus948/dat to access the information.